Nature Hikes in the White Mountains

An AMC Nature Walks Book

Robert Buchsbaum

APPALACHIAN MOUNTAIN CLUB BOOKS
BOSTON, MASSACHUSETTS

Cover Photograph: *Tuckerman Ravine Trail, near Crystal Cascade, Pinkham Notch.* Jerry Shereda

Drawings by Nancy N. Childs

All photographs by the author unless otherwise noted.

Book and Map Design: Carol Bast Tyler

Distributed by The Globe Pequot Press, Inc. Old Saybrook, CT.

Published by the Appalachian Mountain Club. No part of this publication may be reproduced or transmitted in any form or by any means, electronic or mechanical, including photocopying and recording, or by any information storage or retrieval system, except as may by expressly permitted by the 1976 Copyright Act or in writing from the publisher. Requests for permission should be addressed in writing to Appalachian Mountain Club Books, 5 Joy Street, Boston, MA 02108.

Library of Congress Cataloging-in-Publication Data

Buchsbaum, Robert.
    Nature hikes in the White Mountains/Robert Buchsbaum.
      p. cm.
    "An AMC nature walks book."
    Includes bibliographical references and indexes.
    ISBN 1-878239-37-6 (alk. paper): $12.95
      1. Hiking—New Hampshire—White Mountains—Guidebooks.
  2. Hiking—Maine—White Mountains—Guidebooks. 3. White
  Mountains (N.H. and Me.)—Guidebooks. 4. Nature trails—New
  Hampshire. 5. Nature Trails—Maine. I. Title.
GV199.42.W47B83 1995
796.5′1′097422—dc20
                                    94–42245
                                        CIP

Due to changes in conditions, use of the information in this book is at the sole risk of the user.

Printed on recycled paper using soy-based inks.

Printed in the United States of America.

10 9 8 7 6 5 4 3 2   95 96 97 98 99

Contents

This book is dedicated to all the volunteers who build and maintain the trail, allowing us to enjoy more intimately the wonderful vistas, waterfalls, flowers, and creatures of the mountains.

Acknowledgments

I WANT TO THANK the Appalachian Mountain Club for giving me the opportunity to write this book and AMC Editor Gordon Hardy for his faith, encouragement, advice, and good humor throughout the process. Other AMC staff contributed in many ways to this book. Carol Tyler generated all the maps on the computer. Walter Graff and Nancy Ritger of the Education Department provided very helpful recommendations on trails appropriate for children, and contributed some basic ideas on how to approach this topic. Much of what I have learned about the White Mountains comes from my association with other AMC naturalists.

I thank Lesley Rowse of the White Mountain National Forest and Gary Inman for advice on trails, particularly in Evans Notch, for sharing their knowledge of the White Mountains, and for letting us invade their home on numerous occasions. Rebecca Oreskes and Patti Dugan of the White Mountain National Forest also provided valuable information. I am also extremely grateful to Ed Quinlan, Leslie Nelkin, and their children, Suzanna and Michael, for sharing their house with us and accompanying us on a number of hikes.

Suzanna and Michael were two of our primary "field testers."

Helpful comments on various sections of the manuscript were made by E. Dykstra Eusden, Betsy Colburn, Peter Dunwiddie, and Steve Weisman. Of course the author takes all responsibility for any errors.

Very special thanks are due to my wife, Nancy Schalch, and daughter, Alison. Nancy was my chief hiking companion, cheerfully doing more than her share of the child care on our trips so I could concentrate on taking notes and photographs. She provided continual encouragement and logistic support and read and made very useful comments on the entire manuscript. It simply would not have been possible to complete this book without her. Alison went on her first hike when she was two months old and, fortunately for us (and for this book project), instantly took a liking to being out on the trails. I also thank Nancy and Alison for tolerating me on weekends and evenings when I would disappear to work on the manuscript.

Introduction

MY FIRST MEMORIES of the White Mountains are of a family vacation when I was seven years old. Since we all liked model trains we naturally took the Cog Railway to the summit of Mount Washington. For the first time in my life I looked down on puffy clouds. Trails, marked by mysterious piles of stones, snaked off in the distance over rugged, barren peaks, and signs pointed the way to wondrous-sounding destinations like Lakes of the Clouds and Tuckerman Ravine. Later I would actually hike on those trails and visit those destinations many times, but nothing can replace that first impression.

To me, the Whites have always been a fantasyland of bald mountain summits, extensive views, exotic plants, dark mossy enchanted evergreen forests, and cold mountain streams tumbling over boulders in fantastic patterns. My fondness for this region provided the original inspiration for this book. A second inspiration was many years of hiking, first with friends, then with families. Third were my experiences leading nature walks in the White Mountains, many as an AMC naturalist where I enjoyed watching kids and adults discover the natural world. And a fourth, very compelling inspiration was my own impending fatherhood. My wife and I would soon have a new companion on our hiking trips, a companion who would not have our abilities or interests but whom we definitely wanted to brainwash into loving the outdoors. It worked, too, because by the time we finished researching the hikes, our daughter was running along the trails, throwing stones in the water, talking to the gray jays, and trying to pick the wildflowers (our first conservation lesson).

As the book developed I was encouraged by parents who wanted a White Mountain guide that was directed toward young families and others for whom bagging a 4,000-footer is just not as important as getting out and experiencing the natural world of the mountains. Some of these parents had been rigorous hikers themselves BC (before children) and now wanted a guide to trails that were less physically demanding but still interesting to themselves and their children.

This book describes forty-four hikes appropriate for adults traveling with children. Really, though, they are for *anyone* interested in exploring the nature of the White Mountains. The hikes were selected to be right for kids, but they are also great for anyone who wants shorter, less strenuous, nature-oriented hikes. You don't have to be a child, or have young children, to enjoy these walks.

How to Use this Book

This book includes trail descriptions grouped by geographic region within the White Mountains. At the beginning of each regional chapter is a summary of local facilities such as stores, restaurants, and camp-grounds. Then each recommended trail is described in detail, with:

- General features, the length of the trail, how long it should take, elevation gain, the degree of difficulty for children, and options for shorter or longer walks.
- What's in it for kids: a list of potential activities, natural features, and other items of special interest to children.
- Getting there: how to get to the trailhead from major roads and towns.
- Detailed hiking directions for the trail.
- A general trail map showing the locations of various features.
- Highlights of the trail: natural history, scenery, and special activities such as swimming or exploring a quarry.

Also included in this book is an illustrated introduction to nature in the White Mountains and advice on hiking in the Whites in general and hiking with children in particular. The chapter on hiking with children is based on our experiences and those of AMC staffers and friends. The chapter on natural history in the White Mountains emphasizes things that are visible on most trails and likely to be appreciated by both adults and children.

To use this book, we recommend that you read through the trail descriptions before starting out to decide if the hike is right for you. Be sure to scan the

"What's in it for kids" and "Highlights" sections to see if there's something you and your kids might especially like. If you want to know more about a particular tree, plant, or other feature, you can refer to the illustrated nature section at the front of the book.

Finally, in the back of the book you will also find a chart summarizing each trail according to its features: running water, great vistas, rocky ledges, wooden bridges, and so on. This chart will give you a "snapshot" view of the trail so you can match its features to you and your children's favorite trailside pastimes.

Remember that the advice in the trail description on "degree of difficulty" and the length of time a hike should take naturally required some subjectivity. Trails labeled "easy, for all ages" may be manageable at least in part by children as young as two or three years old. They are usually flat and wide with few rocks or other obstructions. Trails labeled "challenging for kids" require a steep ascent, some scrambling on rocks, and are typically longer. On average, they are appropriate for kids above age six. Trails designated as "moderate for kids" are in-between. The estimated times are based on the assumption that you'll take your time and make frequent stops but do not factor in additional time for picnics, blueberry picking, and other activities. All hikes in this book are appropriate if you have an infant in a backpack, weather permitting.

We hope you enjoy this book and that it is a useful companion on many great hikes in the White Mountains. Most importantly, we hope children experience the same sense of wonder about this special region that has inspired you and us.

What to Bring

The *AMC White Mountain Guide* recommends the following for day hikes: extra clothing, hat, mittens, rain gear, windbreaker, food (including high-energy snacks), water, small flashlight, waterproof matches, map and trail guide, compass, pocketknife, first aid supplies, needle and thread, safety pin, nylon cord, trash bag, and toilet paper. Carry these all in a comfortable day pack. It is important to fill your canteen before you start your hike because water in mountain lakes and streams is not considered safe to drink without purification. Consult the *AMC White Mountain Guide* for more details.

Clothing: Dress in layers so that you can peel off or add an item easily. Remember that cotton clothes are very comfortable when dry but lose their insulating properties when wet. Wool or synthetics like polypro or pile are better. You'll need windbreakers and extra clothes because summit ledges even at low elevations are likely to be cool and windy compared to the forest. All of the hikes in this book except one (Alpine Garden) are below 3,000 feet in elevation, so you are not likely to face the potentially extreme weather conditions that characterize life above tree line. Nevertheless, the weather in the White Mountains can be notoriously fickle even at lower elevations, and the extra clothes will help you enjoy exposed summits and lunch breaks.

Good hiking boots are a critical element of a successful hike, especially for the more strenuous ones. Make sure yours have sturdy soles, good ankle support, and are well broken in before you set off.

Protection from insects is essential for certain hikes all summer and for all hikes during blackfly season (mid-May through mid-June). Bring along insect repellent or dress in light, long-sleeved shirts and pants if you prefer to avoid using repellents. And if you expect to spend much time in the sun, remember **sun hats and sunscreen.**

First aid kits are available from outdoor and sporting goods stores, but you can easily put together your own. It should include Band-Aids and sterile gauze pads, adhesive tape, small scissors, tweezers, an Ace bandage, antiseptic ointment, aspirin or other painkiller, small bar of soap, moleskin for blisters, and any special medication anyone requires.

A **flashlight and matches** are especially important if you start your hike in the afternoon.

What to Bring Especially for Kids

First of all, you should bring along all the items that are necessary even for hikes without children. A child who is cold or hungry is not going to be a good hiking companion. Remember that children are more likely to get chilled if you end up carrying them, so have extra clothing, especially for backpack-sized babies.

An important safety item is a **whistle.** Hopefully you will have trained children beforehand to stay within sight and won't need it. However, each child should have a whistle and know that if they are separated from the group, they should stay right where they are and blow on the whistle at regular intervals. Remind them that the whistle is not for play but should be used only when they sense they are lost from the group.

Food is another critical ingredient of a successful hike with kids. Lunch is a great motivator and reward.

Occasional snacks such as granola bars, fruit, or cookies can nip the start of any crankiness before it goes too far.

Have kids carry a **pack** of their own when they are old enough. In addition to extra clothes and perhaps a small canteen, make sure each child's pack has something essential for one of the group activities—a special snack, bags for blueberries, a lunch treat. If the kids insist that they won't wear extra jackets, suggest that they will be great to sit on during lunch.

Consider bringing along a **child carrier,** especially for the longer hikes. It is a lot easier than carrying a tired child on your shoulders and safer too.

Other small items good to have: a hand lens or magnifying glass aids in examining small things; binoculars are great if your destination is a view; a tea or soup strainer can make searching for aquatic life along ponds and streams more fun; and a bug box enables a child to examine insects closely. Last, have younger children bring a favorite toy or stuffed animal in their own daypacks.

Following the Trail

Getting lost with children is even less fun than getting lost alone. The trails in this guide are generally well marked with signs and frequent blazes (painted spots on tree trunks or rocks). Nonetheless, always carry a trail map and a compass and read the trail description before you depart so that you are prepared for any quirks. The maps in this guide are designed to give you a general idea of the trail but they are not as definitive as a detailed contour map; you should also review the maps and trail

Wooden bridges: a perennial hit with kids.

descriptions in the *AMC White Mountain Guide* in addition to this book. Most trails in the White Mountains are well marked; however, intersections with logging roads and unmarked trails might lead to some confusion. If you think you are off the trail, the best thing to do is to backtrack until you find the last blaze. Keep track of the blazes as you hike, a job that you might share with the children so they feel responsible for the successful navigation of the trip (of course, be sure you pay attention, too, so a child doesn't lead you innocently down the wrong path). Remember, too, to keep the whole family on the trail, not only for safety but also to protect the plants and other wildlife near the trail.

Hiking with Children

HIKING WITH CHILDREN requires flexibility, a sense of humor, and patience. You need to slow down and encourage children to explore the natural world around them—the sights, the sounds, and the smells—even if it means that you might not make it to that scenic overlook or waterfall. You have a wonderful opportunity to enjoy nature as your child sees it.

Our recommendations are based on our experiences and those of many AMC staffers and friends, but please keep in mind that it's difficult to generalize about what a child can handle at a given age. Some precocious and energetic five-year-olds are ready for a 4,000-footer. Other six- or seven-year-olds may not be willing to hike very far at all.

Don't be afraid to start your kids early. Our daughter slept through her first hike in a front carrier at two months of age. Hiking with a one-year-old in a backpack is actually much easier than negotiating with a toddler. Pack diapers, baby food, and other items as you would on any daylong outing and be prepared with extra clothes.

What Kinds of Hikes do Kids Like?

With the right spirit, every trail can be fun for adults and children alike, but some will engage children more easily than others. In our hikes with our daughter and other children, we've noticed a few especially winning features.

Children love to be around **water.** The White Mountains have an abundance of waterfalls and lakes that are popular destinations for family hikes. You can go swimming or wading, look for small critters, create rings with pebbles, throw stones in the water, or have a picnic or snack on big, flat boulders while dangling feet in the water. It is also much more fun to hike along a river or a small babbling stream than through a monotonous woodland.

Children love to walk on **wooden plank bridges** that cross streams and wetlands and on split logs that traverse muddy areas. Covered bridges are even better, but there are only a few in the White Mountains.

Kids like **blatantly exciting places and activities** that provide lots of stimulation. The Flume, Lost River, and the Mount Washington Auto Road are natural surrogates for video games, arcades, tourist traps, etc. They make a great compromise.

Kids like to stop and look at **little things,** like an odd-looking bug crossing the path, or a colorful leaf in autumn, or a brightly colored fungus. One friend remembered her nephew's fascination with small conifer trees that were his own height. Take the time to enjoy those things with them rather than hurrying off to the next destination.

Kids like to climb on rocks and explore the **big boulders** that are so common along many trails in the White Mountains. Especially intriguing are those that form caves or overhang the trail. Beginning hikers will proudly show you how they have "conquered" even a small rock in the middle of a trail.

Kids love scrambling around **rocky ledges** particularly after they have been hiking through a dense forest. They may enjoy scrambling on the ledges at scenic overlooks even more than they enjoy the scenery itself. (Of course, if their parents oogle over enough views, children will eventually start oogling too.) Rocky ledges are like a substitute jungle gym. Just keep your eyes on them, since there are no railings on most trails.

Most kids love picking and eating **blueberries.** They may not persevere long enough to collect a stash for tomorrow morning's blueberry pancakes, but they will certainly enjoy it for a while. The summits of many of the smaller mountains listed in this book are loaded with ripe blueberries toward the end of July and in August. Huckleberries, blackberries, and raspberries are also there for the picking.

Some kids love **wildflowers,** although others may not notice them. Keeping children from picking flowers may be the hardest job you'll have on the trail, but once they get into the habit of just looking, they'll keep it for life.

Kids like to see **animals.** Insects, fish, tadpoles, and mammals are usually the most popular animals in a child's bestiary. Trees riddled with woodpecker holes, bark stripped by moose, or trees scarred by bear claws are great things to show them.

Birds are hard for children to enjoy because they are much more often heard than seen in the White Mountains. Encourage them to listen to the beautiful birdsongs in the forest, but don't push it. You'll likely

It's never too early to take your child on a hike.

be more successful if you show them either big birds of open spaces and wetlands, such as hawks, herons, and ducks, or sassy, tame birds like gray jays and chickadees.

Before we had children, many of us sought out quiet, backcountry trails to get a refreshing break from our hectic work lives and our urban or suburban existence. Children are less likely to feel the need for such a **wilderness experience** than their parents. In fact, they may rather enjoy the crowds at such places as the Flume or Glen Ellis Falls.

Few people enjoy walking through an **endless tunnel of trees** with no scenic or watery breaks. Adults can tolerate those kinds of trails in anticipation of a reward at the end in the form of a summit or a waterfall. When you are hiking with children, however, there is no guarantee that you will make it to the end, so pick a hike that won't be disappointing even if you turn around before completing it.

Navigating can be a fun challenge. Some younger kids will be motivated by the responsibility of spotting the next blaze. Older kids may want to learn how to read trail maps and use a compass. They may enjoy helping to plan the hike as well.

Favorite Distractions

Inevitably, on some hikes somewhere, the kids will hit a low point. Here's where you need to be creative and prepared.

Some children love **singing songs** on the trail, no matter what the vocal abilities of the hikers. Camp songs and songs they have learned in school are great for those seemingly endless distances between highlights. Let them pick out the songs, but be ready with your own.

Stories and tales of what you did when you were their age work wonders at distracting children. Ask them a **nature question** they can answer along the hike—look at the hike descriptions for suggestions. Often there's something close at hand that can be made into a game, such as balsam blisters, spruce gum, or jewelweed.

Make the hike into a **scavenger hunt.** Have a list of items kids can search for and be ready to pull it out at the

The view of Mount Adams from Lowe's Bald Spot in Pinkham Notch.

strategic moment. Possible items are mushrooms, spiderwebs, Indian pipes, pinecones, maple leaves, or whatever you can glean from reading the "Highlights" section of the particular hike. You can also impart a valuable conservation lesson if you encourage them to leave the items in the forest rather than collecting them in a bag.

Additional Thoughts

Be flexible and allow plenty of extra time. Always be ready to change your plans in midhike and always encourage the kids to investigate the natural world. Time spent watching a moose feeding on water plants or a moth caught in a spiderweb will likely be remembered much longer than whether or not they made it to that last waterfall.

Be goal-oriented if getting to that waterfall can stimulate your children to overcome those first pangs of tiredness or lack-a-wanna, but be ready to bail out if it isn't working or if the children get engrossed in little things they see along the trail and time runs out. The idea is to have fun, not to make this into a forced march. On the other hand, don't necessarily turn back at the first complaint either, particularly if there is something you're sure they'll really enjoy with just a little more effort. And be liberal with praise for how well they are doing.

Just about all the trails described in this book have interesting things for both adults and children to see along the way so that the trip will be worthwhile even if you do not complete the entire hike. In the text, you'll find logical points to turn around before reaching the end, such as a nice view or swimming hole.

Remember, it is much more important for you to instill an appreciation for the natural world in the kids than to impart facts about nature. Sooner or later, a kid will ask something that even the most expert naturalist can't answer. If the kids find something that no one can identify, make it into a game and help them look it up in a field guide. A pad and pencil is useful to record field notes and questions.

Your own enthusiasm for the hike will rub off on them. Enjoy your hikes and the mountains!

Natural History of the White Mountains

THE WHITE MOUNTAINS are a special place, not only for its scenery and outdoor recreational opportunities but also for its wonderful diversity of natural history. Here is a brief description of the geology, plants, and animals of the region. Additional information is in the hike descriptions. Keep in mind that a complete guide to the natural history of the White Mountains would take up several volumes, so check the bibliography if you want to know more.

Geography

The White Mountains of north-central New Hampshire and western Maine are the largest expanse of mountains in New England. Forty-three peaks exceed 4,000 feet in elevation and seven exceed 5,000 feet. Most of the region is included in the White Mountain National Forest and several state parks. The area has an extensive network of hiking trails, maintained by the National Forest and volunteer organizations, such as the Appalachian and Randolph Mountain clubs.

Because of their elevation, the White Mountains have a cooler climate and a more "northern" ecology than one would expect from their latitude. Snow remains in some of the mountain ravines even into June, and trees generally do not grow above 4,500 feet. The higher peaks are notorious for damp misty weather, which on the positive side contributes to the lush, almost rain-forest-like aspect to some slopes and makes you particularly cherish a great summer day when there are extensive views.

A major geographic feature is the north-to-south-running valleys (called notches) that separate the major mountain ranges. From west to east, these are Franconia Notch, Zealand Notch, Crawford Notch, Pinkham Notch, and Evans Notch. All except Zealand are traversed by roads.

Geology

Where did the White Mountains come from? The story is one of enormous collisions and rifts of ancient continents drifting across the earth. Eons ago there was a sea here instead of mountains. About 400 million years ago, the thick layers of sands and muds at the bottom of this sea were squeezed between two colliding continents. Under this immense pressure, these layers hardened to form the schists, gneisses, and quartzites of the Presidential Range and then were uplifted. A second major geologic event occurred 230–180 million years ago when the granite that is the bedrock of much of the rest of the White Mountains solidified from molten rock deep within the earth as ancient continents split apart. Subsequent uplift and erosion of layers of softer overlying rocks brought the granite to the surface. Volcanic eruptions at that same time created additional rocks.

The rocks along the trails in the White Mountains are almost all granites or schists. Both have a salt-and-pepper appearance because they are comprised of different-colored minerals. Granites are composed primarily of crystals of feldspar (whitish or pink) and quartz (translucent white or gray). Usually there are smaller amounts of mica flakes (biotite if brown or black, muscovite if white or silvery) and hornblende (black). Schists were originally formed from sand and mud that accumulated under the sea before the mountains rose. The mineral crystals in schist are smaller than those in granite.

Gleaming white quartzes and glossy mica flakes are evident along just about any trail. Rock hounds will especially enjoy a visit to one of the abandoned mines, such as on Lord Hill or on North Sugarloaf. At these mines you can find large crystals of mica and feldspar, and if you look hard enough, topaz, garnets, beryl, smoky quartz, and even amethysts.

When hiking through White Mountain forests, you will undoubtedly come upon some monstrous boulders. Jumbles of boulders at the base of mountains, such as on the Ethan Pond Trail at Whitewall Cliff or on the Boulder Loop Trail, probably tumbled down during landslides. Isolated boulders may be glacial "erratics," carried to their destination by glaciers and left behind when the glacier melted. You'll find large glacial erratics at the Flume, the Trestle Trail, "The Boulder" near the Cascade Path in Waterville Valley, and Glen Boulder near Pinkham Notch.

Many of the hikes take you past huge outcroppings of exposed bedrock. Famous profiles such as the Old Man of the Mountain and the Elephant Head are outcrops of bedrock visible from highways.

On most outcroppings of bedrock, you can find narrow bands of white or black rocks called dikes crisscrossing the grayer granite. Dikes were formed when molten rock, heated by forces deep within the earth, flowed into cracks in the granite and then cooled. Pegmatite dikes are typically white and contain relatively large crystals of feldspars and sometimes other minerals. Basalt dikes are black and do not appear to have any crystalline structure at all. In a basalt dike, the magma (molten rock) flowed near the surface of the earth and cooled rapidly, not allowing time for crystal formation. Narrow, steep-sided gorges called flumes form where flowing water has eroded away the softer dike and left the relatively harder granite walls.

The erosive action of glaciers had a profound effect on the White Mountain landscape. Mountain glaciers high up on the sides of peaks carved the famous, bowl-shaped ravines (called cirques) in the Presidential Range. These include Tuckerman, Huntington, and King ravines and the Great Gulf. Mountain glaciers also carved the sharp, narrow ridge of the Franconia Range.

The continental glaciers that covered much of North America during the last Ice Age had an even more widespread impact than the mountain glaciers. Four separate advances and retreats of glaciers occurred between 1 million and 10,000 years ago. The last glacier even covered Mount Washington with several thousand feet of ice. Its erosive action smoothed out the summits of the Presidentials and carved out U-shaped valleys such as Crawford and Zealand notches. Pine Mountain is a good place to see scratches in the bedrock etched by stones dragged along by the movement of ice.

Forests and Plants

The White Mountains are densely forested, a fact many easterners may not appreciate unless they have spent time in the Sierra Nevada or other western ranges. Many walks described in this book pass through two different types of forest: the northern hardwoods at lower elevations and the boreal forest higher up.

Northern hardwoods forests are dominated by three broad-leafed trees: sugar maple, American beech, and yellow birch. Canadian hemlock, a needle-bearing tree, is very abundant along streams in shady gorges. Hobblebush and striped maples are common in the understory. Northern hardwoods cover a wide band of the northern United States and southern Canada from Maine through Minnesota. This forest glows with beautiful colors in autumn, a great, bug-free time to hike.

As you ascend above 2,000 feet, you will notice an increasing number of conifers—cone-bearing trees with needle leaves. The two most common species are red spruce and balsam fir. Spruce and fir, along with pines, are often called evergreens because they keep their needles year-round; however, conifer is a better term because some broad-leafed shrubs, such as rhododendrons, are also "evergreen."

Above 2,500 to 3,000 feet, a dark forest of conifers, the **boreal forest,** completely replaces the northern hardwoods. Boreas, the Greek god of the north wind, was portrayed in mythology as blowing a cold wind across the land, and indeed the boreal forest occurs in colder places such as the middle latitudes of Canada and Russia. An ascent of several thousand feet in the White Mountains is ecologically equivalent to driving several hundred miles north of Montreal or Toronto. Thus, the summit of Mount Washington, the highest point in the White Mountains at 6,288 feet, is roughly equivalent to the environment of northern Labrador.

The boreal forest, also called the spruce-fir forest, is a fantasyland of dense Christmas trees with a soft, dark, mossy understory. Red spruce tends to be more abundant in the lower part of the boreal forest (below 3,500 feet), while balsam fir predominates higher up. Scattered throughout the forest, particularly in clearings, are a few broad-leafed trees and shrubs such as paper birch and mountain ash. The upper part of the boreal forest grades into a realm of dwarf trees and scrub near tree line.

Humans have had a major impact on the character of White Mountain forests. Red spruce at lower elevations was heavily logged in the late nineteenth and early twentieth centuries. Since then, northern hardwoods forests have grown up in many places spruce once dominated.

Fire has been the other major human impact. The most famous fires occurred during the logging era in the Zealand and Wild River valleys, but very few areas were not touched by fires at one time or other. Many of the lower-elevation summits below 4,000 feet are now "bald" because the forest cover was burned off. (The true alpine zone, where weather conditions are too harsh to support the growth of trees, begins between 4,200 and 4,800 feet in the White Mountains. The Alpine Garden Trail is the only hike in this book that takes you into that realm.)

On summits trees are often contorted into odd shapes. This is the result of wind exposure. "Flag," or "banner" trees, with branches on one side only, occur when the combination of ice and wind kills the branches that attempt to grow into the prevailing winds, which are generally from the west or northwest. The surviving branches point away from the wind, just like a flag rippling in a stiff breeze.

Common trees

Identifying different types of trees can seem intimidating at first but there is a logical way to proceed. Here are some simple steps that will help you narrow down the possibilities. These steps are also helpful for shrubs and wildflowers. Encourage the kids to get involved, too, because it really is like solving a puzzle.

1. Determine if the tree has needles or broad leaves. This will distinguish the two main groups of trees, conifers and the broad-leafed deciduous trees.

2. Examine the shape of the leaves. Do the leaves have lobes like maples and oaks? Are they rounded at the base like paper birch or heart shaped at the base like yellow birch, or do they

taper at both ends like beech? Are the edges of the leaves distinctly toothed like beech or smooth like a rhododendron?

3. Closely examine the needles of conifers. If the needles are relatively short (less than 1 1/2 inches) and are attached singly to a branch then it is a spruce, balsam fir, or hemlock. If the needles are longer and attached to branches in clusters of two, three, or five, then it is one of the pines. If the needles are in bunches of twenty or so, then it is a larch. If the needles are tiny scales along the branches, it is a juniper or white cedar.

4. The bark on some trees is a good key to identification. The white, peeling bark of paper birch and the smooth gray bark of beech are two examples.

5. Check the descriptions and illustrations of the common species in the next section and in selected hikes. If a tree or leaf does not fit any of the descriptions, refer to one of the comprehensive field guides listed in the bibliography.

Sugar maple is one of the major trees of the northern hardwoods forest. Its leaves have three or five lobes, somewhat like the palm of a hand, and are attached to branches in pairs (opposite-leaves). Maple seeds are winged "keys" that delight children as they spin like little helicopters to the ground. If you are interested in distinguishing sugar maples from other maples, see page 311.

Striped maple (moosewood) is common in the understory of the northern hardwood forest, although it can occasionally grow up to be a tree. Leaves are often quite large and have three lobes that end in narrow points (resembling a goose's foot, hence its name, goosefoot maple). Branches and young stems are distinctly marked with beautiful green and white stripes.

American beech has distinct, smooth gray bark. The combination of smooth bark and long, pointed buds makes this an easy tree to identify, even in winter. Leaves are tapered at both ends and are toothed along the edges, with prominent parallel veins running to each tooth.

Yellow birch has yellowish brown or gray bark lined with distinct horizontal pores called lenticels. The bark peels in horizontal layers. Leaves are heart shaped at the base and serrated along the edges. Small twigs taste like wintergreen when chewed for a while.

Paper birch has unmistakable white bark that peels into horizontal strips. Please resist the temptation to peel the bark, since the scar may never heal. Leaves are toothed and rounded at the base. Paper birch is often the first tree species to colonize an area clear-cut by loggers.

Canadian hemlock is a sprawling conifer of cool ravines and stream-sides at lower elevations. It has short, half-inch needles with two white lines underneath. The needles are flat, a trait they share with bal-sam fir. Hemlocks produce small cones at the tips of branches.

Balsam fir is one of the two major trees of the boreal forest. Its wonderful balsam fragrance will remind you of Christmas. Like hemlock, the needles of balsam fir are flat, have two whitish lines underneath, and occur individually on branches. Balsam fir needles are longer (up to 1 1/2 inches) than hemlock and are fragrant when crushed. It is the only conifer with cones that sit upright on branches. The trunk is covered with  balsam blisters that if popped are sure to leave a sticky, sweet resin on hands and clothes. Dwarfed balsam firs are a major component of the scrub forest that occurs near tree line.

Red spruce is the other major tree of the boreal forest. Its 3/4- to 1 1/2-inch needles are attached singly to branches and are square in cross section. If you can roll a needle between your thumb and forefinger, it is a red spruce. If you can't (because the needles are flat), it is a hemlock or balsam fir. Spruce needles are sharp to the touch, so remember that to **spruce up** is to look **sharp.**

White pine has needles in bunches of five. The three-to-five-inch needles are soft and flexible so they won't "prickle" you. White pines can grow up to 150 feet tall, making it one of the largest trees in the White Mountains. It's a great tree to snooze under, since its soft needles make a comfy bed on the forest floor.

Larch, also called tamarack, is a tree of open boggy areas. It is less widespread than the other trees in this list, but it is a personal favorite. Larch is a beautiful, distinctive conifer, with lacy, curved branches that give it an oriental look. The one-inch needles grow in clusters of ten to thirty. The larch is unique among conifers in that it drops its needles

in the fall, after they turn a beautiful bright yellow. Once again this illustrates the point that "conifer" is a better term than "evergreen" for this group of trees. Look for larch on Blueberry Mountain or in the wetlands along the Kancamagus Highway near the Passaconaway Campground.

Common shrubs

Blueberries are probably everyone's favorite White Mountain shrub. They are very common on open, low summits and ledges where they are often less than a foot high. During July and August, the tasty berries are a great focal point for several hikes described in this book. Delicate white clusters of small bell-shaped flowers in May and June precede the berries. There are several different kinds of blueberries here. Low-bush blueberry, the most common species, has leaves that are edged with tiny teeth (use hand lens if you have one). Leaves of sour top blueberry lack toothed edges and are somewhat hairy underneath.

Hobblebush is the most abundant shrub in the forest understory of most hikes. It is easy to identify. Rounded, paired leaves with toothed edges and heart-shaped bases run along straggling stems. The thin, often horizontal stems form impenetrable tangles in the forest, giving rise to the name hobblebush and other names: tangle-legs and witch-hobble. Hobblebush produces flat-topped white clusters of flowers in May and clusters of inedible red berries during the summer.

Raspberries and blackberries may be as delicious as blueberries, but picking them can be a scratchy affair. These plants grow as thin, arching "canes" covered with thorns and prickles. White flowers appear in June and the fruits in July and August. Raspberries and blackberries are colonizers of forest clearings, roadsides, and recently logged areas.

Labrador tea is a small (one-to-two-foot) shrub of bogs and boggy shorelines of ponds. Its dark green, leathery leaves are rolled underneath at the edges and remain on the plant all year. Turn the leaves upside down for a surprise; the bottoms of the leaves are covered with dense rusty hairs (sometimes white on new leaves). In June, Labrador tea produces spherical clusters of white flowers at the tips of branches.

Wildflowers

Like much of New England, the White Mountains abound with wildflowers. The peak time for seeing the greatest variety of native woodland wildflowers in the mountains is in May and early June. This great floral display also coincides perfectly with blackfly season, a time when even hardened natives of New Hampshire avoid journeying in the woods. As a result, most people miss the best wildflower time.

Why does this springtime schedule of woodland wildflowers coincide so poorly with that of human visitors? Many wildflowers produce new leaves and flowers before the tree leaves come out and block the sunlight. Once they are under the dark canopy of the forest, some wildflowers, such as trout lilies, completely shrivel up.

Do not despair, however, if you cannot get to the White Mountains before July 4th or if you really can't stand the thought of blackflies. There are some pretty summer wildflowers, both in the woods and fields and on open summits. Also, some of the spring wildflowers produce showy berries in midsummer. And remember that flowers bloom later in the season at higher elevations, so you just might catch that last goldthread in bloom if you are willing to hike up.

If you are interested in identifying wildflowers, don't forget to take note of the habitat in which they grow. Some plants are characteristic of wetlands, others occur only in the northern hardwoods forest, and still others are partial to the mossy understory of the boreal forest. The flowers of fields and roadsides grow well in direct sunlight and do poorly in the partial shade of woodlands.

Here's a brief description of some wildflowers you are most likely to encounter on just about any hike in the appropriate habitat and season. Additional flowers are mentioned in the trail descriptions.

Spring wildflowers

Clintonia is a lily with large, shiny, smooth-edged leaves that hug the ground. A single flowering stalk produces several yellowish green flowers with six "petals" in late May through June. Summer visitors are more likely to see the glossy blue-black berries that give rise to its other name, bluebead lily. Do not eat the berry. Clintonia is common in the forest understory at both low and high elevations.

Painted trillium is one of the grandest of the White Mountain woodland wildflowers. It is unmistakable, containing a whorl of three leaves on a one-foot stem. The stem is topped with a single white three-petaled flower with a purple center. In summer, the flower is replaced by a large, single red berry.

The petals of **red trillium** are completely wine red. If you take a whiff of red trillium, you will smell why it is also called stinking benjamin. Its foul odor attracts flies as pollinators.

Canada mayflower, a small plant, is abundant in many woodlands at both low and high elevations. It has two or three smooth-edged, heart-shaped leaves. Its white, fuzzy spike of small flowers develop first into a white-and-red speckled berry and then into a red berry by late summer.

Pink lady's slipper is another eye-catching flower. Its single flowering stem arises from two large, wide, smooth-edged leaves. You might mistake its leaves for those of clintonia but for the distinct parallel veins running lengthwise. The hanging flower is shaped like a shoe or moccasin. In the White Mountains, the flower of the pink lady's slipper is almost as likely to be white as pink.

Goldthread is a small flower of shady, mossy woods. For most of the year, it is recognizable by its three small rounded leaflets, each with scalloped edges. In spring, a single, delicate, white flower with five to seven petals arises from a separate stem. Goldthread is named for the bright yellow underground stem that connects different individual plants. Before the advent of modern medicines, goldthread was used to relieve the pain of toothache and to combat dyspepsia (what our great-grandparents called indigestion) and "the drinking habit."

Starflower is an easy one for kids to guess since its delicate white flowers really do resemble stars. Typically, two white "stars" with six to eight petals are on top of a whorl of five to seven narrow, pointed leaves on a four-to-eight-inch stem.

Wild strawberries grow along roadsides and power line rights-of-way and in sunny clearings. Their three leaflets with sharply toothed edges form dense colonies. Flowers have five white petals surrounding numerous yellow stamens. The tiny berries, ripe around July 4th, are much more delicious than their larger manufactured, cultivated relatives.

Alpine wildflowers have always been a key enticement for climbing to higher elevations in the White Mountains. There are a number of showy species that bloom in early through mid-June. See the description in the Alpine Garden Trail (pages 273–276).

Summer wildflowers

Bunchberries are cheery white wildflowers that usually occur in large colonies on the forest floor. The flower is also called Canada dogwood. As with the flowering dogwood tree, the four white "petals" of bunchberries are not true petals but are modified leaves that surround a cluster of tiny green flowers. Bunchberries produce a whorl of four or six smooth-edged leaves. Six-leafed plants almost always produce flowers and four-leafed plants almost never do. A good game to play when they are in bloom is to see if you can find any exceptions to this six/four rule. Bunchberries bloom in June at low elevations and early July at higher elevations.

Mountain wood sorrel, another wildflower of the forest floor, will remind you of a shamrock. Its three leaflets, notched at the apex, are a common sight in cool woods. Despite the resemblance, wood sorrels are unrelated to clovers. Mountain wood sorrel has attractive, delicate white flowers with five petals inscribed with thin pink lines and (usually) a pink circle surrounding the center. They bloom in late June through August.

Twinflower is a small plant with rounded, paired leaves on a stem that trails along the ground. The plant

18   Natural History

is named for the two pink flowers that bloom from a single stem in late June and early July. This small, delicate flower was a favorite of Carolus Linnaeus, the Swedish biologist who devised the system of using two Latin words, the genus and species names, to denote each type of organism on earth. Twinflower was given the Latin name *Linnaea borealis* in honor of Linnaeus, who was often pictured holding this plant.

Indian pipes occur in isolated small groups in the forest. They are odd-looking, easily mistaken for a fungus because of their ghostly white appearance and lack of green leaves. Droopy, dull white flowers are produced on top of six-to-eight-inch stems. Indian pipes get all their nutrition from organic matter on the forest floor and therefore have no need for green leaves.

Bluets are small plants, less than three inches high, that seem to reflect the color of the sky. Individual flowers have four light blue petals surrounding a yellow center. They are less than half an inch in diameter but grow in dense colonies that can be quite showy. Bluets sometimes occur in sunny areas along trails but are more likely to be found along roadsides and fields.

Sharp-leafed aster is a very common flower in the northern hardwoods forest in mid-August through September. The leaves are tapered at both ends, coming to a long point at the tip. The plant is also called whorled wood aster because the coarsely toothed leaves appear to be whorled around the stem. Flower heads are daisylike, consisting of white (occasionally light purple) rays and a brown center. Blue asters you may encounter in the forests in late summer include **heart-leafed aster** and **large-leafed aster.** Both have heart-shaped leaves, but those of the latter are especially wide.

Goldenrods are showy late summer flowers of fields, roadsides, and occasionally sunny spots in forests. Distinguishing the many species is something even professional botanists find challenging, so just enjoy the bright yellow color they add to the landscape in August and September.

Turtleheads are tall plants (two to three feet) common around the edges of wetlands. Just about every swale crossed by a bog bridge at low elevation in August or September has at least a few stems. White, oddly shaped flowers, named for their resemblance to the head of a tortoise, are in clusters. Paired, toothed leaves attach to the stem opposite each other.

Orange hawkweed looks like a small orange dandelion. It is not native to North America but nonetheless provides a striking splash of orange color along roadsides and in cultivated areas, such as ski trails and around AMC huts. It is also called devil's paintbrush. **King devil** is a closely related yellow hawkweed that often grows in the same places as orange hawkweed.

Ferns, club mosses, and mosses

Ferns have attractive, feathery leaves called fronds that are divided into leaflets called pinnae. Most pinnae are further subdivided into pinnules. Spores used for reproduction occur in clusters that are fun to examine with a hand lens. A number of different species are abundant in the damp forests of the White Mountains:

Long beech fern is very common in the woods and on ledges around waterfalls. It is roughly triangular in shape with its two lowest pinnae pointing downward.

Rock fern, also called Virginia polypody, grows right on rocks wherever enough soil has accumulated. It is a small (one foot) evergreen fern whose fronds are only divided once. Look at the underside of a frond to see the round spore clusters.

Interrupted fern is a large (three-to-four-foot) fern. It gets its name from the brown, spore-containing section of fertile fronds, which occurs between (and therefore interrupts) the green pinnae along the stem. This fern grows in wet areas, often in clearings and along roadsides. A similar species, **cinnamon fern,** has dense tufts of rusty hairs where the pinnae joins the stem.

Hay-scented fern is a very lacy, medium-sized fern that grows in dense colonies in small clearings, such as those created by falling trees. They give off a sweet smell of freshly mown grass in late September and October when the fronds have dried out.

Bracken fern is a robust fern that has a triangular frond divided into three parts. Unlike most ferns, it grows in sunny, weedy locales, such as along roadsides.

A number of types of **wood ferns** are common on the forest floor. These have finely cut fronds and brown scales along the stem.

Club mosses are not really mosses but plants whose ancestors were the size of trees in the time of the dinosaurs. Modern club mosses are usually less than eight inches tall. They grow on the forest floor in colonies that can be quite large and conspicuous. **Ground pine** looks like a tiny six-inch tree. It is used as a Christmas decoration because it resembles a conifer. Others, such as the very common **shiny club moss,** have upright or horizontal unbranched or occasionally branched stems covered by small, needlelike leaves. Most species have conelike structures on top of stalks for reproduction.

Mosses are small, primitive plants that provide a beautiful cover of greenery in the damp forests. In the boreal forest, they cover rocks, logs, and old stumps, often being the only understory vegetation.

Haircap moss is one of the most common
woodland mosses. Its upright branches are
covered with small, needlelike leaves. This
moss gets its name from the hairy cap
that covers the spore-containing capsules. The capsules, located on stalks on
top of branches, are often quite obvious
even to the casual observer. The spores
are shot out of the capsule as it dries.

Piggyback moss, also called
fern moss, is very feathery
and fernlike. Smaller plants
grow by "piggybacking" on
top of larger ones.

Sphagnum moss, or peat moss, is the most economical-
ly important moss. It covers bogs with green
or red colors depending on the
particular species. Sphagnum
mosses have a tremendous
capacity to hold water, which
is why they are so useful as a
soil conditioner.

Fungi

The odd shapes and occasional bright colors of fungi
are something children are sure to notice. Fungi are like
icebergs—what you see is only a small part of the
whole. The visible, aboveground portion, such as a
mushroom, is the reproductive structure. Below
ground, myriad fungal filaments break down dead

plant matter, helping to create soil. Without these decomposers, all the trails in the White Mountains would be knee-deep in dead leaves and logs. Other types of fungi penetrate plant roots, where they aid the plants in the essential process of taking up nutrients from the soil.

Mushrooms are the most well known of the fungi. They have a fleshy, umbrella-shaped cap and may have gills on the underside that radiate around a central axis, like myriad spokes of the umbrella. Typically, a mushroom first appears as a "button" on the ground. As the mushroom develops, the button grows upward on a stalk and expands. Eventually, the mature, open mushroom releases its spores from the gills.

The best time to find a variety of mushrooms in the White Mountains is in late summer. Russulas are among the most common. They have a stout stem and a broad, brightly colored cap that may be red, yellow, or white and six inches across. Mycenas are much smaller and delicate, with a conical grayish brown cap on a thin stem. They tend to grow in clumps. Amanitas are intermediate in size between russulas and mycenas. They are usually white, although some have colored caps or turn brown with age. The base of the stem is enclosed with a cup (you may have to dig through leaf litter to see it) that may be quite ragged at the end of summer. Virtually all amanitas are deadly poisonous.

Mushrooms can be dangerous. They are a challenge to identify, often changing shape as they develop. *Do not pick or eat wild mushrooms.* Leave that to the experts.

Bracket fungi form massive horizontal, dull white lumps on dead trees and fallen logs. Their bottom surfaces are covered with small pores rather than gills.

Puffballs look like balls made out of brown paper. The ball contains billions of spores. They are fun to toss around when they reach maturity because the spores come out in a brown dusty cloud.

Witch's butter is a bright yellow-orange jellylike fungus that grows on decomposing logs.

Coral fungus looks like someone dropped a piece of coral on the forest floor. They have upright, fingerlike bodies that are often branched.

Lichens are fungi that have trapped cells of an algae within their bodies. The tiny algal cells produce food for the organism, and the fungus provides the algae with some nutrients and with protection from the environment. Lichens can live in harsh places that no other organisms can tolerate, such as the bare rocks above tree line, because they provide for their own nutrition and have an amazing ability to resuscitate after being almost completely dried out. Lichens grow so slowly and live so long that individuals can be used to track the slow, frost-induced movement of rocks upon which they live.

Lichens are abundant on rocky ledges, summits, and drier forests of the White Mountains. They come in three general shapes: crusty, leafy, and bushy.

Map lichen creates pretty green and yellow splashes of color with a black background on boulders on open ledges and summits. These brightly colored lichens grow as flat crusts in patches that resemble the patterns of rivers, oceans, and islands on a map (thus the scientific name for map lichen, *Rhizocarpon geographicum*). Because it is so flush on the rocks, it appears to be part of the rock itself, rather than an independent, living organism.

Rock tripe is a leafy lichen that is abundant on boulders in the forest. It looks like overlapping pieces of black or dark brown rubber, each one to two inches across and irregular in shape. Each piece is attached to the rock by a central stalk.

Reindeer lichen is bushy, with many pale yellow-green entangled branches arising from individual stalks. It grows on open, scrubby ledges, often in large patches that look so neat and well manicured that you might think that a gardener deliberately planted them there. Farther north, these lichen are consumed by caribou and reindeer.

British soldier lichen is named for the bright red tips located on top of thin, upright, pale green stalks. Each stalk arises from a leafy mass covering a rock or log. The red balls are the reproductive structures.

Animals

Insects, spiders, and related invertebrates

Insects and spiders often catch a child's attention, whether it is a colorful damselfly darting over a pond or a brown bug ambling across a trail. When your child stops to follow the path of an insect, make sure you take the time to stop and enjoy this fascinating group of animals.

There might be many admirers of the insect clan were it not for the two most notorious insects of the White Mountains, blackflies and mosquitoes. Knowing something about their lives won't make their bites any less annoying, but they do have an interesting story. Both lay eggs in or near water and have aquatic larval stages. **Blackfly** larvae attach their hind ends to rocks in flowing waters and feed by filtering small organisms from the water. Sometimes the larvae are so dense, hanging on in the swift current, that they darken the rocks over which a riffle or cascade flows. After they pupate into adults and mate, female blackflies search for a blood meal to insure the optimum development of their eggs.

Blackfly season runs from early May through mid-June, a time when only the brave or the foolish dare go into the woods without a liberal dousing of repellent or long sleeves and a head net. Generally, open summits are good places to escape from blackflies but only if there is a breeze. Blackflies are less likely to be out on damp, cool days but unfortunately, so are we.

Just when the blackflies are tailing off, **mosquitoes** pick up the slack. Mosquito breeding areas are typically stagnant, isolated pools of water. These could be temporary pools of water created in small depressions in the woods, permanent shallow swamps, or even water that has collected in tree holes. Mosquitoes can be a real annoyance along swampy, lowland sections of trails in the White Mountains but aren't as bad at higher elevations.

If you can get beyond blackflies and mosquitoes, you will find many attractive insects in the White Mountains. **Butterflies** are high on everyone's list. Tiger swallowtails are certain to catch your eye. They are yellow with black stripes and two "tails," one projecting from each hind wing. They are sometimes called flying flowers, a tribute to their lovely colors and perhaps also their affinity for feeding on nectar. Boldly patterned mourning cloaks, yellow with a black border to the hind wings, are fun to watch as they dart from flower to flower.

Dragonflies and **damselflies** are common around the edges of ponds. They are large and are often colored with iridescent blues and greens, particularly on their elongated abdomens. Both are strong fliers, moving straight ahead rapidly on out-

spread wings like little airplanes and
changing direction quite abruptly.
Dragonflies hold their wings horizontally when at rest whereas damselflies
bring their wings together over their bodies. Both
are predators on other insects, which they catch on the
wing. Both have long immature stages in water, where
they breathe through gills before becoming adults.

Water striders are fascinating to watch as they
stand on the surface of small pools and
skate about gracefully. Like all insects, they
have three pairs of legs, but only the back
two pairs are in contact with the water.
Tiny hairs on their "feet" enable them to
stand on the water without falling through.
The front legs are used to capture prey.

Large black **wolf spiders** are often observed scurrying
across rocks on open summits and ledges. These eight-
legged relatives of insects are predators on other insects.
Unlike most spiders, wolf spiders catch their prey without the use of a web. In the woods, the children will
enjoy searching for the more traditional spiderwebs and
examining what's been snared.

Fallen trees often harbor a variety of invertebrate life
that aids in decomposing the tree and recycling nutrients. **Ants** and **termites** create networks of chambers
under bark and scatter wildly when you uncover them.
Centipedes and **worms** of various sorts often take up
residence in decaying logs. Make sure you return any
logs you overturn to their original positions.

Reptiles and amphibians

The long, cold winters and damp summers of the White Mountains do not make an ideal climate for reptiles. These scaly, egg-laying vertebrates are more diverse in drier, warmer climates. There are no poisonous snakes in the White Mountains.

If you do find a snake, it is likely to be an **eastern garter snake.** It is brownish with three yellow stripes running along the entire length of its body. Although harmless, this snake won't like being picked up and may rub a very stinky fluid on you if you try (you can hardly blame it). Garter snakes feed on insects and small vertebrates.

Painted turtles are occasionally seen basking on rocks and logs in ponds at lower elevations. Their heads are marked with short yellow stripes and their shells are bordered with red. You may not get a good look at these markings without binoculars, because painted turtles are very wary and will plop into the water if you get too close.

Amphibians, which include frogs, toads, and salamanders, are much more tied to water than reptiles. They lay their eggs and develop as tadpoles with gills in water. Many species remain in or close to water as adults even though they breathe air.

The **American toad** is the most wide-ranging amphibian in the region. You'll often find them along trails in the forest far from water, as high up in elevation as tree line. They blend in very well with the dead leaves of the forest floor, and your first clue of them is a rustling sound as they move about. Their leathery, warty skin allows them to wander farther from dampness than most amphibians, although they return to water to lay their eggs.

Frogs of various kinds inhabit ponds and wetlands of the White Mountains. It is much easier to identify them by their sounds than to actually see them. In early spring, the birdlike chorus of **spring peepers** is a familiar sound. Since early spring is a relative term in the White Mountains, choruses of spring peepers can be heard in April at low elevations and in July in high elevation ponds. **Green frogs,** which sound like someone plucking a string of a banjo, are heard from in midsummer.

Salamanders are creatures of damp woods, mountain streams, and ponds. They generally remain hidden and are difficult to see unless you look under dead logs in the woods or flat stones by water. Despite their secretive habits, the abundance of some species makes them very important to the ecology of the soil and leaf litter of White Mountain forests.

The **red-backed salamander** is an extremely abundant woodland species that lives under dead logs and leaf litter. It is long and thin with dusky sides, a rusty red back, and small legs. If you examine the underside of fallen logs in damp woods, you will likely run into quite a few of them.

The only salamander bold enough to cross a trail out in the open is the **red eft.** This bright red salamander with greenish spots can afford to be more brazen than other salamanders because it is very toxic. The red color is a warning to predators to keep away. The red eft is actually a juvenile land stage of the red newt, an aquatic salamander that is sometimes kept as a pet. Red efts are sometimes quite abundant in the mountains, particularly after a summer rain.

Birds

Birds are more often heard than seen in the White Mountains. Nonetheless, a few will catch a child's attention. Also, young and old alike should stop periodically to enjoy the lovely songs of thrushes, winter wrens, white-throated sparrows, and other birds in June and July.

The handiwork of woodpeckers is evident in dead trees riddled with holes. A softball-sized hole in a tree is probably the doorway to the nest of the largest wood-pecker in the White Mountains, the **pileated woodpecker.** Pileated woodpeckers are the size of crows and are black and white with a flaming red crest. Look for large chips of wood under trees they have chiseled as they probe the bark for insects. The little **downy woodpecker** is the woodpecker you are most likely to actually see. It is about the size of a cardinal and is speckled with black and white. Downies have a lively chatter when they land.

Woodpeckers are essential to the ecology of the forest because their holes are used as homes by many different kinds of birds and mammals. Because of this, the Forest Service has a policy of protecting "wildlife trees."

Black-capped chickadees are a favorite of children, because they are perky, relatively tame, and are constantly saying their own name. You'll see them on most hikes.

Dark-eyed juncos are small, sparrowlike gray birds with white bellies and white outer tail feathers. They spend much of their time on summits and ledges.

Many different kinds of birdcalls and songs fill the forests and summits of the White Mountains, but a few are particularly characteristic and easy to identify:

White-throated sparrows sing a number of clear, sweet whistled notes varying in pitch followed by several wavy notes. The song sounds like "See old Sam Peabody, Peabody, Peabody" and is very easy to imitate.

Winter wrens have a loud, bubbly song that varies in pitch and is quite extensive. It makes a lot of noise for such a small bird.

The song of the **hermit thrush** is flutelike, languid, and ethereal. It starts with a single long note and then gradually modulates up the scale. Usually they sing from shrubs or lower branches of trees.

Ovenbirds belt out a raucous, booming two-syllable "t'cher t'cher, t'cher," which increases gradually in volume. These warblers sing from the ground.

Ravens make a hoarse "caw caw" or a series of piglike snorts as they fly overhead.

Mammals

In the White Mountains it is not easy to see large animals. Unlike western mountains, there are no large herds of antlered animals that prance across alpine meadows. Nonetheless, you will see ample signs of mammals in the holes in trees, scratch marks on bark, and the myriad beaver dams. Other than the ubiquitous red squirrels and chipmunks, consider the sighting of mammals as an extra treat.

Beavers are abundant here. Many of the trails take you by beaver ponds where you can see their wooden lodges, dams of sticks and mud, canals, and chewed trees. The animals themselves can sometimes be seen around dusk or dawn. Lost Pond in Pinkham Notch has been a good place to see beavers in recent years.

Red squirrels are the most frequently encountered mammal in the White Mountains. They scold hikers entering their realm with a rattling chatter usually delivered from a red spruce or balsam fir. They can be little thieves at campgrounds.

Chipmunks are also popular campground rodents. Chipmunks chirp like birds and scamper on the forest floor over fallen logs and into holes in the ground much more than squirrels.

Snowshoe hares look somewhat like cottontail rabbits with slightly larger ears and feet that appear a bit too big and gangly for their bodies. Their large feet act as snowshoes, helping them to stay afloat on deep snow in the winter. Snowshoe hares are also called varying hares because they turn white in winter and are brown in the summer.

Moose watching is becoming a popular pastime in the White Mountains as their population has increased. These largest members of the deer family can occasionally be seen along roadsides around dusk. They are not as timid as deer but may slowly amble off into the forest if too many cars stop. The wetlands along the Kancamagus Highway near the Passaconaway Historic Site are particularly good places to look for moose. In the fall rutting season, males can be ill-tempered, so give them a wide berth. Moose leave characteristic stripe marks on trees with their teeth.

These teeth marks were made by a moose.

Black bears are rarely encountered by hikers on the trails, but you may see the claw marks they leave on trees to mark their territories. Bears are omnivores, feeding on a variety of mammals, insects, fruits, and nuts. In recent years, one of the most reliable places to see bears is on the open ski trails of Cannon Mountain, where they browse on berries.

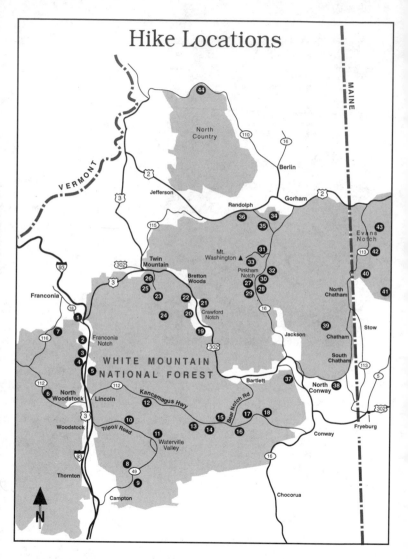

Hike Locations

Key to Hike Locations

Franconia Notch Region

THE FRANCONIA NOTCH REGION is the western-most part of the White Mountains. It includes the Kinsman Range, Franconia Notch, and the Franconia Range. The latter, with beautiful cone-shaped peaks, rises to greater than 5,000 feet, making it the second highest range in the White Mountains. Most of the hiking opportunities described for this region are in Franconia Notch and are easily accessible from I-93. There are numerous waterfalls, unique geological formations, and terrific scenery. The Franconia region is a popular tourist destination and includes such well-known features as the Old Man of the Mountain and the Flume.

Facilities

Supplies. The village of Franconia is at the north end of Franconia Notch off I-93, and Lincoln and North Woodstock are a few miles to the south. These have grocery stores, pharmacies, gasoline, restaurants, motels, and country inns. Those traveling to the Notch from the north on U.S. 3 may find it more convenient to stop for supplies in Twin Mountain, about twelve miles away.

The Flume and Lost River have visitor centers with tourist information, snack bars, rest rooms, and gift shops. The Flume Visitor Center also has a restaurant. At Profile Lake, there are rest rooms, a small interpretative nature center, and a snack bar that serves ice cream and other treats. Echo Lake has a small snack bar and rest rooms, and there are rest rooms at the Basin.

Camping. Lafayette Campground, in Franconia Notch State Park, has more than 200 sites as well as picnic tables for day use, rest rooms, water, a small camp store with limited groceries, information on trails, and ranger naturalist programs. A number of National Forest campgrounds are within a thirty-minute drive. The Zealand and Sugarloaf campgrounds (the latter providing limited facilities for people with disabilities) are near Twin Mountain. The Big Rock and Hancock campgrounds are at the western end of the Kancamagus Highway. The Wildwood Campground on N.H. 112 west of Lincoln is particularly close to Lost River. There are also a number of private campgrounds in the North Woodstock, Lincoln area.

Other. For fishing enthusiasts, Profile Lake is stocked with trout. Nonmotorized boats are permitted. The Pemigewasset River is also popular for fishing.

Bald Mountain and Artist's Bluff

- **1.5 miles, 300-foot elevation gain**
- **1–2 hours**
- **moderate for kids**

Bald Mountain and Artist's Bluff command magnificent views of Franconia Notch for relatively little effort. This is an ideal family outing because it is short, has a well-defined goal, and begins and ends near Echo Lake, a picturesque swimming beach.

This has been a popular family destination for decades. Before the age of Vibram soles and Gore-tex® parkas, hikers in long, frilly dresses, starched collars, and neckties walked up Bald Mountain and Artist's Bluff from the Profile House in Franconia Notch and other grand hotels that have long since disappeared.

This trail is very close to the scenic "attractions" in Franconia Notch State Park: the Old Man of the Mountain, Echo and Profile lakes, Cannon Mountain, the Basin, and Eagle Cliff. Despite the crowds, these natural wonders are worth a stop before or after your hike. Echo Lake has a snack bar, rest rooms, information, and picnic area.

Although the elevation of Bald Mountain and Artist's Bluff is only about 2,300 feet, these summits are exposed. Bring a windbreaker, particularly if you plan to have a picnic at either site.

What's in it for kids_____

- Great views for little effort.
- Open ledges to scramble out on.
- Some impressively large rocks alongside the trail.
- Your eventual destination (Artist's Bluff) is visible from below.
- Swimming at Echo Lake.
- Flag trees.

Getting There

The trail to Bald Mountain and Artist's Bluff forms a semicircle with both ends on N.H. 18 about a half-mile apart. From the south, take the Franconia Notch Highway, the extension of I-93 through Franconia Notch. As you approach the north end of the Notch, the cliff of Artist's Bluff looms ahead. Take the exit for N.H. 18, Echo Lake, Peabody Slope, park in the parking area for Echo Lake (fee charged), and walk up the road about 0.3 mile to the west trailhead. Alternatively, you can drive the 0.3 mile and park for free on the side of N.H. 18 by the parking lot for Peabody Slope Ski Area of Cannon Mountain. The west trailhead is at the far end of the parking lot. The east trailhead is very near the Echo Lake parking area.

From the Twin Mountain area, follow U.S. 3 south toward Franconia Notch, and pick up N.H. 18 at the entrance to the Notch where N.H. 3 and I-93 come together and then follow the above directions.

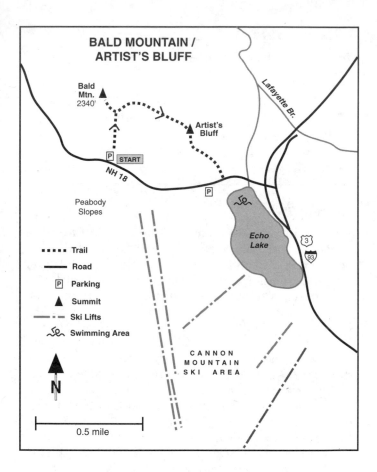

**BALD MOUNTAIN /
ARTIST'S BLUFF**

Bald
Mtn.
2340'

Artist's
Bluff

P START

NH 18

P

Lafayette Br.

Peabody
Slopes

Echo
Lake

3

93

•••• Trail
—— Road
P Parking
▲ Summit
—·—·— Ski Lifts
🏊 Swimming Area

N

0.5 mile

CANNON
MOUNTAIN
SKI AREA

The Trail

The trail, marked with red blazes, is fairly steep initially but relatively wide. After about ten minutes of steep climbing through northern hardwoods, you reach the trail junction with the spur trail that takes you to the summit of Bald Mountain. Follow this to the left and continue ascending, now through a forest of red spruce and balsam fir. A short distance farther, the vegetation becomes scrubby, and a little bit of scrambling on rocks is required before you reach the summit of Bald Mountain 0.3 mile from the trailhead.

After enjoying the view, retrace your steps back to the trail junction. If you have had enough for the day, take the right fork and descend to the parking area. For

The hike to Artist's Bluff provides a quick reward.

Artist's Bluff follow the left fork. The trail descends to a gravelly gully, passes a huge boulder, and then ascends to the junction with the short spur trail on the left that takes you to Artist's Bluff.

From Artist's Bluff the trail descends steeply, first on some conveniently placed rocky stairs. In about ten minutes it ends on N.H. 18, a short walk to your car across the road at Echo Lake.

Highlights

The views are not only breathtaking, but they also reveal something about the **geological history** of the Franconia Notch. From Bald Mountain the Peabody Slopes of the Cannon Mountain Ski Area are immediately across from you to the south. Farther to the east (your left) is the glacially carved valley that is Franconia Notch. From Artist's Bluff, Echo Lake is immediately below, and you look directly down the Notch.

Try to imagine this area completely covered by ice thousands of feet thick as recently as 10,000 years ago. The glacier acted like a giant piece of sandpaper, grinding and smoothing the walls of the valley as it moved slowly through the region. North-south valleys in the White Mountains were particularly well scoured by the north-south movements of the continental ice sheet and so have characteristically broad bottoms and steep sides.

Mount Lafayette, at 5,260 feet the highest mountain of the Franconia Range, forms the eastern wall of Franconia Notch. You will immediately be struck with how "pointy" the summits of Mount Lafayette and other peaks of the Franconia Range are compared to the broad, smooth summits of the Presidential Range. This is because the tops of the Presidentials were flattened out by the massive continental glacier while, in contrast, the Franconia Ridge was scoured from the sides by mountain glaciers. The freezing and thawing of the ice literally plucked out chunks of rock from both sides of the Franconia Ridge, leaving behind a narrow ridge.

Another noteworthy feature of Mount Lafayette is the steep ravine formed in the side of the mountain by the rushing water of Lafayette Brook. This was formed in postglacial times. Eagle Cliff is the dramatically rugged shoulder of Mount Lafayette. Legend has it that golden eagles used to nest there, and in recent years peregrine falcons have taken up residence (very hard to see even with binoculars).

Looking east, you will see evidence of clear-cutting on Big Bickford and Scarface mountains. Beyond that is Mount Garfield, a picturesque cone-shaped peak.

The Notch is a great north-south divide between two completely different **drainage patterns**. Tell the children about drops of water falling as rain and the paths they take to reach the sea. Echo Lake below you has an outlet to the northwest that flows into the Gale River, which joins the Connecticut River and flows into Long Island Sound. Profile Lake is just a little south of Echo Lake, on the other side of an almost imperceptible rise in the land. A drop of water falling in Profile Lake flows south through the Pemigewasset River to the Merrimack River and eventually reaches the Atlantic Ocean at Newburyport, Massachusetts.

Watch for the **changes in the forest** as you hike up. Northern hardwoods, including some good-sized yellow birches, dominate at the beginning of the trail. Past the junction of the spur to Bald Mountain, you enter red spruce-balsam fir forest. The spruce and fir trees grow shorter as you ascend. At the summit the ledges are covered with stunted spruce and firs and shrubs such as mountain holly and blueberries. Note the three-toothed cinquefoils growing in cracks in the rocks where some soil collects. This and bunchberries cover the ledges with pretty white flowers in mid-June. At Artist's Bluff you will also find wild raisin and mountain alder.

Show your children the **"flag trees,"** with branches just on one side of the trunk. Let them guess how that happened. The answer lies in the prevailing winds that, in combination with ice, kill buds on that side of the trunk before they even have a chance to sprout. On Bald Mountain, most of the flag trees point east, indicating that the wind is usually from the west. Exceptions do occur, perhaps where the winds whip around the side of the mountain.

The **understory vegetation** is particularly lush between the two overlooks with abundant ferns, mosses, clintonia, club mosses, false Solomon's seal, mountain wood sorrel (particularly near the junction with the Bald Mountain spur), red and painted trillium, and pink lady's slippers (both pink and white-flowered varieties). Striped and red maples are common understory shrubs. Other plants to look for are bristly and wild sarsaparilla, goldenrods, rattlesnake root, wild oats, and Canada mayflower.

Echo Lake and Franconia Notch from Artist's Bluff.

If you are lucky, you may see one of the White Mountain's largest and most charismatic animals, at a distance so safe that you'll need binoculars. In recent years, **black bears,** often a mother bear with cubs, have taken to foraging on berries in the open ski trails high up on Cannon Mountain during daylight. This is about as good a chance as you'll have to see bears in the White Mountains, since they normally are secretive. The bears' presence along the ski trails shows that these trails are not without value to some wildlife.

A Hike to Lonesome Lake

- **3.2 miles round-trip, 900-foot elevation gain**
- **4 hours**
- **challenging for kids**

Lonesome Lake is a beautiful lake perched on a shoulder of the Kinsman Range on the west side of Franconia Notch. It is popular with families because it's relatively easy to reach and offers swimming and beautiful views. The AMC's Lonesome Lake Hut at the south end of the lake provides overnight accommodations and very hearty meals (reservations required). Day hikers can use the rest rooms and buy trail snacks, hot and cold drinks, trail maps, t-shirts, and other supplies. Soup is sometimes available midday.

This hut is especially popular among parents of young children because it requires a relatively short walk and is laid out so that families staying overnight can often have a room to themselves. An AMC naturalist may be there to present an evening program and to discuss your questions about the mountains. Day hikes starting from the hut include a short, self-guided nature trail or a longer network of trails that take you around the lake to Cannon Mountain or to other destinations.

The Lonesome Lake Trail is a short, somewhat steep climb. The Around Lonesome Lake Trail then takes you past the hut on a complete loop around the lake. Allow about one and a half hours to ascend to the hut, about an hour or so to stroll around the lake, and one hour to descend. The Cascade Brook Trail, part of the Appalachian Trail, offers a longer, more gradual ascent from Franconia Notch.

What's in it for kids

- Swimming in a shallow, clear lake with relatively warm water and great views.
- A chance to visit and maybe even stay overnight at an AMC hut.
- Lots of wooden bog bridges.
- Beaver dams.

Getting There

The Lonesome Lake Trail starts at the Lafayette Campground in Franconia Notch State Park. From the north, take the Franconia Notch Highway through the Notch, to the exit for the campground about 1.5 miles south of the Old Man of the Mountain. If you are coming from the south through Lincoln and North Woodstock, exit at the trailhead parking about 1.5 miles north of the Basin, then cross over to the west side through a foot tunnel.

The Trail

The trail begins at the picnic area at the campground's south parking lot on the west side of the highway. There is a large sign for the trail and yellow blazes to help you make your way past the picnic area, across the Pemigewasset River and through the campground without getting off track. After leaving the campground,

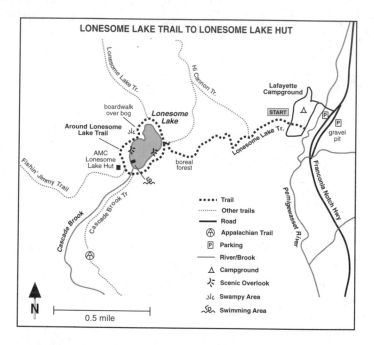

LONESOME LAKE TRAIL TO LONESOME LAKE HUT

Lonesome Lake Tr.

Hi Cannon Tr.

Lafayette
Campground

START

boardwalk
over bog

*Lonesome
Lake*

**Around Lonesome
Lake Trail**

P

gravel
pit

AMC
Lonesome
Lake Hut

Fishin' Jimmy Trail

boreal
forest

Lonesome Lake Tr.

Cascade Brook

Cascade Brook Tr.

Franconia Notch Hwy

Pemigewasset River

- - - - Trail
······· Other trails
——— Road
Ⓐ Appalachian Trail
Ⓟ Parking
——— River/Brook
△ Campground
⅄ Scenic Overlook
⌇ Swampy Area
～ Swimming Area

N

0.5 mile

the Lonesome Lake Trail follows an old bridle path once
used to reach a private camp on the lake. In ten minutes
(0.3 mile), make a sharp left turn and cross a wooden
plank bridge over a stream that tumbles down the
mountainside. At 0.4 mile, the Hi Cannon Trail exits right
toward the summit of Cannon Mountain. The Lonesome
Lake Trail then ascends moderately steeply via three
switchbacks for the next 0.8 mile, then descends slightly
through a pretty boreal forest before reaching the lake at
the junction with the Cascade Brook Trail (1.2 miles).

At this point, begin your loop around Lonesome Lake on the Around Lonesome Lake Trail. (This trail incorporates sections of the Cascade Brook, Fishin' Jimmy, and Lonesome Lake trails.) Since it's a loop, you can take it in either direction, but we recommend going clockwise. Turn left on the Cascade Brook Trail and follow the southeast shoreline of the lake toward Lonesome Lake Hut. From vantage points along the shore you can see North and South Kinsman mountains and the Cannonballs. At 1.4 miles, turn right on the Fishin' Jimmy Trail. In another 0.1 mile you pass the outlet of the lake and then the dock area of the Hut (1.6 miles) where the best swimming is. On a hot summer day, after sweating mightily on the way up, there will be nothing better than a swim.

At this point, you can visit the AMC hut by following the Fishin' Jimmy Trail to the left. Ask at the hut for information on the self-guided nature walk, which uses the next portion of the Around Lonesome Lake Trail.

The Around Lonesome Lake Trail continues clockwise along the western shore of the lake. The trail goes through an open boggy area on split rail bridges and planks and about 0.3 mile from the hut reaches the junction with the Lonesome Lake Trail. Turn right on the Lonesome Lake Trail to complete the loop in another 0.2 mile. From here you could either descend to your car at Lafayette Place on the Lonesome Lake Trail or walk back to the hut.

Parts of the Around Lonesome Lake Trail may be soggy, particularly in the spring. Even so, children will enjoy having to jump from plank to plank to keep their feet dry (or not).

Highlights

The highlight of this hike is **Lonesome Lake.** Other than a few stream crossings and some nice choruses of hermit thrushes and winter wrens, the ascent is not noteworthy. It runs through a dense northern hardwoods forest without any views until you reach the lake.

The fun begins at the height of land, where the trail levels out and you walk through a **beautiful boreal forest** with red spruce and balsam fir and a lush understory of mosses, goldthread, mountain wood sorrel, and clintonia. The terrain here is very hummocky—it looks like the kind of place where elves might pop out from behind the trees.

If the weather is cooperative, you should jump into the lake for a **swim,** but keep an eye on the kids since there are no lifeguards. The lake is about twenty acres big and averages three to six feet in depth with a maximum depth of twelve feet. Technically it's a tarn—a mountain pond scoured out of the mountainside by the glacier. This may be the best place in New England to get a beautiful view while practicing your backstroke. Across the Notch is Mount Lafayette and other peaks of the Franconia Range. Walker Ravine in Mount Lafayette appears as a deep V in the mountainside.

While sitting around the lake, you will likely see **dragonflies** hovering and darting above the water. Dragonflies are strong fliers and active predators on other insects around the lake. Dragonfly behavior is fun to watch. Although you might see dragonflies chasing prey, much of their activity is related to mating. Territorial males alight on favorite perches and chase intruding males away. Males and females mate on the wing and you may even see two dragonflies in such a "tandem flight." The female then deposits her eggs in the water by hovering above the water and touching it periodically with the tip of her abdomen.

You can fish for **brook trout** at Lonesome Lake. Contact the New Hampshire Fish and Game Department for the appropriate license.

Very tame **snowshoe hares** hang out around the dock and the hut. These hares change colors to match the season, brown in the summer and white in winter. This camouflages them although their tameness around the hut leaves the impression that they are not too worried about predators. The grassy areas around the hut provide them with forage during the summer. In winter they feed on twigs and bark.

Shrubs growing by the dock include sheep laurel, wild raisin (withe rod), sweet gale, and mountain ash. See if the kids can tell the difference between red spruce (square needles) and balsam fir (flat needles).

If you stay at the hut in June, you will have a chance to awaken to a **symphony of birdsongs.** These might include Swainson's thrush, winter wrens, and white-throated sparrows. Yellow-rumped warblers, chickadees, and dark-eyed juncos are also around.

Beavers have played a large part in creating the landscape around Lonesome Lake. Although they no longer inhabit the lake itself, their legacy remains in the extensive boggy wetlands created by their dams, particularly on the western and northwestern shore. You can still see the old dams, too. Beavers are now active downstream from the outlet and upstream of the northwestern shore.

The dock at Lonesome Lake.

The open wetlands created by the beavers on the west and northwestern shore support a number of **wetlands plants.** As the self-guided nature trail describes, the wooden planks protect your shoes from the dampness, while at the same time protecting the plants from your shoes. The most abundant shrubs in the wetland are sheep laurel, sweet gale, and leatherleaf. The pink flowers of sheep laurel, produced in early July, look like smaller versions of those of mountain laurel, a close relative. Crushed leaves of sweet gale smell as sweet as those of its close relative, the bayberry.

Ask your children to examine the **undersides of leaves** of several of the shrubs, with a hand lens if possible. Sweet gale leaves have tiny yellow resin dots. The undersides of the thick leaves of leatherleaf are covered by rusty scales. The best leaf "underside" to show them, however, is Labrador tea, a shrub with thick leathery leaves whose undersides are covered with dense reddish brown woolly hairs.

In the same area, look for **larches** between the plank trail and the lake. This relative of pines, spruces, and firs is partial to bogs. Unlike pines, which have needles in bunches of two to five, larches have needles in bunches of twenty or so, which give its branches a delicate, lacy appearance.

Challenge your children to see if they can find carnivorous **sundews** in the wetland. These are tiny bog plants that capture small insects using sticky hairs on the tips of spoon-shaped leaves. The insects are digested and provide nutrients to the plant. The low nutrient conditions of bog soils make them a haven for carnivorous plants, but it takes a sharp eye to find sundews.

On the northwest shore, near the junction with the Lonesome Lake Trail, there are many upturned trees whose intricate root systems are exposed to view. It reveals graphically how shallow the root systems are, due to the thinness of the soil. Here you will also find the large cabbagelike leaves of Indian poke and an extensive cover of sphagnum moss.

When you are looking for these various wetlands plants, you cannot help but notice your idyllic surroundings. There are a few rocks on the shoreline where you can sit and contemplate the lake and the view across Franconia Notch to Mount Lafayette with background music provided by thrushes and other birds. And you can top it off with a swim.

Pemi Trail

- **4 miles one-way, 500-foot elevation gain**
- **2–3 hours**
- **moderate for kids**

The Pemi Trail is a relatively level hike that runs along the Pemigewasset River through Franconia Notch. It divides roughly into two sections, from the Basin north to the Lafayette Campground, and from the Campground north to Profile Lake. The elevation gain from the Basin to Profile Lake is so gradual that it really does not make much difference which direction you hike. With two cars, you can spot one car at the end of the trail to avoid backtracking.

The combination of flowing water, dense forest, wildflowers, occasional views, and possible wildlife sightings makes for a very pleasant walk. Since you are in a dense "tunnel" of forest most of the time, this is a good trail for a hot summer day (and you can swim at Echo Lake after you finish). You do hear traffic noise for much of the walk, particularly from Lafayette Campground to Profile Lake, but the wonderful views of the cliffs and talus slope of Cannon Mountain make it worth it.

What's in it for kids _____

- Level walk along a stream with a number of wooden bridges.
- Chance to poke along the stream for aquatic life.

- Beaver dams.
- Great view of the cliffs of Cannon Mountain.

Getting There

This description assumes you are hiking from the Basin to Profile Lake. Park at the Basin parking lot on either side of I-93 and follow the signs to the Basin. The first sign for the Pemi Trail is a short distance beyond the Basin, near the trailhead to the Basin-Cascade Trail. There are a lot of little trails in the area, but you should have no trouble finding the Pemi Trail.

(To get to the trailhead at the Profile Lake end, exit the Franconia Notch Parkway at the exit for the Cannon Mountain Tramway and follow the signs to the viewing area for the Old Man of the Mountain. Find the trailhead by climbing up a set of stairs at a point where the road loops behind the parking lot. The first Pemi Trail sign is at the top of the stairs.)

The Trail

The trail is marked with blue blazes and parallels the Pemigewasset River, the Franconia Notch Highway, and a bike path through the Notch for its entire length. The trail is not too heavily used, so the path tends to be softer on feet than many White Mountain trails. At various points in the first section you walk on sandy soil of the river's floodplain.

After two miles (about an hour) you reach Lafayette Campground. The exact route of the trail is hard to follow within the campground, but if you walk along the

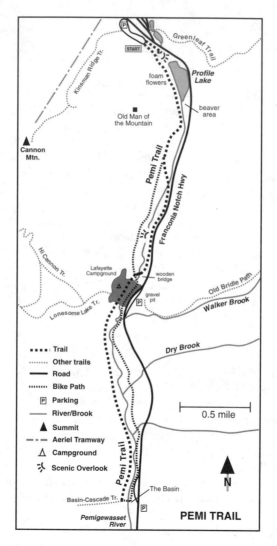

Legend

- **▪▪▪▪** Trail
- **⋯⋯** Other trails
- **▬▬▬** Road
- **▪▪▪▪▪** Bike Path
- **P** Parking
- **▬▬** River/Brook
- **▲** Summit
- **▬ ▪ ▬** Aeriel Tramway
- **△** Campground
- **⚹** Scenic Overlook

Map labels: START, Greenleaf Trail, Kinsman Ridge Tr., foam flowers, Profile Lake, Old Man of the Mountain, beaver area, Cannon Mtn., Pemi Trail, Franconia Notch Hwy, Hi Cannon Tr., Lafayette Campground, wooden bridge, Old Bridle Path, gravel pit, Walker Brook, Lonesome Lake Tr., Dry Brook, 0.5 mile, N, Pemi Trail, The Basin, Basin-Cascade Tr., Pemigewasset River, **PEMI TRAIL**

58   Franconia Notch Region

road closest to the river, you'll eventually pick up the blue trail blazes again. The campground is a convenient place to use rest rooms, have a lunch at the picnic grounds, refill your canteens, or end your walk if you've had enough. Visit the small camp store to pick up soda, snacks, and worms and crawlers for fishing before resuming the second half of the walk.

After departing the Lafayette Campground, the trail passes over the bike trail and enters a boggy area with lots of sphagnum moss. It traverses over the slowly moving water on wooden boards, then crosses to the east side of the Pemigewasset River on a wooden bridge. Soon after, a left fork of the trail takes you to a wonderful vista of the cliffs of Cannon Mountain.

Pass back to the west side of the river on another bridge. The trail joins up with the paved bike path for a short distance, becomes a dirt path again, and passes a series of beaver dams near the south end of Profile Lake. The trail then follows the west shore of Profile Lake with great views of Eagle Cliff and Mount Lafayette. At the north end of the lake, a right turn at a side trail takes you across a marshy area to the viewing area for the Old Man of the Mountain or you can continue straight for a more direct route to the parking lot.

Highlights

Because the hike is in a floodplain, this is a good place to teach children about **rivers.** The sand they see in the floodplain between the Basin and the Lafayette Campground may seem out of place in the mountains, but it reveals the handiwork of the river. When snow melts and heavy rains fall in the spring, rushing water erodes the sides of the mountains, carrying all kinds of soil particles into the river. The smaller particles of silt and clay are carried farther down the river, leaving the heavier sand behind. In the spring, the river typically overflows its channel, in some very wet years covering the entire floodplain. Evidence of this flooding is the sandy soil underneath your feet on the trail.

Between the campground and Profile Lake, the banks of the river are steep-sided with no obvious floodplain. This is an area where the gradient of the river is steeper and the rushing water is still eroding a channel through newly exposed bedrock.

The river is a mixture of pools and riffles with many downed trees that make natural bridges. This is ideal habitat for **brook trout,** a prized game fish of cold streams. Look for them in the deeper pools and under fallen logs. You may also see schools of minnows in shallow water along the shore. Little anglers may want to bring their fishing poles, but check with the park authorities about fishing regulations.

Fish that inhabit the Pemigewasset River feed on aquatic insects, such as mayfly larvae, that are abundant in the river. You and the kids can "fish" for these insects and other aquatic life along the river using a soup strainer. Try looking for salamanders under rocks along the edge of the river.

The trail has a particularly rewarding view of the Cannon Mountain cliff. Unlike the crowded lookouts on the highway, you will likely have this vista all to yourself—and the kids may appreciate this view even more for having hiked to a special place for it. The huge pile of broken rock, called talus, at the base of Cannon cliff is formed from rocks plucked from the cliff by the freezing and thawing action of water in cracks in the cliff.

The forest is northern hardwoods for much of the trail, and the understory is dominated by hobblebush. Look for a stand of large red spruce near the Basin. Hemlocks grow along the edge of the river.

If you hike in the spring, you'll see a good assortment of White Mountain **wildflowers** in bloom. This is a particularly good trail to find foamflower, a low plant with three lobed leaves and clusters of small, white

A brown sedge, common in damp spots along the Pemi Trail.

flowers with feathery stamens that give it a foamy appearance. Foamflowers tend to grow in colonies, so if you find one, you are likely to see quite a few. This species and another you might see on this trail, the early saxifrage, are both types of saxifrages. "Saxifrage" means rock breaker, which tells you what these plants do to survive in thin soils.

Chipmunks and **red squirrels** are the most obvious wildlife in the area. The **beavers** that made the dams near the outlet of Profile Lake are hard to see unless you are there at dawn or dusk and get lucky. You will also see a number of trees riddled with **woodpecker holes** and may even catch a glimpse of a crow-sized pileated woodpecker, a starling-sized downy woodpecker, or other species sized in-between working on a tree. These holes are home to many animals.

Point out to your children that the woodpeckers, beavers, and the river itself are all working to shape the landscape around Franconia Notch.

The Basin-Cascade Trail and the Basin

- **2.4 miles round-trip, 400-foot elevation gain**
- **1–2 hours**
- **easy at beginning and challenging at end for kids**

This trail should be on every waterfall-lover's list. It follows Cascade Brook in Franconia Notch State Park beginning at the Basin (an interesting destination in its own right). You then ascend gradually past Kinsman and Rocky Glen falls and a whole series of smaller waterfalls, rapids, and potholes with large flat, sunny rocks just right for family picnics.

This is really a three-tiered hike. The first section, which takes you a little beyond the Basin, is very easy and suitable for even the youngest child. The second section is moderate but should present no serious problems for children above five. The third is more challenging because the footing is rough. Hiking boots have caused severe erosion here, exposing tree roots and rocks in many places. Entering into this last part of the trail also requires that you cross over a narrow, rickety footbridge. Use your judgment and be careful, particularly in wet weather.

While you are in the area, save a few minutes to see the Basin, one of the largest, most impressive glacially carved potholes you will ever see. The Basin is wheelchair-accessible from the parking lots. There are rest rooms but no other facilities.

What's in it for kids _____

- Waterfalls and lots of running water.
- A bridge that is bound to terrorize parents.
- Many good rocks along the stream for picnics.
- The swirling waters of the Basin.
- A number of places to wade in the brook.

Getting There

Park at the parking lot for the Basin, a well-marked exit off the Franconia Notch Highway. If you approach from the south, the exit is about 4 miles north of the Lincoln/North Woodstock exit and 1.5 miles north of the Flume. After parking your car on the east side of the highway, follow the signs to the Basin via a walkway under the highway. If you are heading south through the Notch from the Franconia or Twin Mountain area, the exit for the Basin is about 1.5 miles south of the Lafayette Campground, and the parking area is on the west side of the highway.

Walk past the Basin itself following the Pemigewasset River downstream, cross over a bridge, make a right turn at the first fork, and pick up the signs for the Basin-Cascade Trail. There are lots of paths in the area, but you should have no trouble finding this one from the Basin.

Those who want to return south from the Basin after their hike need to drive north for three miles on

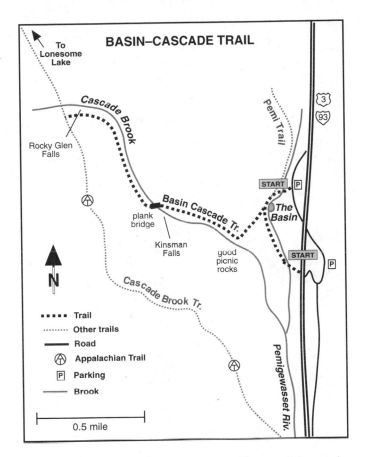

BASIN–CASCADE TRAIL

To Lonesome Lake

Cascade Brook

Rocky Glen Falls

Pemi Trail

3
93

START   P

The Basin

Basin Cascade Tr.

plank bridge

Kinsman Falls

good picnic rocks

START   P

Cascade Brook Tr.

N

Pemigewasset Riv.

▪▪▪▪▪ Trail
⋯⋯⋯ Other trails
▬▬▬ Road
Ⓐ Appalachian Trail
P Parking
— Brook

0.5 mile

Franconia Notch Highway to the Cannon Mountain Tramway exit to a turnaround, since there is no place to reverse direction at the Basin itself. Those returning north can reverse direction at the Flume exit.

The Trail

Almost immediately after departing the Basin, you come to a large flat slab of rock in the streambed of Cascade Brook. Unless water levels are unusually high, this is an excellent place for a picnic or snacks. Families with very young children may want to use this spot as their turnaround point, visiting the Basin on the way back. If you go on, you will find numerous other places along the trail where short side paths lead you to the stream. At 0.6 mile (about fifteen minutes past the Basin), a rough, unmarked side path leads down a slope to the base of Kinsman Falls. Shortly thereafter (0.7 mile), you

The Basin–Cascade Trail is a delightful walk along the water.

reach the rickety footbridge. This is another good spot to turn around if you find the bridge unnerving, especially since the trail beyond becomes somewhat rougher. At the time we crossed it, the bridge was made of single split logs with a railing for balance. If you do proceed, the trail passes through a beautiful small canyon just beyond the bridge with a pool deep enough for a swim. In about another 0.2 mile, you cross over a small bridge two logs wide and then cross a gentle tributary stream that runs into Cascade Brook. This is a pretty spot with lush mosses and small pools for young waders. In another fifteen minutes (0.5 mile above the footbridge), the trail passes Rocky Glen Falls then becomes more level. A small canyon is a convenient place to turn around. (The Basin–Cascade Trail ends just beyond at the Cascade Brook Trail.)

Highlights

The Basin Cascade Trail is an excellent place to show children the action of water on seemingly impenetrable rocks. The **Basin** is a pothole in a curve of the Pemigewasset River, about thirty feet in diameter and fifteen feet deep. It was scoured out and polished into a smooth, round surface by sand and small stones thrashing about in water rushing from snowmelt around the time the last continental glacier departed the region (within the past 25,000 years). Take a moment to read the sign describing how it was formed. (After his 1858 visit Thoreau wrote in his journal, "This pothole is perhaps the most remarkable of its kind in New England.")

Kinsman and Rocky Glen falls are two beautiful waterfalls that the whole family will enjoy. Just above Rocky Glen Falls, a **small rectangular canyon** was carved out by a tributary to Cascade Brook. It looks like someone deliberately created a box canyon, but in fact it's an entirely natural fracturing of the rock by the action of water.

Many **large flat rocks,** perfect for sunning, picnicking, or wading, are spread throughout the streambed. Some have great views of the Kinsman and Franconia ridges.

The **forest** along the trail changes from northern hardwoods to red spruce as you ascend. Hemlocks thrive along the brook, creating a cool, shady environment. There are some **huge white pines** too. The cooler atmosphere at the brook creates a "refrigerator effect," causing spring wildflowers, such as clintonia and Canada mayflower, to bloom several weeks later than in surrounding uplands. Right above Rocky Glen Falls, there is a particularly good display of bunchberries. Ask the kids to find a tree seemingly growing out of rock about five feet above the ground in the same area.

Chipmunks are particularly common along the Basin-Cascade Trail. Listen for the harsh, birdlike chirp of this children's favorite. You'll probably see a few as well, with their distinctive striped faces and backs and their habit of carrying their tail straight up when they dash about. Your children will certainly enjoy them, along with all the watery things along the Basin Cascades.

The Famous Flume
of Franconia Notch

- **2 mile loop, minimal elevation gain**
- **2 hours**
- **easy for all ages**

If you like the idea of strolling along rushing water on a boardwalk through an extremely narrow gorge bounded by straight, vertical sides, then you should not miss the Flume. The Flume is a popular tourist destination in Franconia Notch State Park and is a perfect half-day outing. Your children will be thrilled as they dash up and down stairs and across bridges. In addition to the 800-foot boardwalk through the Flume, the park has an easy loop trail that takes you past waterfalls, a giant pothole, huge boulders, and two covered bridges. You can walk all or only one section of the trail. You can even cut out some walking distance by hopping on a school bus. (You'd be surprised how enthusiastic the kids will be for a school bus when they're not in school!)

In addition to the walk, there is a large visitor center, a trout pool, and a self-guided nature trail at the Flume. There is a six-dollar charge for admission to the park for adults, three dollars for children six to twelve. The visitor center has a cafeteria, picnic tables, snack bar, gift shop, and rest rooms.

The Flume is well advertised, so expect crowds of tourists. But don't be discouraged. This is definitely a fun place for families.

What's in it for kids _____

- •Spectacular walk on a boardwalk through the Flume.
- • Rushing water everywhere and many waterfalls.
- • Two covered bridges.
- • Huge glacial boulders.

_____

Getting There

The parking area for the Flume is at Exit 1 of the Franconia Notch Highway, the extension of I-93 through Franconia Notch. The exit is very well marked and is about four miles north of the exit on I-93 for North Woodstock, Lincoln, N.H. 112, and the Kancamagus Highway.

You can start your hike right at the Flume visitor center or cover the first 0.7 of a mile on the school bus. If you take the bus, you will miss walking past a three-ton glacial erratic boulder, but you can see that on the way back.

The Roaring River Nature Trail begins near the far end of the southernmost parking area (the parking area to the left if you are standing at the visitor center).

The Trail

The State Park provides a short pamphlet that contains a map and a description of the major features of the Flume. It also has a pamphlet on the self-guided Roaring River Nature Trail.

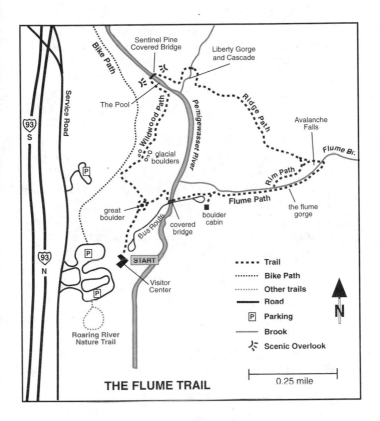

THE FLUME TRAIL

Map legend:

- ----- Trail
- ········· Bike Path
- ········· Other trails
- —— Road
- P Parking
- —— Brook
- ⅄ Scenic Overlook

0.25 mile

Map labels: Bike Path, Sentinel Pine Covered Bridge, Liberty Gorge and Cascade, The Pool, Wildwood Path, Pemigewasset River, Ridge Path, Avalanche Falls, Flume Br., 93 S, Service Road, glacial boulders, Rim Path, Flume Path, the flume gorge, great boulder, Bus Route, covered bridge, boulder cabin, 93 N, P, START, Visitor Center, Roaring River Nature Trail, N

The paths at the Flume are mostly hard-packed dirt and are wide enough to walk several people abreast. They are very well marked and patrolled by park staff. As a cautionary note, there are a number of overlooks with steep drop-offs so parents should keep an eye on younger children, especially those who like climbing on split rail fences.

Starting from the visitor center, you pass a huge glacial erratic after 200 yards. Follow the path through the Flume Covered Bridge, to the Boulder Cabin, where the bus leaves you off if you ride. The 0.3 mile from the Boulder Cabin to the Flume is a pleasant, bridge-sprinkled walk along Flume Brook. The walk through the Flume to Avalanche Falls is mostly on boardwalks, stairs, and more bridges. At this point, you can take a shorter loop back toward the visitor center on the Rim Trail or continue to the Pool on the Ridge Path (the Pool is as spectacular as the Flume). The Ridge Path leads to the Pool and the Sentinel Pine Covered Bridge over the Pemigewasset River in about 0.7 mile (mostly down-hill). From there it is 0.6 mile back to the visitor center, through a forest laced with boulders.

The Roaring River Nature Trail is an easy 0.3-mile, self-guided loop trail past ten marked stations. There is a gazebo at the midpoint in the walk.

Highlights

Why are the walls of the **Flume** so straight? The Flume was formed by erosion of a basalt dike within the granite. Two hundred million years ago the granite, which tends to crack in straight lines, fractured vertically at the Flume. Lava from deep within the earth then flowed into the fractures, forcing the granite apart and solidifying to form a seam of basalt from twelve to twenty feet wide. Eventually water began to flow over the granite and basalt, eroding the softer basalt and leaving the steep granite sides of the Flume. The narrowness of the gorge reflects the width of the original basalt dike. The straightness of the walls shows the fracture planes of the granite. In some places, you can still see remnants of the black basaltic rock.

From overlooks 130 feet above the **Pool** you look down on a giant pothole 150 feet wide and 30 to 40 feet deep within the Pemigewasset River. The Pool was formed by the scouring action of sand and small stones blasted against the rock over a millennia of winter snowmelts and floods.

The **Sentinel Pine Covered Bridge** crosses the river right at the Pool. Make sure you see the fallen 175-foot

The Sentinel Pine Covered Bridge spans the Pemigewasset River.

white pine that forms the base of the bridge. The best view is from a short spur trail to the left after you pass through the covered bridge.

Along the last stretch of the trail between the Pool and the visitor center, you'll pass through an **area of large boulders** interspersed with the dense forest. These boulders are glacial erratics, carried to the area and then left behind by the last glacier. Some of the boulders are piled up together to form caves that look large enough for bears.

Ask your children how the **trees, perched precariously on top of rocks,** can grow seemingly without any soil. They probably got started in small pockets of soil on the rocks and then sent roots down. See if they can follow the roots around the rocks and into the earth.

The **Roaring River Nature Trail** is a quieter experience than the walk through the Flume. Here, away from the crowds, you can learn about the forces of destruction and renewal that shape the northern hardwoods forest. With the aid of the pamphlet, you can identify the four major trees of the forest: sugar maple, yellow birch, American beech, and eastern hemlock. Small, parallel holes were made in trees by yellow-bellied sapsuckers, a type of woodpecker. A gazebo provides a place to listen quietly to the sounds of the forest while looking out at a view of Mount Flume and Mount Liberty, two 4,000-foot peaks of the Franconia Range.

This view is a great place to end your visit to the Flume, because it shows you the mountains that are the source of the waters that roar along the nature trail and through the Flume.

Lost River

- **0.75 mile loop, 300-foot descent**
- **1.5 hours**
- **easy for all ages**

Lost River was described by one of our friends as "wicked fun for kids." Don't let its status as a New Hampshire "attraction" discourage you from a visit. Despite the hype, Lost River is still impressive—a mysterious river that flows between and beneath large boulders while you stroll easily on a boardwalk or wiggle down narrow passages into candlelit caves. Besides, on some days kids would prefer an "attraction" to a long walk in the woods anyway. Lost River is a sure bet to excite the family and to teach you about nature, too.

In addition to the gorge, Lost River also features a wildflower garden and displays on White Mountain logging, minerals, birds, and mammals. You could easily spend several leisurely hours walking and viewing the exhibits.

Lost River Reservation is owned by the Society for the Protection of New Hampshire Forests (SPNHF) and run by New Hampshire Attractions. It has a visitor center, gift shop, and snack bar. At the time of this writing admission for adults was seven dollars and four dollars for kids under twelve. The Reservation is open from 9:00 A.M. to 5:00 P.M. in May, June, September, and October and from 9:00 A.M. to 6:00 P.M. in July and August.

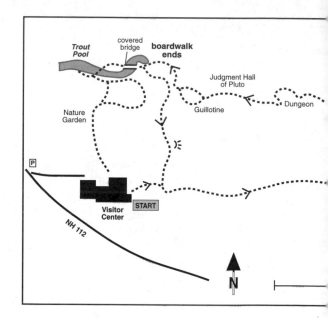

Call for opening and closing dates in May and October, which are weather dependent (603-745-8031). Tickets are sold until one hour before closing time.

What's in it for kids

- Ladders into mysterious caves.
- Giant boulders.
- Extensive boardwalk over rushing water.
- Waterfalls.

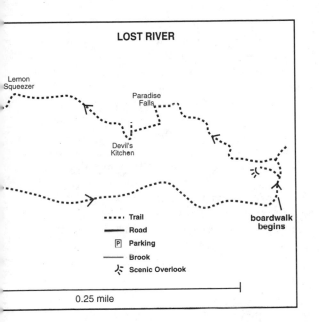

LOST RIVER

Lemon
Squeezer

Paradise
Falls

Devil's
Kitchen

boardwalk
begins

····· Trail
──── Road
P Parking
──── Brook
⋇ Scenic Overlook

0.25 mile

Getting There

Lost River Reservation is easily accessible from North
Woodstock, Lincoln, and Franconia Notch. From I-93,
exit onto N.H. 112 (North Woodstock, Lincoln) and follow N.H. 112 about seven miles west to the Reservation
entrance (very well marked).

The Trail

Pick up a trail map and guide at the visitor center
before you head out on the trail. The trail is one loop so

it is virtually impossible to get lost. The 300-foot descent to the gorge has stairs and plenty of benches. In the gorge itself, the well-maintained boardwalk insures easy walking despite rushing water and rocks all around you. You can explore some or all of the caves by scrambling down ladders and through narrow passageways, or you can keep to the main trail if dark, damp places are not for you. Some of the caves may be closed at times due to high water levels. The descriptions at each cave give you some sense of what you will be getting into if you descend. At the end of the gorge trail, you can return to the visitor center either by walking past a lookout with a view of the Kinsman Range or by ambling through a covered bridge, past a trout pool, and then through the Nature Garden.

Highlights

No question that the main attraction here is the **gorge of Lost River.** The caves have names like Thor's Cauldron, The Devil's Kitchen, Cave of Silence, and the Judgment Hall of Pluto. Many are lit by candles, contributing to the mysterious atmosphere. Children will have an easier time than their parents exploring the caves at Lost River. One particular cave, the Lemon Squeezer, is so narrow that it can only be entered by those small enough to fit through a narrow wooden passageway at its entrance. In addition to the caves, the long **boardwalk** built into the gorge is bound to delight children.

The **geology of the gorge** and how it was formed is well described in the exhibits and the pamphlet. In brief, water melting from the last glacier (10,000 years ago) carried with it all sorts of abrasive gravel and sand. These swirled around the river with such force that they carved out the potholes and walls of the gorge. More resistant pegmatite rocks were eroded less than the granite, so they form some of the more distinct features of the gorge. Potholes perched high above the river show that the water level was once much higher than at present.

While walking through Lost River, show your kids the difference between the lighter pegmatite and the grayish granite. A very long time ago, even before the

Wooden walkways aid your exploration of the Lost River Gorge.

glaciers, the pegmatite you see was formed as a dike in the granite: Molten lava from deep within the earth flowed into cracks in the granite, then "froze" to form what you see here.

The final stage in the formation of the Lost River gorge occurred after the glaciers retreated. Over time, huge boulders split off from the walls of the gorge by the freezing and thawing action of water. These boulders tumbled into the gorge, in places burying the "lost" river. The "slag" of loose rocks below the Dilly Cliff, visible at an outlook near the visitor center, was formed by a similar process of freezing and thawing.

The geological processes that formed the Lost River Reservation are still going on. Every winter and early spring, water seeps into cracks in the rocks and then freezes. Eventually new boulders may come tumbling down to create new caves in the Lost River.

Look for **brook trout** in some of the deeper pools in the gorge and in the trout pool at the end of the trail. Brook trout like the cold waters of larger White Mountain streams. They are particularly fond of streams with a mixture of pools, riffles, and fallen trees and brush. Many streams and ponds are stocked with brook trout and, in places, the Forest Service has placed brush and dead snags over streams to enhance their habitat value to trout. It's a good place to tell your kids that wildlife typically abhors prim-looking rivers and well-manicured forests.

The path down to the river is a good place to try identifying a number of common **trees and plants** of the White Mountains. Trees include striped maple (very obviously "striped"), red maple, balsam fir, white

Canada mayflower.

(paper) birch, and yellow birch (very yellow bark). Hobblebush is the dominant understory shrub, but mountain holly, with its tiny spined-tipped leaves, and mountain maple are also present. Herbs of the forest floor include clintonia, painted trillium, red trillium, Canada mayflower, and goldthread. Rock ferns cover some of the rocks. When you reach the **Nature Garden** at the end of the trail, you can see how well you've done. The creators of the Nature Garden have created a swale, forest, field, bog, and even a small alpine area. The plants are labeled and grouped by the habitat in which they typically occur.

Coppermine Trail and Keeper of the Stray Ladies

- **5 miles round-trip, 1,200-foot elevation gain**
- **3–4 hours**
- **moderate for kids**

The Coppermine Trail has an aura of mystery and romance about it. It takes you along Coppermine Brook to Bridal Veil Falls, one of the most beautiful waterfalls in the White Mountains, but the mystery does not come from the waterfall itself. You can give the children a mission: Along the way, if they look hard, they will find a plaque on a large boulder along the brook with an enigmatic inscription,

> In Memoriam to Arthur Farnsworth
> "The Keeper of Stray Ladies"
> Peckets 1939
> Presented by a Grateful One.

For the rest of the hike, you can ponder who Arthur Farnsworth was, whether he met a tragic fate along Coppermine Brook, why the tribute was placed in such an obscure place, and who was this "Grateful One" who chose to eulogize Mr. Farnsworth in this manner (read on and find out!).

The Coppermine Trail itself is a pleasant walk on the western side of Cannon Mountain. Most of it grades gently uphill along Coppermine Brook. The distance from the trailhead to the falls is about 2.5 miles, so plan on a round trip of several hours. The Coppermine Shelter, located near the falls, is an open-ended lean-to with an outhouse nearby.

What's in it for kids

- Walking along a brook to a beautiful waterfall.
- Searching for the mysterious memorial plaque hidden in the woods.
- A picnic at the falls or at the Coppermine Shelter nearby.
- Wading in the brook.

Getting There

The Coppermine Trail is off N.H. 116 about 3.4 miles south of the village of Franconia. If you are traveling north through Franconia Notch, take the Franconia exit on I-93 (Exit 38) and then go south on N.H. 116 for 3.4 miles. Alternatively, from the North Woodstock and Lincoln exit on I-93, travel west on N.H. 112 for about 8 miles and then north on N.H. 116 for 7.7 miles. Look for Coppermine Road on the east side of N.H. 116. Park your car right where there is ample space on Coppermine Road just after turning off N.H. 116 and walk along the road to the trailhead.

The Trail

Coppermine Trail departs from the left side of Coppermine Road approximately 0.4 mile from N.H. 116. It starts out as a smooth dirt road, very easy on the feet,

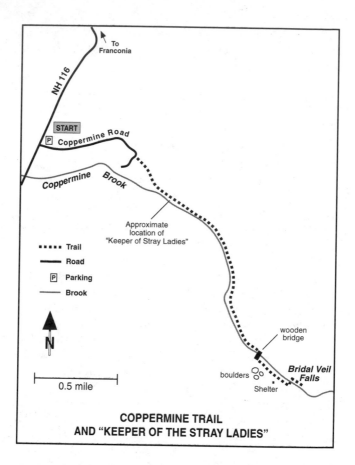

**COPPERMINE TRAIL
AND "KEEPER OF THE STRAY LADIES"**

and then becomes a wide path for most of its length. The trail is enclosed in a pleasant woodland setting of northern hardwood trees for its entire length. Coppermine Brook comes in from the right after a short distance and is within sight or earshot of the trail for practically its entire length. After about an hour to an hour and a half (about 2 miles), the trail crosses over the brook on a wooden bridge, passes the Coppermine Shelter, crosses back over the stream on rocks (no problem), climbs moderately, and then ends at Bridal Veil Falls 0.2 mile after the bridge. The more adventurous can walk up to the top of the falls on the right for a different view.

If you decide to cut the walk short, several places where the trail runs right along the brook make for a pleasant short (or long) stop before turning around.

Highlights

Bridal Veil Falls is really several connected cascades, some forming "shoots" along sloping rock faces and others tumbling over rocks into pools, like the large one at the bottom. Like most waterfalls in the White Mountains, the best time for viewing is when water levels are relatively high, either early in the season or soon after a rainstorm. If you scramble up the side of the waterfall, you will be rewarded with a view of a second, very pretty pool that is not visible from the bottom.

Flowing water, in addition to its pleasant sight and sound, is also a habitat for some of the creatures of the mountains. Encourage your children to see what they can find, particularly under rocks in the water (two-lined salamanders are a possibility). Teach children to be gentle with any animals they find and return any rocks they have disturbed to their original location.

While walking along the dirt road at the beginning of the trail, look for circular clumps of **interrupted fern,** a large fern whose leafy green pinnae (leaflets) are "interrupted" along the stalk by brownish reproductive leaflets. Unfortunately, not all interrupted ferns will be producing these reproductive structures, so the name may be as much of a mystery as the "keeper of stray ladies." Show the kids the **raspberries** growing in disturbed areas near the road. These might make a great treat if birds and other hikers haven't gotten there first.

The **northern hardwoods forest** through which the Coppermine Trail runs is dominated by yellow birch, sugar maples, and American beech. Yellow birch is especially abundant along this trail. Conifers, particularly Canadian hemlock, but also red spruce and balsam fir occur along the side of the brook where the microclimate is shadier, damper, and cooler. The most abundant understory shrub is hobblebush. Mountain maples, with their characteristic arching stems, are at the bridge crossing the brook and around the Coppermine Shelter.

Most **wildflowers** growing along the trail bloom in May and June. These include trout lily, foamflower, rosy twisted-stalk, Canada mayflower, clintonia, false Solomon's seal, Indian cucumber root, jack-in-the-pulpit, starflower, wild sarsaparilla, and shinleaf.

Little caves are created by fern and moss-covered boulders and overhanging tree roots between the bridge and the waterfall. These look like great dens for animals or for weary elves. The small evergreen ferns that grow right on top of the boulders are appropriately named **rock ferns,** or Virginia polypody.

And finally, the mysterious story of **The Keeper of Stray Ladies.** What follows is a summary of an article by Lyn McIntosh in the Autumn 1987 issue of *Magnetic North.* Arthur Farnsworth was a handsome young Vermonter who was employed at Pecketts, a fashionable, year-round resort in the 1930s on Sugar Hill, just west of Franconia Notch. Guests of Pecketts rode on horseback to land owned by the resort on Coppermine Brook for hiking, fishing, snowshoeing, or simply enjoying the beautiful rushing stream. Farnsworth's job was to make guests feel at home at the lodge. In 1939, the famous Hollywood actress Bette Davis came to Pecketts for a period of rest after a particularly exhausting time of moviemaking. In brief, Davis fell in love with Pecketts, the whole region, and Farnsworth. The simple life of the

The mysterious message along the Coppermine Trail. Nancy Schalch.

North Country and the strong, honest gentleman who did not find her fame particularly intimidating was just the antidote the actress needed from her life as a movie star. Legend has it that Bette Davis strayed from a hiking party at Coppermine Brook, knowing that Farnsworth would be sent to find her. They were married in 1940 and lived happily in California, occasionally escaping to the White Mountains. Unfortunately in 1943 tragedy struck. Farnsworth died after he fell down some stairs at their home on Sugar Hill. Davis continued to come back to the White Mountains for a while but sold her home on Sugar Hill in 1961. The plaque mysteriously appeared on Coppermine Brook sometime around then.

The plaque is located about 0.25 mile from the junction of the Coppermine Trail with Coppermine Road (0.75 mile, twenty-minute walk from N.H. 116). Look for a spot where the trail first comes near the brook and there is a steep slope through conifers down to the brook on the right. Between the trail and the brook is a flat area where people often pitch tents. You need to scramble a bit to reach the streambed, and then use caution because the rocks are slippery. Look for the plaque on a big boulder that is on the same side of the brook as the trail. The boulder juts out into the stream roughly halfway along the flat area. The plaque itself faces downstream.

For most trails in this book, we have focused on the mysteries of nature. For the Coppermine Trail, the human mystery is just as intriguing.

Waterville Valley Region

WATERVILLE VALLEY is a beautiful valley tucked in among 4,000-foot peaks. It still feels secluded and quiet despite the presence of a major ski resort and conference center. If you are coming from the south, reach Waterville Valley from I-93 by traveling about eleven miles northeast on N.H. 49 (Campton exit). This is a well-paved scenic road that parallels the Mad River. If approaching from the north, travel about ten miles east through Thornton Gap on Tripoli Road, an unpaved road for much of its length.

The region has the advantage of being a shorter drive from the big metropolitan areas of the East Coast than other parts of the White Mountains and also of warming up earlier in the spring and cooling down later in the fall. The valley's loop hike to Welch and Dickey mountains is one of the most popular family hikes in the White Mountains. There is also an extensive network of easy trails along streams.

Facilities

Supplies. Waterville Valley is a planned, resort community with downhill ski slopes, a convention center, and condominiums. It caters to outdoor activities, so you'll have no trouble buying the latest high-quality fashions to wear on the trail or a prepared lunch to go. You'll also find restaurants for a posthike repast and a small market, Jugtown, with some supplies. There is a gas station on Tripoli Road at its junction with N.H. 49.

If you are coming from the south on I-93, check out the Campton Cupboard just north of N.H. 49 on N.H. 175. If you are coming from the north, you may find it convenient to get your supplies at the Lincoln, North Woodstock exit where there are a number of stores.

Camping. There are two National Forest Campgrounds off N.H. 49. The Campton Campground is closer to I-93 and has fifty-eight sites open in the summer season and a group camping area open year-round. The Waterville Campground, open year-round, is eight miles from I-93 and has twenty-seven sites. Russell Pond Campground is accessible from Tripoli Road. The campgrounds in Franconia Notch and the western part of the Kancamagus Highway are about thirty to forty-five minutes from the trailhead.

Other. In addition to the *AMC White Mountain Guide,* two other guides to Waterville Valley hikes are available. The Waterville Valley Athletic and Improvement Association (WVAIA) includes the Welch and Dickey trails and many shorter walks in its map of hiking trails in the area. This map is sold at Jugtown and at the service station opposite the Waterville Campground. Leaflets describing several of the trails are available at several of the ranger stations in the White Mountain National Forest.

The Welch and Dickey Loop Trail

- **4.4 mile loop, 1,600-foot elevation gain**
- **3.5–5 hours**
- **challenging for kids**

This was probably the single most "suggested" hike when we asked anyone to recommend their favorite family hikes in the White Mountains. Welch and Dickey are two small mountains (2,605 and 2,734 feet) near Waterville Valley whose summits command excellent views. The hike is substantial enough to give you a feeling of accomplishment, yet manageable for most everyone above age six or so. For those with less time or energy, a hike up to the summit of Welch Mountain requires only about an hour one way. The Welch and Dickey Loop Trail is a good choice early in the season, since its lower elevation and relatively southern location insures that snow disappears earlier here than farther north.

The extensive open areas of the summits of Welch and Dickey mountains resemble the alpine zones on the Presidential and Franconia ridges. Although not technically alpine areas because they are too low in elevation, the Welch and Dickey summits have a similar feel: low gnarled trees and shrubs, extensive ledges and boulders, and the presence of some alpine plants. You can see all this without having to worry about the unpredictable, occasionally severe weather that occurs on the higher ridges.

The large areas of rocky ledges near the summits should present no problems for most hikers; however, we do not recommend this trail for a family hike if the weather is wet or if walking on rocks makes anyone in the group anxious. And remember, these summits, despite their low elevations, are still quite exposed, so do not forget windbreakers.

What's in it for kids

- Lots of open ledges with rocks to scramble on.
- Great views.
- A hike along a stream with wooden board crossings at the beginning.
- Blueberry picking.
- Lots of interesting plants.

Getting There

The Welch and Dickey Trail is located off N.H. 49 at the entrance to Waterville Valley. Take I-93 to the Campton, Waterville Valley exit and follow N.H. 49 toward Waterville Valley. Four and a half miles beyond N.H. 175 in Campton, turn left (northwest) on Upper Mad River Road and cross the river. As of spring 1993, there was a sign at the turnoff for Welch and Dickey; however, never trust that such signs are permanent due to the misguided nostalgia of some hikers. Follow this road for 0.7 mile, then turn right on Orris Road. The parking

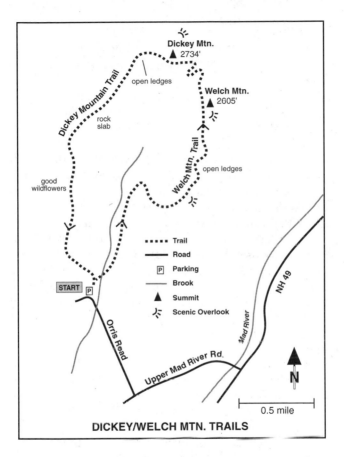

Dickey Mtn.
▲ 2734'

open ledges

Welch Mtn.
▲ 2605'

rock
slab

Dickey Mountain Trail

Welch Mtn. Trail

open ledges

good
wildflowers

······· Trail
——— Road
P Parking
——— Brook
▲ Summit
⁎ Scenic Overlook

START P

Orris Road

Upper Mad River Rd.

Mad River

NH 49

N

0.5 mile

DICKEY/WELCH MTN. TRAILS

area (in 0.6 mile) is not large, considering the popularity of this trail, so you may have to wait for someone to depart before you can get into the lot. Don't despair, the turnover is rapid.

The Trail

The Welch and Dickey Loop Trail does not connect up with any other trail, so it is hard to make a wrong turn. The biggest decision is whether to follow the loop counterclockwise up Welch Mountain first or begin by scaling Dickey. We recommend Welch first because it is a shorter walk to a viewpoint. You can turn around there if going farther is just not in the cards.

The trail up Welch Mountain is well marked with yellow blazes. Take the right fork just beyond the display board and lost-and-found box at the trailhead. Although its popularity has led to erosion in some places, the walk is smooth for much of its length.

The hike up Welch follows a stream through a northern hardwoods forest for about the first 0.5 mile. There are a number of stream crossings on wooden boards. After about forty-five minutes, you reach a switchback with steps and start to ascend more steeply. The trail passes the first open ledge with a viewpoint soon after (0.9 mile). A sign and small stones placed in neat lines urge hikers to avoid stepping on the low vegetation of this and other ledgy areas by remaining on the trail or on exposed rocks. The trail then proceeds upward, past other ledges and through low forests of evergreens, before reaching the summit of Welch (1.5 to 2 hours).

If you want to go on, the trail descends steeply to the saddle between Welch and Dickey and then ascends to the Dickey summit. It takes twenty to thirty minutes (0.5 mile) to hike from Welch to Dickey.

From Dickey, the trail descends through more ledges and is marked with cairns in a number of places.

A half hour or so beyond the Dickey summit, the trail crosses a particularly impressive rock slab and shortly thereafter enters a forest of beech and maple. It's about another mile to the parking lot. Near the end, make sure to stay on the trail as it passes an abandoned road and a logging road.

Highlights

The Welch and Dickey Loop Trail has many highlights, including magnificent views, ledges with alpine plants, interesting geological features, a babbling brook, wildflowers, and wildlife.

The **vistas** are spectacular on a clear day. From the ledges and summit of Welch the prominent peaks are Dickey Mountain, the Sandwich Range (southeast), Mount Tecumseh (north—the major ski area for Waterville Valley), and Mount Tripyramid (northeast). You also have an excellent view of the Mad River Valley and a breathtaking view down into the saddle between Welch and Dickey. The view from Dickey includes the Franconia Range. When you descend Dickey, the impressive cliff on Cone Mountain is straight ahead (southwest).

Ask the children what they think caused rectangular open areas visible in the forest below. These are places where **loggers** have clear-cut the forest. They are in various states of revegetation depending on how long it has been since the area was logged. A dense tangle of shrubs, such as raspberries, blueberries, and huckleberries, will grow up within a few years, followed by early successional trees such as paper birch, aspen, and pin cherry.

Spring wildflowers and ferns are abundant, especially as you descend Dickey Mountain. Look for Canada mayflower, wild oats, clintonia, Indian cucumber root, false Solomon's seal, true Solomon's seal, painted trillium, starflower, and goldthread. Around Memorial Day when the leaves are just emerging, the kids may be curious about **wild sarsaparilla,** a plant with glossy reddish leaves in groups of threes or fives. You might think that they are about to touch poison ivy. Rest assured. Poison ivy does not occur at these elevations. See if they can find **pink corydalis** on the back side of Dickey. It has ferny leaves and small, pink flowers that resemble the heads of birds. **Partridgeberry** is a small, low plant with paired, dark green leaves that hug the ground and are occasionally punctuated with bright red berries. The distinctive, arrowhead-shaped leaves of the **rattlesnake root** are present throughout the year, but its flowers do not appear until late summer.

Near the summits, you enter a red spruce forest with some balsam fir. In open areas these species are joined by oaks and white pine, species that thrive in sunny locations. **Jack pine,** a rare tree in the White Mountains, occurs on ledges near the summit of Welch Mountain. You can identify it by its short, stiff needles occurring in bunches of two. Why it occurs on Welch but not in similar habitats on Dickey is a mystery.

Recovery areas for small plants on the ledges are delineated by lines of small stones. **Two tiny alpine species** protected by this effort are mountain cranberry and mountain sandwort. The thin soil, exposure to the winds, and absence of trees mimic the alpine conditions normally found above about 4,500 feet in the White

A plant restoration area marked by stones on Welch Mountain.

Mountains, allowing these plants to thrive on Welch and Dickey. Three-toothed cinquefoil, whose small white flowers bloom in June, is probably the most abundant plant in the recovery areas. Each of the three leaflets of this low plant has three teeth on their outer edge.

Shrubs are a major component of the vegetation on the open ledges. **Blueberries** are a popular midsummer attraction, but please make sure your picking does not destroy them or any other vegetation in this fragile habitat. If the kids are careful observers, they might see bumblebees pollinating blueberry flowers.

Around Memorial Day, **rhodora,** a type of rhodo-dendron, will be in glorious bloom, particularly on Welch. It has large pinkish purple flowers and bluish green leaves. Labrador tea, chokeberries, shadbush, and bush honeysuckle are other shrubs on the ledges.

In the saddle between Welch and Dickey, there is a particularly attractive example of **boreal forest plants.** Where the shading from the red spruce is not dense, bunchberries and reindeer moss (a lichen) grow in patterns that look like they were designed by a rock gardener. Mountain holly, wild raisin, the white form of the pink lady's slipper, clintonia, and haircap moss grow under the spruce canopy as well.

As you hike along show the children the large **glacial erratics** scattered throughout the woods. These are often covered with mosses and rock tripe, the latter a type of lichen that, although edible, looks and tastes like a piece of shoe leather. Two other particularly interesting geological features are a jumble of rocks that forms a cul-de-sac tunnel with a natural bridge, and a very prominent large granite rock slab a mile below the summit of Dickey. This is laced with stripes that are sills of dark gray basalt formed from molten lava that penetrated cracks within the granite.

As you approach the summit ledges, see if anyone can spot a **raven.** These large, completely black members of the crow family are considered among the most intelligent of birds. They are frequently observed soaring around ledges in the mountains and sometimes cavort with each other and even fly upside down. Their voice is a hoarse call that sounds like a cross between a crow and a hog. A much smaller bird you are likely to see at higher elevations is the **dark-eyed junco,** a slaty gray, sparrow-sized bird with a white belly and white outer tail feathers.

Smarts Brook Trail

- **2.6 miles round-trip, 300-foot elevation gain**
- **1.5–2.5 hours**
- **easy for all ages**

The Smarts Brook Trail is a very pleasant woodland walk along Smarts Brook on an old logging road. In the right season you will see lots of pink lady's slippers and other wildflowers. You can wade in a beautiful swimming hole beneath a small waterfall and then explore an open pond and meadow area created by beavers—a nice contrast to the "closed in" feeling of the forest. This is one of the easiest places to walk out on a beaver dam in the White Mountains.

This is a "southern" trail (relative to others in the White Mountains) and is at low elevation, so snow melts and plants bloom earlier in the spring than elsewhere. It's a good choice on a hot summer day because of the dense forest and accessibility of the stream. Bring mosquito repellent because it can be buggy.

What's in it for kids

- Easy walk on a very broad trail.
- A pretty swimming hole.
- A chance to poke around a stream for salamanders and other aquatic life.
- A great beaver dam to explore.
- A glacial erratic shaped like a boat.

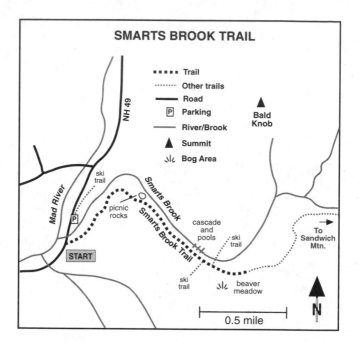

SMARTS BROOK TRAIL

Legend:
- ▪▪▪▪ Trail
- ⋯⋯⋯ Other trails
- ▬▬▬ Road
- P Parking
- ── River/Brook
- ▲ Summit
- � Bog Area

NH 49

Bald Knob

Mad River

ski trail

picnic rocks

Smarts Brook

Smarts Brook Trail

START

cascade and pools

ski trail

To Sandwich Mtn.

ski trail

beaver meadow

0.5 mile

N

Getting There

From I-93, take the Campton Waterville Valley exit and follow N.H. 49 toward Waterville Valley. The parking area for Smarts Brook Trail is on the southeast side of N.H. 49, 3.8 miles east of its intersection with N.H. 175 in Campton. Walk back across the bridge over Smarts Brook to the trailhead. Do not confuse with ski trail.

From Waterville Valley, the trailhead is 0.5 mile past the intersection of N.H. 49 with Upper Mad River Road, 5.2 miles from the junction of N.H. 49 and Tripoli Road.

The Trail

The trail is a wide logging road to the pool and beaver meadow. Beyond there it narrows to a path and gets a lot steeper. A number of well-marked cross-country ski trails, which are not on any hiking map, intersect with this trail at various times, so be careful to stay on the main path.

The trail begins by ascending a few log steps. Fairly soon, a cross-country ski trail marked with blue diamonds comes in and runs together with the trail for a while. After another logging road enters from the right (keep this in mind for your return trip), you start picking up yellow blazes that mark the trail.

After about thirty to forty minutes, the trail approaches the bank of Smarts Brook. There are some flat rocks here so it is a good place for a picnic or to turn around if you have had enough. Continuing along the brook, the swimming "pool" and cascade are only a few minutes farther.

Just beyond the falls, the Tri Town cross-country ski trail comes in from the right, then departs shortly to the left. Where it departs, a sign for the Smarts Brook Trail points you to the left across the stream. This is a loop that eventually rejoins the main trail, but we recommend you ignore it and follow the main path to the beaver meadow a few minutes ahead.

About 0.2 mile beyond the pool, you cross a tributary stream over some wooden boards. You can see the beaver dam and meadow through the woods to the right, but continue a bit past it for easiest access.

The Smarts Brook Trail continues on for another 4 miles to the Sandwich Mountain Trail, but we recommend that after exploring the beaver meadow, you retrace your steps and make your way back to N.H. 49 and the parking area. Just remember to follow the trail to the right when you reach the point where the logging road forks to the left about 0.2 mile from the trailhead.

Highlights

The delightful series of **pools and small waterfalls** are not only fun for kids to splash in but also contain interesting aquatic critters. The largest pool is about four feet deep, not bad for a swim in a mountain stream. There are smaller "kiddie pools" and good flat sitting rocks for picnics just upstream.

As you walk along the Smarts Brook Trail, you will encounter a number of **aquatic insects** that are common in streams, ditches, and temporary woodland pools of the White Mountains. Some of these, like water striders and whirligig beetles, will instantly catch children's eyes.

The **crane fly** is a graceful fly with very long legs. It is likely to be seen hovering above the water, occasionally landing on your children and causing instant panic because it looks as if the world's largest mosquito is about to bite. But don't worry, crane flies are harmless.

Mosquitoes begin life in small, temporary pools, such as those that form in depressions on the path after a period of heavy rains or in holes in trees. They survive best in these isolated pools because they are rather easy prey for fish, salamanders, and just about everything else that lives in more permanent bodies of water. See if your children can find any of the larvae in flooded ditches along the sides of the path. Their reaction is likely to be something between "ooooooh" and "yuck." The wormlike "wrigglers" tend to hang down from the water surface, feeding on detritus and scattering toward the bottom when your shadow or any other "threat" appears over their little pool.

Crane flies and mosquitoes are both airborne as adults, but the **predaceous diving beetle** spends most of its life in water. You might find these at the big pool in Smarts Brook or in smaller pools in ditches along the side of the trail. They are blackish and oval and swim strongly underwater, feeding on invertebrates and even larval fish. Don't try to pick one up with your hands, because they can give a surprisingly nasty bite (their larvae are named "water tigers"). Adults can fly, which is how they reach some of those out-of-the-way pools in the woods.

A perennial favorite of children is the **water strider.** These insects literally walk on the surface of water, supported by surface tension—the same force that keeps cocoa powder on the surface of the hot water until it is stirred. Tiny hairs on the bottoms of their legs repel water and prevent them from breaking through. If for some reason their legs do fall through the surface, then the insect "falls" underwater and must crawl up on some vegetation to dry off before it can walk on water again. If the lighting is just right, make sure the kids see how the shadow of a water strider appears to have foot pads under their legs. These are actually indentations of the water surface itself under the weight of the bug.

Humans are much too big and heavy for surface tension to hold us up, but for many small creatures, the water surface can be an impenetrable barrier. Water striders feed on small invertebrates that fall onto the surface film and get stuck. They lay eggs underwater, and the newly hatched young must swim to the surface and break through to survive.

Whirligig beetles spin around in dizzying patterns on the surface of the water, particularly when they are disturbed by your presence. They actually have two pairs of eyes, one that can look up at the sky to detect predators and the other that looks into the water. They hold their antenna on the water surface, and are very sensitive to vibrations that might indicate potential prey struggling on the water surface.

Encourage your children to look for salamanders under loose stones at the water's edge. We found a two-lined salamander around the large pool. This small amphibian (2.5 to 4 inches) has two stripes on either side of its yellowish back.

Take time to explore the **beaver-created wetland** at the end of this hike, because you won't often have such a good opportunity to inspect their handiwork so closely. You can walk right out on one of the old dams. See if the kids can figure out the construction materials used by the beavers. They should be able to see the combination of small branches and mud underneath the new plants that now grow on top of the dam. The dam that you are walking out on is actually one of the oldest in a series. The beavers have moved farther downstream over the years as they have chopped down the more

It's easy to discover where beavers have been.

upstream trees. The part of the wetland they have abandoned has since silted in.

The open wetland created by the beaver provides a good lesson on how different kinds of habitats attract different types of plants and animals. The wetland plants, such as marsh St. Johnswort, steeplebush, and sedges, must be tolerant of full sunlight as well as wet soil. Birds attracted to the open spaces of the beaver meadow are tree swallows, flickers, blue jays, and hawks such as the broad-winged hawk. You may also find moose tracks in soft muddy areas of the wetland and hear green frogs calling "glunk" as if someone had just plunked a banjo string.

In contrast to the open beaver meadow, most of the Smarts Brook Trail is within a northern hardwoods forest, with yellow birches particularly abundant. Hemlocks and haircap mosses thrive in the damp areas near the brook, and the understory is dominated by hobblebush and striped maple. Wildflowers are abundant in spring and the most common birds are thrushes and warblers.

About halfway to the falls, you will pass a **huge glacial erratic** that looks like a boat. Its top is covered with rock ferns (Virginia polypody). The overhang provides a great hiding place and rest stop before you continue down the trail.

East Pond and Little East Pond

- **5.2 miles round-trip, 800-foot elevation gain**
- **4–5 hours**
- **easy to moderate for kids**

East Pond and Little East Pond are two gems nestled behind Mount Osceola and Scar Ridge at 2,600 feet. The entire loop may be long for younger children, so you can shorten the hike by walking only to East Pond and back, a relatively level 1.4 mile walk in each direction. One can easily spend all day at East Pond, picnicking, swimming, enjoying the scenery, and observing the natural history of the pond shores. Little East Pond is smaller, shallower, more remote, and very scenic, too. The trails themselves are enjoyable and interesting, passing through rich woodlands carpeted with wildflowers, ferns, and mushrooms and crossing over a number of streams. *Ponds and Lakes of the White Mountains* by Steven Smith (Backcountry Press) is a good reference for additional information about the ponds.

What's in it for kids

- A visit to one or two beautiful mountain ponds.
- Throwing stones in water.
- Swimming.
- Raspberries.

- Hunt for witch's butter and doll's eyes.
- How did Tripoli Road get its name?

Getting There

The East Pond Trail is off Tripoli Road, about 5.4 miles from its junction with I-93. If you are coming from Waterville Valley, the trailhead is about 6 miles west of the junction of Tripoli Road and N.H. 49. Stay to the right when the road to the ski area splits off to the left. The parking area for the trail is on the north side of the road.

The Trail

The East Pond Trail starts out on an old wide logging road. After a few minutes, the logging road swings off to the right, and the East Pond Trail continues straight, still on a wide path. Look for the yellow blazes that mark the trail.

After 0.4 mile, you reach the junction of the Little East Pond Trail, which goes off to the left. At this point, it is 1.1 miles to East Pond and 1.7 miles to Little East Pond. This description assumes that you are heading to East Pond. From East Pond, you can either complete the counterclockwise loop to Little East Pond or simply return the same way you came.

The trail to East Pond continues along the old logging road straight ahead on a gradual uphill. It remains wide and for the most part easy walking. At about 0.7 mile from the trailhead, you cross East Pond Brook, which could be difficult if water levels are high. Even in

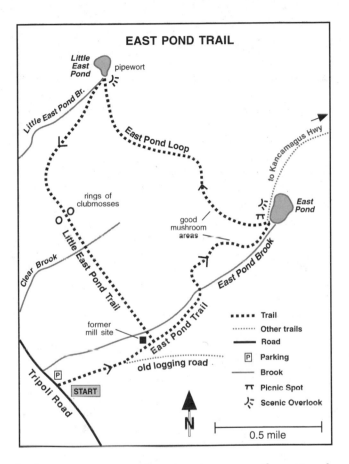

EAST POND TRAIL

Little East Pond

pipewort

Little East Pond Br.

East Pond Loop

to Kancamagus Hwy

rings of clubmosses

good mushroom areas

East Pond

Clear Brook

Little East Pond Trail

East Pond Brook

former mill site

East Pond Trail

old logging road

Tripoli Road

P

START

▪▪▪▪	Trail
····	Other trails
▬▬	Road
P	Parking
▬▬	Brook
ᴫ	Picnic Spot
⅄	Scenic Overlook

N

0.5 mile

low water, use care when stepping across the wet rocks. At 1.4 miles, just below East Pond, the East Pond Loop Trail diverges left toward Little East Pond. Take a side path to the right to reach the shore of East Pond at an open, meadowy area. This is the best spot to view the pond and to swim and picnic.

For some different perspectives of the pond, the East Pond Trail continues along the west side of the pond for a couple of hundred yards. (It eventually swings away and meets the Kancamagus Highway in 3.7 miles.) Explore some short spur paths to informal camping areas near the pond shore.

If you want to hike the entire loop, return to the trail junction and head west on the East Pond Loop. It is about 1.5 miles (one hour) from East Pond to Little East Pond via the East Pond Loop. The trail has a few minor ups and downs but almost no overall change in elevation.

The East Pond Loop passes mainly through a forest of paper birch with an understory of red spruce and balsam fir. There are a number of sunny, open patches caused by blowdowns where you get partial views through the trees of Mount Osceola, Scar Ridge, and the Sandwich Range. After about 0.9 mile, you cross a streambed that is likely to be dry in mid- to late summer. The trail reaches the junction of the Little East Pond Trail at the south end of Little East Pond, which is also the best vantage point.

From Little East Pond, return to your car via the Little East Pond Trail (1.7 miles) and the East Pond Trail (an additional 0.4 mile). The trail descends gradually for the first 0.7 mile, initially along a small ravine. It then makes a sharp left turn, levels out, and follows the grade of an old logging railroad. The trail crosses Clear Brook, East Pond Brook, and other smaller brooks, eventually reaching the trail junction with the East Pond Trail. Turn right to get back to the parking area.

Highlights

East Pond is a scenic mountain pond of about 6.5 acres. A saddle in Scar Ridge forms the backdrop of the pond as you look out from the southern end. The pond is shallow by the gravelly "beach" area but then grades off to a depth of twenty-seven feet.

There's much for everyone to enjoy right at the edge of the pond. Swimming is good, but be aware that the pond reportedly contains leeches. The kids can **toss stones** and watch the ripples. The pond is also a good spot for observing wildlife and other creatures. A **beaver dam** is nearby at the outlet, and a lodge is visible near a big rock on the opposite shore. **Dragonflies** patrol the shores of the pond for unwary insects, and **water striders** skim across the pools in the small outlet creek near the informal camping area. Keep a watchful eye skyward for birds that may fly over the pond. **Ravens** are likely and hawks a possibility.

Little East Pond (3.5 acres) is shallow and dotted with water lilies and pipeworts. **Pipeworts** look like hat pins, with small, white rounded balls on top of thin stalks. The "pinheads" are the flowers. The shoreline of Little East Pond is boggy, with abundant sphagnum, leatherleaf, mountain holly, and marsh St. Johnswort. Right by the trail sign look for a pretty patch of snowberries and bunchberries growing under small balsam fir and red spruce.

There is plenty to see along the trails too. For your children, make the hike into the great hunt for **witch's butter.** Witch's butter is a bright yellow or yelloworange fungus that grows on dead logs. It is also called jelly fungus because it looks like a blob of jelly on a log and is somewhat sticky. Like most fungi, witch's butter gets its nutrition by breaking down dead organic matter, such as the log upon which it rests. You will find lots of witch's butter and a variety of brightly colored **mushrooms** along the upper part of the East Pond Trail and the East Pond Loop.

The **forest dynamics** are also particularly interesting. Much of the forest was logged in the past and is now dominated by paper birch. See if your children can find places where there is a canopy of paper birch and an understory of balsam fir and red spruce, particularly along the upper part of the East Pond Trail and the East Pond Loop. Fir and spruce were dominant before logging and will eventually replace the paper birch. Point out that when they come back in ten or twenty years, the forest will look quite different than it does now.

This area is a good place for kids to learn that nature is not static. There are many **small gaps in the forest** created by trees that have fallen, particularly along the East Pond Loop. Gaps in the forest are often colonized by **hay-scented fern,** a large, lacy fern that smells like fresh-cut grass when it dries out in the fall. Hay-scented fern grows as a dense colony because new individuals are produced from old ones by underground runners. So the patch you see is really a clone, technically one individual because the ferns are all connected underneath.

On the Little East Pond Trail where it follows the old logging railroad bed you walk through a rich northern hardwoods forest. Along with the typical hobblebush and striped maples, notice the **many young sugar**

maples coming up. Unlike many species of trees, which will die if they are kept in the shade too long, sugar maple saplings are able to survive under the forest canopy, biding their time and waiting for their moment in the sun when one of the giants around them falls. Then, finally bathed in full sunlight, the little trees grow fast toward the forest canopy. Slower ones are shaded out by the faster ones. Sounds like material for a children's story—the little maple that could.

A mill once stood at the junction of the East Pond and Little East Pond Trails. The mill no longer exists, but it is a good spot for **doll's eye.** Doll's eye, also called white baneberry, has pyramidal clusters of tiny white flowers in the spring. Kids will particularly appreciate the fruits in mid-summer that look like white plastic

Shiny club mosses grow in circles along the East Pond Trail.

beads, each with one dark spot. (Do not let them eat these, however!)

There are striking **"fairy rings" of shiny club moss** along the Little East Pond Trail. These are almost round patches of a dark green low plant with small, dense, needlelike leaves on upright stems. Like the hay-scented fern described earlier, this growth habit is the result of one individual spore germinating and then sending out runners that create new upright plants.

And for our last question: How did Tripoli Road get its name? Tripoli (or tripolite) is a rock, also called diatomaceous earth, that can be made into a fine powder used as a polish in toothpaste and in industry. Tripoli is composed of the silica derived from the skeletons of diatoms, which are microscopic marine algae. The rock was mined from the bottom of East Pond in the early part of the twentieth century and hauled down to the aforementioned mill for processing. So before East and Little East Pond existed, and before doll's eyes and witch's butter were here, an inland sea covered this region, depositing the microscopic organisms that would eventually give Tripoli Road its name.

Cascade Path

- **3 miles round-trip, 300-foot elevation gain**
- **3 hours**
- **moderate for kids**

This is a pleasant, relatively easy walk to a beautiful series of small waterfalls in Waterville Valley near the resort community. In the spring (through mid-June) an added bonus is the rich assortment of wildflowers. It's a perfect family outing, easy except for a few short uphills. There are a whole series of connecting trails maintained by the Waterville Valley Athletic and Improvement Association (WVAIA) that could make for a longer outing. If the Snow's Mountain ski lift is operating, you can ride to the top and walk downhill to your car, cutting your walking time in half.

What's in it for kids

- A beautiful series of small waterfalls, rapids, and pools.
- A number of wooden bridges.
- A relaxing, easy walk along a brook.

Getting There

Waterville Valley is at the end of N.H. 49 about eleven miles northeast of the Campton exit of I-93, or about ten miles east of I-93 through Thornton Gap on Tripoli

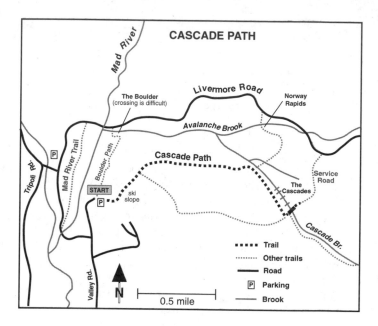

CASCADE PATH

Mad River

Livermore Road

The Boulder
(crossing is difficult)

Norway
Rapids

Avalanche Brook

Cascade Path

Service
Road

The
Cascades

Mad River Trail

Boulder Path

Tripoli Rd.

P

START

P

ski
slope

Valley Rd.

Cascade Br.

N

0.5 mile

•••• Trail
••••• Other trails
—— Road
P Parking
—— Brook

Road. To find the trailhead, continue on N.H. 49 past the town square and turn right on Valley Road, following the signs to Snow's Mountain Ski Area. Park in a lot a little past the tennis courts and a corral, right near the ski lift.

The Trail

Be warned that the trail map produced by WVAIA and that by DeLorme are not entirely in agreement on this trail, probably because they were written at different times. Development in Waterville Valley has forced relocation of some trails, so it's good to have your information as up-to-date as possible. Also, be careful not to follow ski touring trails (separate map available). But if you follow the route we suggest, you shouldn't get lost.

The Cascade Path begins by climbing up a ski slope (the steepest uphill of the trail) and enters the woods on the left (north) side after about 0.3 mile. Signs warn you not to turn off too soon on a cross-country ski trail. The trail, marked with yellow blazes, passes the Elephant Rock Trail (0.5 mile), crosses over a series of small wooden bridges, and reaches Cascade Brook (about 1 mile). You could turn around here, although the cascades are not much farther and are really worth seeing. Note the old logging road that angles in from the left at this point, and be careful not to use it if you return by retracing your steps. The Norway Rapids Trail heads left across the brook, but keep walking straight. After about ten more minutes (0.4 mile), you reach the first cascade.

The trail then becomes a little rougher as it climbs the right side of the brook. There is a trail on the left side as well, but the right one is the "official" route. Keep walking until you run out of cascades. When you reach the unpaved maintenance road for the Snow's Mountain Ski Area, you can either retrace your steps back to your car or turn right to descend on the ski slope.

Highlights

The **series of cascades** on Cascade Brook is the major highlight. They go on for a good distance, shooting through small gorges and tumbling into deep pools. Just when you think you've reached the last waterfall, you walk up a little farther and discover yet another.

At least one of this pair did not have to work hard to enjoy the Cascades.

Although pools below several of the cascades may look inviting, care and common sense should be used. Some are difficult to reach because of the steep sides of the bank. Others show signs of erosion where too many people have scurried down the sides to get to them, inadvertently destroying the vegetation.

Much of the streambed around the cascades (and around the Norway Rapids, too) consists of flat slabs of granite. A flat slab just below the bridge at the top of the trail is a great lunch rock. Note there and elsewhere how the granite fractured along smooth joints when eroded by streams.

Where the trail runs right along Cascade Brook, tell your kids to try their luck at finding **salamanders** by turning over some stones along the water's edge. Two species they may find here are the two-lined and dusky salamanders. Although they are more at home in water than on land, both breathe air through their moist skin rather than through lungs. The two-lined is more common and is usually yellowish with two dark lines running the length of its body along the side. It can be quite speedy in beating a hasty retreat if you uncover its hiding place. The dusky is variable but is typically grayish or brownish and somewhat chunkier (and slower) than the two-lined. Even if they fail to find salamanders, kids

An amanita mushroom.

will still be rewarded with water striders (very abundant) or other small critters.

Small rivulets running down into Cascade Brook are crossed on the trail by a number of **wooden bridges.** Growing as a carpet right on the mud by the second bridge is a small, innocuous plant with the much too glamorous name of golden saxifrage. There is nothing particularly golden about this plant, and its flowers are even more inconspicuous than its leaves, but if you have a hand lens your kids might be able to turn it into a tiny bouquet.

Soon after you reach the brook, you will pass by a marvelous example of a **tree that grows on top of a rock.** Ask your children how they think this tree can survive and how it ever got started.

The **woods** along the trail are dominated by northern hardwoods—beech, sugar maple, and yellow birches. Not long after entering the woods from the ski trail, you will walk through a section that has been recently cleared. The giveaway is the growth of spindly young yellow birches, none taller than about twenty feet.

Spring wildflowers abound along the trail. There are particularly pretty displays of red and painted trillium, clintonia, Canada mayflower, goldthread, and mountain wood sorrel. In late summer, most of the flowers are gone, but the rich woods are a great habitat for mushrooms. Amanitas, most of which are deadly poisonous, are particularly abundant. There are also boletes, which have tiny pores instead of gills on their undersides.

All in all, the Cascade Path is a great place to spend an afternoon.

Kancamagus Region

THE KANCAMAGUS HIGHWAY (N.H. 112) is a scenic highway running east-west for about forty miles between the towns of Conway and Lincoln. It provides access to many trails. The highway follows the Swift River in its eastern section and the East Branch of the Pemigewasset closer to Lincoln, so you are never far from rushing water. The area is heavily wooded and particularly beautiful (and crowded) during fall color season. Here you and your children can enjoy waterfalls, mountain ponds, and several small mountains that have excellent views for relatively little effort. The White Mountain National Forest maintains a number of picnic areas, campgrounds, and recreation areas along the highway.

The highway is named for a Native American who became chief of the Penacooks in 1685. Kancamagus was the grandson of Passaconaway and the nephew of Wonalancet, two other Penacook chiefs who also had mountains named after them. Angered by the continued intrusion of white settlers, Kancamagus led the last uprising of the Penacooks. Eventually he and the scattered remnants of his tribe emigrated north to Canada.

Facilities

The Saco Ranger Station of the White Mountain National Forest is on the Kancamagus Highway at its eastern terminus at N.H. 16. The Lincoln Woods Ranger Station is on the highway about four miles east of Lincoln. Stop in for trail information and to pick up the descriptive pamphlets for the guided nature hikes along the highway. The ranger stations also have water, rest rooms, and displays of the local natural history. Information on trails and rest rooms can also be found at the Passaconaway Historical Site about three miles east of Sabbaday Falls. There are rest rooms at the Rocky Gorge and Lower Falls scenic areas.

Supplies. There are no stores or gas stations along the Kancamagus Highway, so make sure you are well supplied with lunch, snacks, and gas before heading out. If you are coming from the east, Conway and North Conway have stores, gas stations, restaurants, motels, hot tubs, crafts, factory outlets, and other amenities. Along N.H. 16 south of Conway, there is a small general store in Chocorua and a few others between Chocorua and the Kancamagus Highway.

If you approach from the west, there is a shopping center with a supermarket on N.H. 112 right in Lincoln. Those coming from Crawford Notch will want to stop in Bartlett before traveling south on Bear Notch Road to the Highway.

Camping. The Kancamagus Highway has six campgrounds (over 250 sites) and six picnic facilities, spread conveniently along the entire length of the highway. White Ledge Campground, also run by the National Forest, is off N.H. 16 a few miles south of the highway. The campgrounds do fill up on popular weekends, so check at the information board on N.H. 112 just off I-93 in Lincoln (west end) or at the Saco Ranger Station (east end) on availability before you start your drive on the highway.

Greely Ponds

- **3.2 miles round-trip to the upper pond or 4.6 miles to both ponds, 300-foot elevation gain**
- **2–4 hours**
- **moderate for kids**

The two Greely Ponds are classic mountain ponds bordered by rugged heights that descend abruptly to the shoreline. Set dramatically near the height of Mad River Notch between Mounts Osceola and Kancamagus, the ponds are reached by a relatively easy trail that crosses numerous split-log bridges over muddy sections. This hike can easily provide a full day of swimming, picnicking, and fishing.

The Greely Ponds Trail (going south from the Kancamagus) is generally suitable for all ages, with perhaps a little assistance and encouragement from parents. Two-to-four-year-olds may need a ride in a backpack part of the way. If you are at the bribery stage with your kids, do not count on making it to the lower pond, particularly since the upper one has better swimming and picnicking potential. Be prepared for some mud, although the worst sections are bridged.

What's in it for kids

- Beautiful ponds in a dramatic setting.
- Sandy areas for swimming at the upper pond.

- Lots of split-rail bridges over wet areas.
- Darning needles and turtleheads.

Getting There

The parking area for the Greely Ponds Trail is on the south side of the Kancamagus Highway (N.H. 112) about nine miles east of I-93 in Lincoln. It's at a hairpin turn in the road. The lot is small, and given the popularity of this trail it may be full.

Be careful not to be confused by the winter ski trail to Greely Ponds, which is about 0.25 mile west of the hiking trail and is also marked with a sign for Greely Ponds. We ran into several unhappy hikers who had walked the ski trail by mistake and had been slogging knee-deep in mud. You will find the hiking trail muddy enough to satisfy whatever craving for goo you and the kids might have. If you park at the ski trail lot because the hiking trail lot is full, walk along the road to get to the correct trailhead.

If you are heading west on the Kancamagus Highway, the trailhead is about 0.25 mile west of the Hancock Scenic Overlook. The distance from N.H. 16 in Conway is about 25 miles.

The Trail

The Greely Ponds Trail, marked with yellow blazes, is a gradual uphill until it reaches the height of land in Mad River Notch. It then descends gently to the ponds. Particularly at the beginning, it's heavily eroded with lots of exposed tree roots. The cross-country ski trail, marked

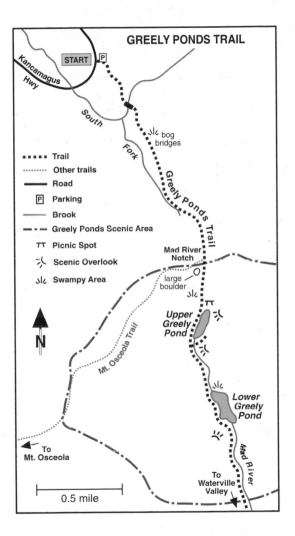

GREELY PONDS TRAIL

START

Kancamagus Hwy

South Fork

bog bridges

Greely Ponds Trail

- **••••** Trail
- •••••• Other trails
- ▬▬ Road
- P Parking
- ▬ Brook
- –•–•– Greely Ponds Scenic Area
- ⊤⊤ Picnic Spot
- �☆ Scenic Overlook
- ☀ Swampy Area

N

Mad River Notch

large boulder

Mt. Osceola Trail

Upper Greely Pond

Lower Greely Pond

To Mt. Osceola

Mad River

To Waterville Valley

0.5 mile

with blue diamonds, intersects the hiking trail several times.

The trail starts out through a dense forest of balsam fir. You soon cross over two streams and a number of small wetlands on a series of wooden bog bridges.

The trail enters the Greely Pond Scenic Area and reaches the height of land near where the Mount Osceola Trail comes in from the right 1.3 miles from the trailhead. (The Mount Osceola Trail climbs very steeply and is not an appropriate family walk.) Just beyond this junction, you pass a huge boulder that probably tumbled down from the cliffs of East Peak. Stay right at the next fork (with the ski trail again) and cross over another bog bridge.

At 1.6 miles (1–1.5 hours) a short side path to the left leads to the north end of the upper pond. There is a flat sandy area here, great for a picnic unless the water levels are too high. If there's time, walk around to the open areas on the southeast shore. To get there, continue along the main trail to the south side of the pond and take the short side trail leading left.

It takes ten to twenty minutes along the Greely Pond Trail to hike from the south end of the upper pond to the lower pond. There is an interesting open area at the north end, but hike a little farther to a small cove near a stand of paper birches for the best vista.

Retrace your steps for the return trip, but be careful at the various intersections with the ski trail. Just beyond the big rock, make sure you stay right at a fork or else the ski trail might take you to the Osceola Trail. If you find yourself ascending very steeply, turn around and walk back to the junction of the Greely Pond Trail.

Highlights

The Greely Ponds are named after Nathaniel Greely, who ran an inn in Waterville Valley in the nineteenth century when the valley was still a quiet, secluded place. He was one of the pioneer trail builders in this part of the White Mountains.

There are a couple of neat things for kids on the way to the pond, including **wooden bog bridges** and a **huge rock** just beyond the height of land. We used the rock as an incentive for some slower younger hikers, because whoever hurried up and got to it first could hide there, then jump out and scare the rest of us. Growing around this boulder are a big balsam fir and a birch whose trunks almost merge together as they twist around each other. Near the boulder at the junction of the Mount Osceola Trail, ask the children to find a large yellow birch with a split trunk that looks dead. The tree was evidently struck by lightning, but on top it is still alive. Hopefully it won't topple before you can see it.

The two **Greely Ponds** provide an interesting contrast. The upper one is deeper with steeper shorelines and better swimming. The lower one is shallower, boggy, and shows much evidence of beavers.

There are three areas for hanging out at the upper pond. The best vista is from the two areas at the southeast corner of the pond—the craggy East Peak of Mount Osceola is particularly impressive. You can get a sense of how the glacier that swept through this valley plucked rocks from the side of the mountain, creating the cliff you now see.

It's easy to spend a leisurely day at the Greely Ponds.

The upper pond is a beautiful place to **swim.** Obviously, you need to keep a close eye on the children because there are no lifeguards. The shoreline grades off gradually so that younger nonswimmers can still splash around and have a great time. By August, the water temperature may even be tolerable (the loudest screech I ever heard was from someone who boldly dove into Greely Pond in mid-June). Watch out for snags in the water. You may also discover a few leeches, or they may discover you, but don't let them deter you. The Greely leeches are small and innocuous and won't likely bother you if you keep moving.

The snags that stick out of the water are great perching spots for **black-winged damselflies** and dragonflies. Black-winged damselflies are boldly marked with unmistakable electric green bodies and black wings, striking colors that you might expect more in a tropical jungle rather than here. Damselflies hold their wings vertically when at rest, unlike dragonflies, which hold their wings horizontally.

The lower Greely Pond is less than 100 feet lower in elevation than the upper pond. The vistas from its two vantage points are not as dramatic as those of the upper pond, and it is too shallow for swimming but is equally interesting from a natural history perspective. The children will be able to find much evidence of beaver activity, particularly lots of standing dead trees in the water indicating recent flooding.

At the north end of the lower pond there is a **boggy area** with lots of sphagnum moss. Leatherleaf, Labrador tea, tall meadow rue, and sweet gale are the most

Red eft on a pincushion moss. Photo courtesy Massachusetts Audubon/H.B. Kane

obvious shrubs and cotton grass, white turtleheads, marsh St. Johnswort, bog club moss, and twig rush the most common nonwoody plants. Cotton grass, actually a type of sedge, has dense balls of white, cottony hairs that surround its inconspicuous flowers. Maybe the kids can even guess its other name, hare's tail.

Help the kids carefully inspect the sphagnum mats for **sundews,** tiny plants whose rounded leaves are bordered with sticky hairs that trap insects. Bogs are low in nutrients, so the sundew feeds itself in a very unplant-like way—catching and digesting insects. Be careful to avoid trampling the sphagnum when you hunt for sundews.

The forest along the Greely Pond Trail contains a rich assortment of **woodland wildflowers,** particularly in the section between the two ponds. There are lots of clintonia, goldthread, painted trillium, hobblebush, rosy and clasping-leafed twisted-stalks, sharp-leafed asters, and rattlesnake roots (the latter having big bizarre leaves in three parts and drooping, greenish flowers in late summer). Snowberries, whose tiny rounded leaves smell like wintergreen when crushed, are particularly abundant at the side trail at the south end of the upper pond. In wet swales, there are white turtleheads, sedges, sphagnum moss, hobblebush, and (just beyond the big boulder), New England asters. Look for blue-colored algae growing on damp, moldy wood, the bright blue looking more like paint than a living thing.

If you look up, you may see ravens flying by. They roost on cliffs, such as those on East Peak of Osceola. And keep your eyes and ears open for the passage of guilds of small birds in the forest. Except for the red squirrels, animals are much less predictable than plants.

Sabbaday Falls

- **0.6 mile round-trip, minimal elevation gain**
- **30–60 minutes**
- **easy for all ages**

The short walk to Sabbaday Falls off the Kancamagus Highway has been one of the most popular in the White Mountains ever since tourists first started to frequent the region. It is an ideal walk for families with very young children. At the falls, it's easy to spend a long time watching the patterns of water rushing over granite ledges, through a narrow flume, and into deep, clear pools. Expect to have plenty of company on this trail.

No swimming or wading is permitted at Sabbaday Falls but the parking area has picnic tables, rest rooms, and an old hand pump for water.

What's in it for kids

- Short walk along a brook.
- Great cascades.
- Walk on stone stairs through a narrow flume.
- Hand pump for water at picnic area.

Getting There

The trailhead for Sabbaday Falls is on the south side of the Kancamagus Highway roughly fifteen miles west of

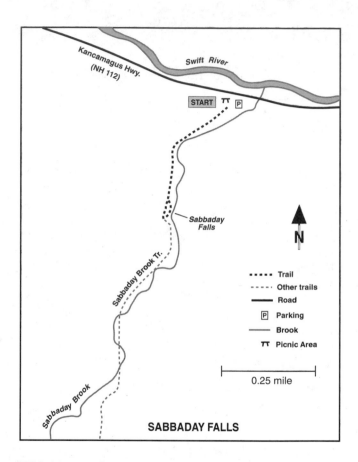

N.H. 16 near Conway and about nineteen miles east of I-93 in Lincoln. For those coming through Crawford Notch or Bartlett, the trail is three miles west of the junction of Bear Notch Road with the highway.

The Trail

Reach the falls via a short, well-marked loop off the Sabbaday Brook Trail. The 0.3 mile between the trailhead and the loop is wide and flat enough for a Mack truck (or at least a station wagon). The trail follows Sabbaday Brook on a slight ascent. The well-marked loop to the falls goes off to the left, passing the lower pool before ascending the stone stairs in the flume. The loop crosses over a bridge, goes past the upper pool, and then returns to the main trail. Turn right for the short walk back to the parking area.

This is a good place to hold your children's hands, since they will probably climb on the railings around the chasm and the falls.

Highlights

Sabbaday Falls contains a number of interesting **geological features** described on informative signs. The gorge, the pools, and the small rounded potholes in Sabbaday Brook were carved out by sand and small rocks carried by meltwater from the last continental glacier about 10,000 years ago. The floods that accompanied the melting of the glacier must have been tremendous, far surpassing anything we see today. Not only did the glacier unload vast volumes of water on the landscape, but it also unloaded sand and gravel that, in combination with the fast currents, acted like sandpaper to grind down rocks, creating waterfalls, new stream channels, and pools.

The narrow, straight gorge, or **flume,** at Sabbaday Falls was formed by the same processes that created the

Water rushes through a narrow flume at Sabbaday Falls. Nancy Schalch.

famous Flume of Franconia Notch (p. 69). A layer of basalt that had intruded into a crack in the granite wore away during the last Ice Age, leaving steep-sided granite walls fifty feet or so above the water. You can still see some remnant of the gray-black basalt within the flume at its lower end where it enters the lower pool.

Both the **lower and upper pools** were formed by scouring action of water melting from the glacial ice and during spring floods. Initially, **the falls** tumbled into the lower pool, but they eventually carved their way back through the basalt dike to form the flume and are now really several falls. At the deep upper pool you can get a feeling for the powerful erosive action of the grit-laden water by observing how the rock underwater has been carved away in a neat curve, creating an overhanging ledge. Keep in mind that the geological processes that created these marvels are still going on today, albeit at a slower rate than in the past because there is no glacial meltwater.

If you walk out below the lower pool, you will see a great example of a **pothole.** It is round and perched above the current level of the water, suggesting that it was carved out during the melting away of the glacier when water levels were higher than today. If it is filled with rainwater, look for mosquito larvae and other aquatic critters.

The trail is in a forest of northern hardwoods. Uphill from the brook, the trees are beech, sugar maple, and yellow birch, but along the brook itself, hemlocks are dominant. Hobblebush is the common understory shrub. Look for mosses and long beech fern growing right on the damp rocks around the falls. They have the best view.

The UNH Trail
to Hedgehog Mountain

- **4.8 miles loop, 1,200-foot elevation gain**
- **3.5–5 hours**
- **challenging for kids**

The UNH Trail is a loop trail off the Kancamagus Highway that takes you to the summit of 2,520-foot Hedgehog Mountain. This small mountain has a number of rocky ledges that provide great vistas of nearby peaks. It is surrounded by 4,000-footers, so you have the sense of being in the mountains rather than on top of them. On a clear day, you can see as far as the Presidential Range.

This is a substantial hike, so it's not suitable for younger children unless they do well in your baby backpack. Friends reported that it was a perfect outing for their eight- and ten-year-olds. The elevation gain is mostly gradual, with a few short steep sections. The trail takes you past three outlooks: the East Ledges, the summit, and Allen's Ledge. If you are short on time, just hike to Allen's Ledge, which is a little over a mile from the parking area.

The UNH Trail should be hiked only when the weather is good for two reasons: First, the ledges around the summit could be hazardous in wet weather; second, you don't want to miss the views.

You can combine this hike with a visit to the Russell Colbath House, a restored 1830s house that shows how some of the first settlers in the area lived. It is about a mile east of the trailhead along the Kancamagus Highway.

What's in it for kids _____

- Several rocky ledges to climb out on.
- A loop trail that is not too difficult.
- Great views and a sense of accomplishment.

Getting There

The trailhead for the UNH Trail is on the south side of the Kancamagus Highway about thirteen miles west of its intersection with N.H. 16. It is also the trailhead for the Downes Brook and Mount Potash trails. Turn left (south) on a gravel road opposite the Passaconaway Campground to find the trailhead. For those coming from the Crawford Notch or Lincoln, the trailhead is about one mile west of the intersection of the Kancamagus Highway and Bear Notch Road.

The Trail

The UNH Trail is named for the University of New Hampshire, whose forestry program uses the buildings you pass early in your hike. The trail runs with the Downes Brook Trail for about sixty yards in an open field, then turns left and enters the forest. The trail is marked with blue blazes, but there are some yellow blazes, too.

After a few minutes (0.2 mile) on an old railroad bed, you reach the junction of the loop. You can take either fork to reach Hedgehog Mountain, but we recommend

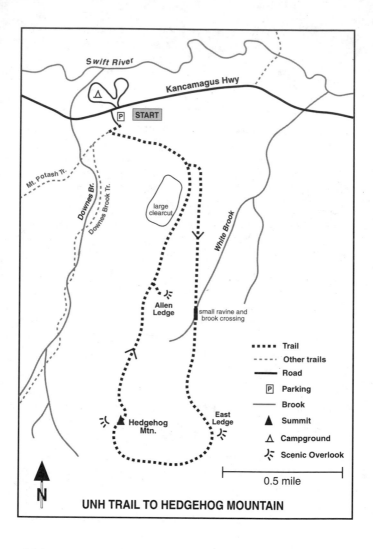

Swift River

Kancamagus Hwy

△

P START

Mt. Potash Tr.

Downes Br.

Downes Brook Tr.

large clearcut

White Brook

Allen Ledge

small ravine and brook crossing

Hedgehog Mtn.

East Ledge

▪▪▪▪	Trail
▪ ▪ ▪	Other trails
▬▬	Road
P	Parking
	Brook
▲	Summit
△	Campground
⅄	Scenic Overlook

0.5 mile

UNH TRAIL TO HEDGEHOG MOUNTAIN

N

hiking the loop clockwise so you can enjoy the view from open ledges on the descent. Also, the east branch ascends more gradually. However, if you only have time for Allen's Ledge, take the right fork of the loop.

For the complete loop, take the left (east) fork, which continues straight ahead from the junction on the railroad bed for another 0.2 mile, then turns right and ascends gradually up an old logging road for a while. It leaves the logging road and continues ascending through a nice stand of hemlocks. At 1.6 miles, the trail descends into a small ravine and crosses a brook. It then ascends more steeply through a red spruce forest and comes out on the East Ledges (2.0 miles, about 1.5 hours). Stop for a while to enjoy the view.

The trail levels, then climbs steeply to reach the summit itself, about 0.9 mile (forty minutes) from the East Ledges and 2.9 miles from the trailhead. Be careful here, because some of the ledges could be slick in wet weather. The best view is not at the summit itself but at ledges a little beyond. Turn left at the trail sign to reach that area.

The UNH Trail descends from the summit of Hedgehog Mountain through open ledges with great views north. In about twenty minutes (0.8 mile from the summit) watch for the turnoff to Allen's Ledge, marked by a sign. Take the side trail back uphill and follow the base of a massive rock to the left.

From Allen's Ledge it is 1.1 miles (about thirty minutes) to the parking area. The trail descends steeply, passing a very large clear-cut. Just before the loop junction, a cross-country ski trail enters from the left. Turn left at the loop junction to get back to your car.

Highlights

Two mountains south of the Kancamagus Highway are named after hedgehogs, presumably because the spires of spruce and fir that cover their rounded summits reminded those in charge of naming things of the spines of a porcupine. You and your children can make a game of this: Have them look at the trail map for other mountains named after animals and ask them why they are so named.

The **three different vistas** on this hike are all distinctive and all will satisfy young ledge scramblers. The view from the East Ledges is the most intimate, looking down over a secluded valley bounded by Mount Passaconaway and Mount Paugus. Chocorua is in the background. Former clear-cuts obviously covered with new growth testify to logging in years past.

The **ledges near the summit** offer spectacular views of peaks to the north and south. Carrigain Notch, bordered by Mounts Carrigain, Anderson, and Nancy, is a wonderful example of a glacially carved U-shaped valley. Mount Hancock to the west of Carrigain is a long ridge. To the west, Mount Passaconaway is particularly massive. Potash Mountain, with a number of clear-cuts, is nearby and roughly the same height as Hedgehog. Behind Potash are the three summits of Mount Tripyramid. The Swift River Valley separates this assemblage of mountains from Carrigain and Hancock.

Allen's Ledge was named for Jack Allen, a White Mountain guide. From here Mount Washington is visible on a clear day. In front of Mount Carrigain, Green's Cliff is prominent. You also see Bear Mountain, Mount Chocorua, and Mount Paugus.

Inspecting the view from the East Ledges of Mount Hedgehog.
Edward F. Sullivan.

This is a good trail to see the passage of a **guild of forest birds** containing a variety of species. Guilds are "teams" of birds of different species that forage together in the forest. The term "guild" comes from the old Dutch craftsmen's associations. You may have noticed on this and other hikes that you usually go a long time without seeing or hearing any birds; then all of a sudden, you are surrounded by chickadees, nuthatches, golden-crowned kinglets, warblers, woodpeckers, and others. If you stop to watch them for a while, they will busily make their way together across a trail and eventually move on.

If you have binoculars, notice that the different species have different ways of feeding. Chickadees and kinglets are acrobats, often hanging upside down as they inspect small twigs for insects or buds. Nuthatches probe the bark of the main trunk and large branches, while woodpeckers poke holes in branches and trunks to catch the insects deeper within the tree. Warblers and flycatchers sally for flying insects, while juncos and thrushes forage among the leaf litter on the ground. By using different feeding methods, these birds reduce competing with each other, although there is undoubtedly some overlap in their menus. The advantage to feeding in guilds is that large numbers of birds are probably more efficient at flushing insects than an individual would be. Also, there are more eyes to watch out for predators, like Cooper's hawks, and to mob a predator if one should appear.

If a bird guild should appear while you are walking through the boreal (spruce and fir) forest, keep your eyes open for **boreal chickadees.** These birds resemble black-capped chickadees, those familiar epicures of sunflower seeds at backyard bird feeders, but they are slightly smaller and have a brown, rather than black, bib. Boreal chickadees inhabit the spruce-fir forests in the White Mountains. At the elevation of Hedgehog Mountain, 2,500 feet, you might very well see both species of chickadees, perhaps even together.

The forest you walk through starts out as northern hardwoods and eventually becomes boreal as you near the ledges. Some understory plants to look for are heart-leafed aster, Indian cucumber root, Solomon's seal, Indian pipes, and shiny club moss. At the summit of Hedgehog Mountain, red spruce, sheep laurel, mountain holly, and bracken fern grow.

When you finish this hike, the kids may be a little weary but they'll be proud of their accomplishments.

Rail 'n River Nature Trail

- 0.75 mile loop, no elevation change
- 0.5 hour
- easy for all ages

The Rail 'n River Nature Trail is an easy, short, self-guided nature trail off the Kancamagus Highway at the Passaconaway Historical Site. This pleasant walk is suitable for even the earliest walkers. The trail is a wide path through a forest with some very tall trees and includes a short section on the banks of the Swift River. Past logging activity and the old logging railroad that used to run here are major themes of the nature walk. The trail brochure also describes interesting trees, the river, and evidence of local wildlife.

You can combine this walk with a visit to the Russell Colbath House, where people in period dress describe how the early settlers lived. The house also serves as a National Forest Information Center. Swimming is five miles east at Lower Falls.

What's in it for kids

- Short, easy loop trail.
- Exploring the Swift River.
- Some very tall, straight white pines.
- Glacial erratic.
- Searching for evidence of the old railroads that were here almost a century ago.

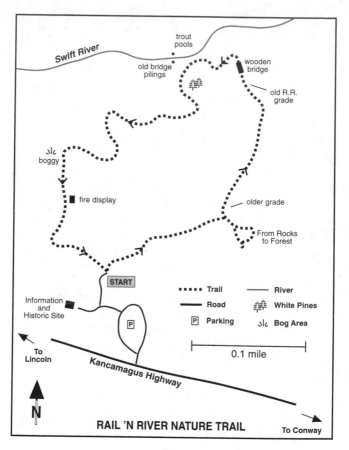

Swift River

trout
pools

old bridge
pilings

wooden
bridge

old R.R.
grade

boggy

fire display

older grade

From Rocks
to Forest

START

Information
and
Historic Site

P

••••• Trail	—— River
—— Road	🌲 White Pines
P Parking	⟱ Bog Area

0.1 mile

To
Lincoln

Kancamagus Highway

RAIL 'N RIVER NATURE TRAIL

To Conway

N

Getting There

The Passaconaway Historic Site is just west of the junction of the Kancamagus Highway and Bear Notch Road. From N.H. 16 in Conway, it's a little over twelve miles west on the Kancamagus Highway (N.H. 112). From the Crawford Notch area, take U.S. 302 to Bartlett, turn right on Bear Notch Road, then right on the Kancamagus Highway for less than a mile. From Franconia Notch and Lincoln, the historic site is about twenty-two miles east of I-93 on the Kancamagus Highway.

The parking area is on the north side of the Kancamagus Highway. Follow the path toward the historic site, and turn right toward the rest rooms. The Rail 'N River Nature Trail starts just beyond.

The Trail

The last time we walked this trail, very few of the numbered stations listed in the nature leaflet were actually marked in the forest. The Forest Service may be revamping the trail in the near future, so you might check in at the information center about its status before using the brochure. Of course, it might be fun to try to figure out where the stations should be, given the information in the brochure. The walk is still a good family outing even without a trail guide.

The Rail 'N River Nature Trail is a loop that is very wide and easy. Parents will have no trouble holding hands with their children. We will describe it going counterclockwise as recommended in the trail leaflet.

After walking a few minutes, partly over an old railroad grade, you reach a short side trail that leads to the "From Rocks to Forest" area. Here, there are a number of interpretive signs.

Back on the main trail you reach the Swift River after walking across a wooden board bridge. Old pilings poking up in the river are a remnant of an old railroad bridge.

The trail turns away from the river and reaches a junction. Follow the main trail straight ahead past some very large white pines, an open boggy area, and a display of firefighting equipment. Soon you are back at the loop junction.

Highlights

Look for evidence of the **logging railroads** that traversed this area in the late nineteenth and early twentieth centuries. The Bartlett Land and Lumber Company Railroad was the first one in the area and hauled logs to Bartlett. Later, the Swift River Railroad brought lumber to mills in Conway. Have the kids look for raised areas running off into the woods. These were elevated embankments for tracks. Their present overgrown appearance makes them look natural until you realize that no geological process would have made them so straight. There are also depressions where gravel was dug from the side of railroad grades to build them up. The trail brochure is handy for pointing out exact locations, but you should be able to find some yourselves.

The From Rocks to Forest loop is a great place to learn about the **formation of soil.** You first pass a large glacial erratic covered with mosses. Rocks such as this are the raw material from which soil eventually develops. At another station, the Forest Service has dug a hole in the ground to show you a soil profile. The uppermost layer of soil really does look different from lower layers, because materials have been leached from

Exploring the Swift River.

the top by water infiltrating down over centuries. The information panels tell you that it takes 1,000 years to make one inch of soil.

The short section **along the Swift River** is a treat. If you are there during dry periods in the summer, the river won't be very swift. The water meanders by slowly, allowing you to see reflections of trees and sky. The bottom is covered with a lush growth of wild celery. In spring when the snow melts, however, the Swift River can be a raging torrent and live up to its name.

Look for a large white pine with a double trunk where the trail turns away from the river. See if the kids can guess how it got its unique shape. Probably an insect destroyed the bud at the tip of the tree when it was a sapling, and two side branches then grew out.

The Rail 'n River Nature Trail is a great place to learn to differentiate **conifer trees.** Five different species grow in close proximity to the trail: white pine, red spruce, balsam fir, hemlock, and larch (tamarack). The white pines, with their long, soft needles in bunches of five, are particularly impressive in size and straightness. Fortunately, both the Bartlett Land and Lumber Company and the Conway Lumber Company must have missed these, so they are now here for us to enjoy. Red spruce, balsam fir, and hemlock all have single needles (not in bunches). Red spruce needles are squarish, so you can twirl them in your fingers. Balsam fir and hemlock needles are flat, therefore not twirlable. Hemlock needles tend to be shorter than balsam fir needles and are attached to the twig by a tiny stalk. Balsam fir needles lack a stalk. Larch has needles in bunches of twenty to twenty-five.

The best place to see larches on this trail is in the open boggy area around station 25, about three-fourths of the way around the loop. It's also a good spot for haircap mosses, sedges, blueberries, huckleberries, and rhodora.

Champney Falls

- **3.5 miles round-trip, 600-foot elevation gain**
- **3 hours**
- **moderate for kids**

The hike to Champney Falls is an ideal family walk: long enough to feel you've accomplished something, yet not so long so that it becomes an ordeal. At the end you are rewarded with two pretty waterfalls that will be especially impressive just after a heavy rain. And getting there is also fun: The trail runs along the brook for much of the walk, passing by some weirdly shaped trees on rocks and a good assortment of White Mountain wildflowers.

What's in it for kids

- Two waterfalls.
- Rocks to scramble around at the waterfalls.
- A wooden bridge over Champney Brook right at the beginning of the trail.
- A good part of the hike is along a stream.

Getting There

The parking lot for the Champney Falls Trail is on the south side of the Kancamagus Highway (N.H. 112) about ten miles west of its junction with N.H. 16 and about two miles east of Bear Notch Road.

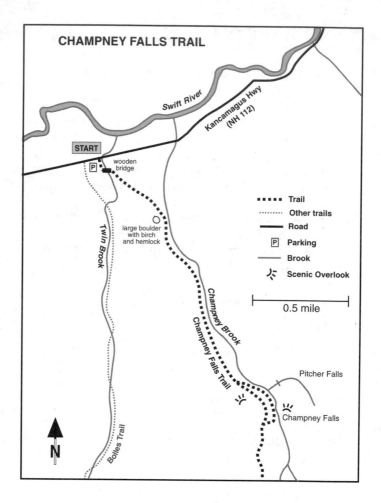

CHAMPNEY FALLS TRAIL

Swift River

Kancamagus Hwy (NH 112)

START

P wooden bridge

Twin Brook

large boulder with birch and hemlock

• • • • Trail
• • • • Other trails
———— Road
P Parking
———— Brook
⅄ Scenic Overlook

0.5 mile

Champney Brook

Champney Falls Trail

Champney Falls Trail

Pitcher Falls

Champney Falls

Bolles Trail

N

The Trail

The Champney Falls Trail is marked with yellow blazes. It is very heavily used and has a large number of exposed tree roots.

The Champney Falls Trail begins by crossing Twin Brook on a wooden bridge with a railing on one side. After about fifteen to twenty minutes, you reach Champney Brook and parallel the west bank of the brook for the rest of the hike.

Take a left at the junction to the loop trail to Champney and Pitcher falls at 1.4 miles (1–1.25 hours). In about ten minutes you pass a small waterfall, more like a shoot, that empties into a pool. Soon after, you reach Champney Falls. After admiring Champney Falls, make sure to walk about 100 yards east between two narrow ledges to the base of Pitcher Falls. Pitcher Falls is more likely to have significant water flowing over it all year.

Continue on the loop trail and ascend the west side of Champney Falls to the top of the falls, where there is a restricted view. Be cautious when scrambling around the rocks because the shade tends to keep them damp and slippery.

Follow the trail away from the falls to the upper junction of the loop trail with the Champney Falls Trail (2–2.25 hours). Turn right and begin the gradual 1.7-miles descent back to your car.

Highlights

The loop trail takes you through a rocky glen to **Champney and Pitcher falls.** Before you reach these falls, you

Pitcher Falls.

pass a small cascade that empties into a pool surrounded by moss-covered rocks. The pool is deep enough for wading, but the shadiness keeps the temperature of the water at penguin level for most of the year. Look for water striders in the pools.

You then come to Champney Falls, named for Benjamin Champney, a White Mountain artist of the nineteenth century. Water plunges (or in dry weather, trickles) over a series of stairlike ledges. There is a large rectangular boulder in the streambed at the base of the falls that has seen the bottom of many young hikers' feet.

Pitcher Falls is a beautiful, thin cascade of water that looks like it somehow got lost and changed its course. You enter a narrow gorge bounded by two almost vertical side walls. Instead of being at the far end of the gorge as you might expect, Pitcher Falls plunges over one of the sides. The stream above Pitcher Falls likely changed its course at some point, since erosion by water created the gorge in the first place.

The top of the falls is another communal stop on this hike. You will likely find other people there, perched out on rocks admiring the brook and the view of nearby mountains. The view is refreshing, particularly after the long walk through a dense forest. There is another good overlook on the section of the Champney Falls Trail between the upper and lower junctions with the loop trail.

The falls aren't the only thing of note on this trail. On the way there are some **natural bridges and dams** created by tree falls. These will be in place for a few years, then will move on during late spring floods, as the trees decompose. Nevertheless, they can trap debris and small stones and create pools that last as long as the trees stay in place.

At the point where the trail first reaches Champney Brook, there is a marvelous **duo of a yellow birch and hemlock** on top of a large boulder. Both trees look like they are growing right out of a rock, and their roots have intertwined as they reach for a foothold in the ground beneath the boulder. It is a good lesson in cooperation.

The **forest** is of northern hardwoods with lots of hemlock early in the trail, particularly along water. Hobblebush and striped maple form the understory. Have the kids find a number of particularly "stripey" striped maples on the Champney Falls Trail between the upper and lower junction of the loop trail.

The Champney Falls Trail has a good assortment of **wildflowers** and other small plants, particularly near the trailhead. Indian cucumber root, partridgeberry, and shiny club moss are particularly common. Also, look for painted trillium, shinleaf, rosy twisted-stalk, jack-in-the-pulpits, and a few pink lady's slippers. Bunchberries, wintergreen, and hobblebush border the brook right at the ledge above the falls.

With the falls and the flowers, you'll have a very satisfying half-day outing.

Rocky Gorge and the Lovequist Loop around Falls Pond

- **0.9 mile loop, no elevation gain**
- **0.5–1 hour**
- **easy for all ages**

This is a short, easy hike right off the Kancamagus Highway. It includes a walk on a bridge over a small gorge on the Swift River and a peaceful walk around a small pond. The Rocky Gorge Scenic Area is a popular destination where families can hang out or have picnics on the abundant flat rocks by the river's edge and perhaps throw a fishing line in the water. Falls Pond is a quiet pond hidden by a dense forest of conifers.

What's in it for kids

- Lots of flat rocks on which to scramble around.
- A bridge over a canyon with rushing water flowing underneath.
- Short loop around a pond surrounded by dense spruce and hemlocks.
- Chance to explore around the edge of the pond.
- A chance to meet a joe-pye weed.

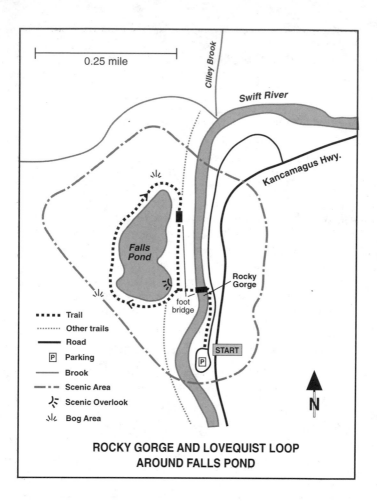

0.25 mile

Cilley Brook

Swift River

Kancamagus Hwy.

Falls Pond

Rocky Gorge

foot bridge

START

P

N

- - - - Trail
- - - - Other trails
──── Road
P Parking
──── Brook
─·─·─ Scenic Area
⚹ Scenic Overlook
⚺ Bog Area

**ROCKY GORGE AND LOVEQUIST LOOP
AROUND FALLS POND**

Getting There

Rocky Gorge Scenic Area is nine miles west of the intersection of the Kancamagus Highway (N.H. 112) and N.H. 16 in Conway. The well-marked turnoff is about three miles west of the turnoff for Lower Falls, another scenic area. You'll find rest rooms right at the parking area.

If you are coming from the Crawford Notch area, take U.S. 302 to Bartlett, turn right on Bear Notch Road, and then left (east) when you reach the Kancamagus Highway. The parking area for Rocky Gorge Scenic Area is on the left in about 3.5 miles.

The Trail

From the parking area, walk northeast on the paved path along the river until you see the footbridge over Rocky Gorge. Cross the river, then stroll up wooden steps through hemlocks to get to the junction with the loop trail. Go straight across to the shore of the pond for a nice view before beginning the Lovequist Loop.

The Lovequist Loop is a short, wide path, essentially free of rocks. Except for one section, you could take a stroller. Return to the junction, make a right turn and head clockwise around the pond. Go up a small hill, then turn right at the next junction (sign saying "around the pond"—straight ahead is a cross-country ski trail). This next section of the Lovequist Loop is particularly pleasant. You are high above the pond, but it's visible through tall spruces with little understory.

At another fork, veer slightly left and start heading downhill. A "caution" sign reveals that the Lovequist Loop is part of the cross-country ski trail system maintained by the Forest Service. Turn sharply right at a boggy area at the bottom of this hill.

The trail then goes through a small section of hardwoods roughly halfway around the loop, then the spruces return. Two short spur trails give you access to the pond shore. Take either or both for a vista from this side of the pond and for exploring pond shore life.

The trail crosses over a stream surrounded by a wetland with lots of sphagnum. Soon after, follow an arrow directing you back to Rocky Gorge. The trail passes over a solid wooden bridge at a rushing stream—the outlet from the pond. At the end of the loop, turn left to return to Rocky Gorge and your car.

Highlights

Rocky Gorge and Falls Pond are the "cohighlights" of this hike. The children will enjoy the excitement of the water rushing through a narrow gorge, which is a nice contrast with the peaceful pond hidden behind hemlocks and spruce. You can experience both in little more than an hour.

When you stand on the **bridge** note that the walls of the canyon are fairly rectangular, at least in part because granite fractures along definite joints. It's a surprise when natural things are organized into such familiar geometric shapes. Notice, too, that the granite rocks are crisscrossed with white pegmatite dikes.

Signs make it very clear that you should not attempt to swim at Rocky Gorge. The strong currents in the gorge make it dangerous. Check out Lower Falls, three miles east for swimming.

Falls Pond, eight acres in area, feels remote despite its proximity to the Kancamagus Highway. For most of the hike, the dominant trees are **red spruce** and white pine. Some of the spruce are massive, particularly along the south shore of the pond. Many young spruce are also in the understory, indicating that this area is likely to remain heavily endowed with spruce for a long time.

Red spruce is presently abundant at midelevations (roughly 2,000 to 4,000 feet) in the White Mountains. This tree is easily recognized by its needles—they are individually attached on twigs (in contrast to pines in

Red spruce dominates the forest around Falls Pond.

which the needles are in bunches of two to five) and feel decidedly prickly when you grab them. Spruce needles are square in cross section, so that you can twirl them between your fingers, unlike the flat, untwirlable needles of hemlock and balsam fir. One way to remember all this is that to "spruce up" is to look sharp, just like spruce needles.

Before the advent of widespread logging in the White Mountains, the red spruce was more common even at lower elevations (1,100 feet at Falls Pond). Unfortunately, spruce were preferred by many loggers, and the forests that replaced them often grew up in northern hardwoods rather than spruce. So appreciate this great stand of spruce and that it is apparently sustaining itself well.

The kids might like to try spruce gum. Find some exuded resin, pick out as much dirt as possible, and start chewing. The taste is pleasant and piney, and after a while, it will become the texture of chewing gum.

Take a look at the shrubs growing in damp, boggy habitats along the pond shore. Common ones include sweet gale (crushed leaves smell like bayberry), Labrador tea (rusty brown fuzz on the underside of leaves), leatherleaf (rusty scales on the undersides of leaves), sheep laurel, and huckleberry.

The **boggy wetland** at the southwest corner of the pond exists because the topography does not allow water to drain. A number of plants historically important to people grow there. **Sphagnum moss** soaks up water like a sponge and creates acid conditions in the bog by secreting hydrogen ions. Because sphagnum absorbs water so well, it has been used as a natural diaper. Its acidity has also led to its use as a sterile compress. And, of course, it is the peat moss that we use to condition the soil in our gardens.

In August, you will be greeted by **joe-pye weed,** a tall plant with large purple or pink flat-topped flower clusters comprised of many small individual florets. Joe Pye, or Jopi, was a Native American who reportedly used the plant to cure typhus and other fevers in colonial times.

Sensitive fern is one of the first plants to succumb to cold weather in the fall, hence its name. The fertile (reproductive) frond of this fern looks like a stalk topped off with clusters of tiny ball bearings. These latter, containing the spores, are often part of dried flower bouquets.

The trees growing in the boggy area are red maples, famous for their brilliant, red fall foliage.

In contrast to the damp habitats of the bog and the pond shore, there are a few drier areas along the Lovequist Loop where the sun shines through to the forest floor. Bracken fern has colonized these areas. Unlike most of its ferny cousins, the bracken does not seem to mind drier habitats and thrives where the canopy of trees is thin. Look for bracken, a robust fern whose main stalk divides into three equal stalks, after you climb up the little hill at the beginning of the loop.

Boulder Loop Trail

- **3.1 miles loop, 850-foot elevation gain**
- **2–4 hours**
- **challenging for kids**

Most self-guided nature trails are simple, short, and flat, usually on a well-manicured path. The Boulder Loop Trail has more ambition. It takes you up about a thousand feet to rocky ledges on a shoulder of the Moat Range where there are fine views across the Swift River valley to a number of 4,000-footers south of the Kancamagus Highway. The loop is appropriate for younger hikers who have some experience on trails or for nonhikers who can be easily carried in a backpack. The trail lives up to its name by passing jumbles of huge boulders deposited by landslides. Along the way, you pass eighteen numbered stations at sites of particular geological or ecological interest. An informational leaflet available at the Saco Ranger Station or the trailhead provides a narrative on each station.

*What's in it for kids*_____

- Good scrambling on rocks at the ledges.
- Some blueberries there, too.
- Jumbles of huge boulders from past landslides, some creating caves.
- Eighteen numbered stations to hunt for in the forest.
- A covered bridge near the trailhead.

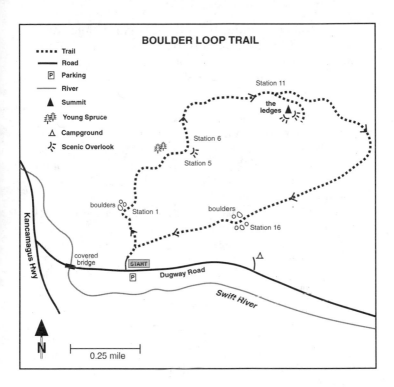

BOULDER LOOP TRAIL

- ∙∙∙∙ Trail
- ▬ Road
- P Parking
- ▬ River
- ▲ Summit
- 🌲 Young Spruce
- △ Campground
- 🎋 Scenic Overlook

Station 11

the ledges ▲

Station 6

🌲

Station 5

boulders

Station 1

boulders

Station 16

Kancamagus Hwy

covered bridge

START

P Dugway Road

△

Swift River

N

0.25 mile

Getting There

The Boulder Loop Trail is six miles west of the intersection of the Kancamagus Highway (N.H. 112) and N.H. 16. Turn right at the sign to the Covered Bridge Campground (Dugway Road) and drive through the Albany Covered Bridge (constructed 1858, renovated 1970). Park in the first parking area beyond the bridge and find the trailhead at the north side of Dugway Road.

If you are coming from the Crawford Notch area, take U.S. 302 to Bartlett, turn right on Bear Notch Road, and then left (east) when you reach the Kancamagus Highway. Dugway Road is about six miles east.

The Trail

The Boulder Loop Trail is marked by yellow blazes. The loop begins 0.2 mile (5 minutes) from the parking area. Turn left to follow the sequence with the numbers of the nature trail. Right away you pass a huge boulder where the trail bends to the right and then a few more impressive boulders. The trail ascends and after about forty minutes enters a clearing (around station 5 of the nature trail) that provides the first vista out over the valley and across to the ledges. In another twenty minutes (1.3 miles), you reach the sign saying "to the view, 0.2 mile" (station 11). Follow the short side trail up the stone steps that takes you to the ledges.

The side trail extends onward in the open for another 0.3 mile beyond the first view. The views are all great, but don't get too close to the edge, particularly if it's rainy, because the drop-off is steep. These ledges, at 1,965 feet, are the highest elevation on the trail. A large yellow X marks the spot where you turn around.

When you return to the main trail, turn right for the one-hour descent. Just below the ledges, you pass a huge rock that is at least as large as ten blue whales. The trail continues downhill, crosses a stream (station 16), and enters another area of huge boulders strewn by a landslide 2.3 miles from the trailhead (station 17). The kids will undoubtedly try to walk through caves created by the jumble of rocks. Beyond this, the trail flattens out and traverses a few small streams. At the loop junction, go straight to return to the parking area.

Highlights

The leaflet for the **self-guided nature trail** provides you with a wealth of information on forest dynamics and geological processes of this area. The two most striking aspects are the giant boulders and the ledges. Although more subtle, the forest dynamics are also quite interesting. Put your children in charge of finding the numbered stations while you read to them from the leaflet.

Two particularly impressive jumbles of **large boulders** are located at station 1, right at the beginning of the hike, and at station 17 near the end. Major landslides formed these jumbles. Station 1 has two especially huge boulders, one with a crack in it that forms a cave and another covered with rock tripe lichens. The most notable formation at station 17 is an overhanging rock that is a good place to get out of the rain and still be able to sit on a flat rock.

Forest dynamics are easy to follow along the Boulder Loop Trail. The trail begins in a northern hardwoods forest with an understory of hobblebush and striped maple. By station 2, increasing numbers of red spruce indicate a transition to the boreal forest. Note the area of young spruce trees (around station 4) growing in a former clearing. At the clearings on the ascent, such as around stations 6 and 7, red spruce are largely replaced by red oak and white pine. Ask the kids to speculate on why this is so, and then have them feel the

Albany Covered Bridge at the trailhead to the Boulder Loop Trail. Nancy Schalch

difference in temperature (if sunny) and soil on the ledge compared to the forest. Oak and white pine survive better than spruce in drier, sunnier, warmer areas, such as these open ledges.

Other things to note about the forest are the large holes made by pileated woodpeckers (in one of the white pines at station 6) and white ash (station 7). White ash is a broad-leafed tree whose leaves are composed of many leaflets and arranged in pairs along the twigs. Its wood is used for baseball bats. Common woodland wildflowers include Canada mayflower, clintonia, pink lady's slipper, false Solomon's seal, spikenard, wild sarsaparilla, silverrod, goldenrod, shinleaf, and sharp-leafed aster. The descent is particularly rich in hobble-bush and spinulose wood fern.

On a clear day, you can see Mounts Chocorua, Passaconaway, Middle Sister, and the Tripyramids from **the ledges.** Immediately below is the valley of the Swift River. This river is a tributary of the Saco River, which flows into the Atlantic Ocean on the coast of Maine.

The ecology at the ledges differs from the lower forest, partly because the thin soil supports only a few trees. Like the clearings described earlier, this area receives more sunlight and is drier so red oaks and white pines are mixed in with some red spruce. Note how the white pines have shorter needles, possibly an adaptation to reduce water loss in this wind-exposed location.

Mountain ash, a small tree of the boreal forest with distinct compound leaves, is common on the ledges. Mountain ash is really not an ash at all but a relative of apples and pears. In June it displays showy white flowers, and in late summer its red berries, borne in flat-topped clusters, are relished by birds. Their twigs are a favorite food of moose.

Low shrubs at the ledges include low-bush blueberries, shadbush, and dwarf juniper. Wildflowers include goldenrods and cow wheat. Reindeer moss, a pale green lichen, forms an ornate border around trees and shrubs.

Crawford Notch/ Zealand Region

THE CRAWFORD NOTCH/ZEALAND REGION lies in the heart of the White Mountains. The area includes two stunning U-shaped valleys and a number of mountains that rise above 4,000 feet. Just getting to this area is a real treat because the drive up U.S. 302 through Crawford Notch and up to the Zealand area is one of the most spectacular in the eastern United States, surpassed only by the drive *down* U.S. 302 in the same area. An early explorer, quoted by the Reverend Benjamin G. Willey in his 1856 book, *Incidents in White Mountain History,* described it eloquently:

> The sublime and awful grandeur of the Notch baffles all description. Geometry may settle the heights of the mountains, and numerical figures may record the measure; but no words can tell the emotions of the soul as it looks upward and views the almost perpendicular precipices which line the narrow space between them....

The hiking trails selected here take you to hidden ponds, breathtaking overlooks, good wildlife viewing, and some of the highest waterfalls in the White Mountains. In the secluded Zealand Valley many trails follow old logging railroads with gentle grades perfect for young hikers.

Facilities

A number of places provide information to hikers as well as an introduction to the rich history of the "Great Notch of the White Mountains." Crawford Notch State Park's visitor center is at the **Willey House Historic Site** off U.S. 302 and has a snack bar, rest rooms, and information. **Crawford Depot,** the old historic train station built in 1891, is now an information center run by the AMC and the Forest Service. This is where guests used to disembark for the Crawford House Hotel, which once stood near the site of the present hostel. The Depot is located just north of the point where U.S. 302 passes through the "Gateway of the Notch," highest and narrowest part of Crawford Notch.

If you really want to go upscale and get a flavor for a bygone era, you could stay at the Mount Washington Hotel in Bretton Woods. This is one of the last remaining grand hotels in the White Mountains and was the site where the Allies met after World War II to set monetary policy.

AMC Crawford Hostel. The Appalachian Mountain Club's Crawford Notch Hostel is located on U.S. 302 at the head of Crawford Notch by Crawford Depot. It offers overnight accommodations in two large bunk rooms (twelve beds each) and two cabins that sleep eight each. Reservations are recommended, particularly for large family groups. You need to bring your own food, but you can use the kitchen facilities, including the stove, utensils, pots, refrigerator, and dishes. There are no grocery stores in the immediate vicinity of the hostel, so it is a good idea to pick up your food in one of the towns you drive through along the way.

The hostel is centrally located for day hikes around Crawford Notch and Zealand. It has a small library there, too. Occasionally, AMC naturalists stay over and present evening programs or lead walks.

Supplies. This is an area of small towns and small stores. For picnic and other supplies, stop at one of the stores you pass on U.S. 302 in Glen, Bartlett, Notchland (in the heart of Crawford Notch), Bretton Woods, or Twin Mountain. The Big Red Barn, 1.6 miles west of Zealand Road on 302, is the closest place for food around Zealand. There are rest rooms and ice cream there, too. The towns of Twin Mountain, Bretton Woods, and Bartlett have a number of restaurants, gas stations, motels, hotels, and tourist cabins.

Camping. The Dry River Campground on U.S. 302 is the only public campground in Crawford Notch itself. It is about 1.5 miles south of the turnoff to Ripley Falls and 5.5 miles south of Crawford Depot. The Zealand and Sugarloaf campgrounds of the White Mountain National Forest are in the Zealand area. The Zealand Campground, with eleven sites, is right at the junction of U.S. 302 and Zealand Road. The two Sugarloaf campgrounds are 0.5 mile south on Zealand Road. They have a total of sixty-two sites and have facilities for people with disabilities. There are private campgrounds near Bartlett and Twin Mountain.

Ripley Falls

- **1 mile round-trip, 400-foot elevation gain**
- **1 hour**
- **moderate for kids**

Ripley Falls is one of the most impressive cascades in the White Mountains, particularly when water levels are high. The hike to Ripley Falls is a good one even for younger children. There is a short, steep section right at the beginning of the Ethan Pond Trail, but then, when you turn off for Ripley Falls, the hike levels out and is a pleasant woodland walk.

The Arethusa-Ripley Trail continues past Ripley Falls to Frankenstein Cliffs and Arethusa Falls, a long 3.8-mile hike with ups and downs. Save that one until the children are older.

A few miles south, **Arethusa Falls,** at over 200 feet the highest waterfall in New Hampshire, can be reached from U.S. 302 via the 1.3 mile Arethusa Falls Trail. Along the way a short side trail, the Bemis Brook Trail, passes by two smaller cascades, Bemis Brook and Coliseum Falls. Arethusa Falls is certainly worth a visit; however, the trail gets very heavy use and was heavily eroded the last time we hiked it. Some stream crossings and other parts of the Arethusa Falls Trail can be quite slippery, so extreme caution is needed. The hike to Ripley Falls is substantially easier.

What's in it for kids

- One of the prettiest waterfalls in the White Mountains.
- Swimming in potholes above the falls.
- Crossing over railroad tracks near a train trestle.
- An exploration of a hanging valley.

Getting There

The trailhead for Ripley Falls is at the site of the old Willey House Station off U.S. 302 in Crawford Notch State Park, about 0.5 mile south of the Willey House itself. There is a sign for Ripley Falls at the turnoff, which leads up a paved road 0.2 mile to the parking area for the trail. The turnoff is roughly 4 miles south of Crawford Depot and the AMC's Crawford Notch Hostel and 12 miles southeast of the junction of U.S. 302 and U.S. 3 in Twin Mountain. If you are coming up through Jackson or North Conway, the turnoff is about 16 miles northwest of the intersection of U.S. 302 and N.H. 16 in Glen.

The Trail

The hike begins with a steep climb on the Ethan Pond Trail, a part of the Appalachian Trail and thus marked with white blazes. Cross over the old Maine Central railroad tracks near a trestle. Avoid the temptation to walk along the railroad tracks and out on the trestle, since the entire rail bed is in poor repair (and it's illegal). After 0.2 mile the Arethusa-Ripley Trail, well marked with a sign, diverges left. You'll appreciate the

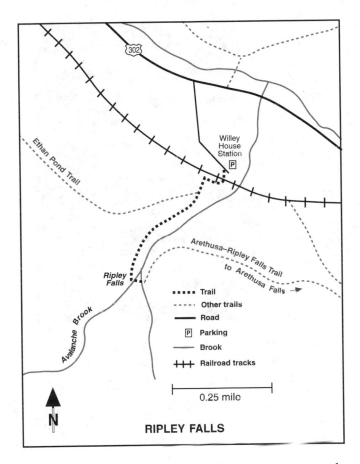

RIPLEY FALLS

Legend:
- **▪▪▪▪** Trail
- **- - -** Other trails
- **▬▬▬** Road
- **P** Parking
- **——** Brook
- **+++** Railroad tracks

0.25 mile

turnoff, since the Ethan Pond Trail continues on steeply whereas the Arethusa-Ripley Trail is quite level.

The Arethusa-Ripley Trail was marked with both yellow and blue blazes at the time of this writing. The

Ripley Falls.

trail proceeds high above Avalanche Brook, perched on the side of a steep slope for much of the 0.3 mile between the Ethan Pond Trail and the falls.

When you reach the falls be careful of the slippery rocks just underneath. The ledges at the top of the falls can also be slippery, so keep the kids away if you explore there.

Highlights

Ripley Falls is 100 feet high and flows gracefully down a slab of granite. The falls are named after Henry

Wheelock Ripley, who reported their existence in the 1850s.

Ripley Falls, like other waterfalls in the area, began flowing after the continental glacier departed from the area about 10,000 years ago. The glaciers that covered New England deepened the large north-south valleys such as Crawford Notch. Valleys of tributary streams that ran east or west, such as Avalanche Brook, were not similarly gouged and so were left high above the valley floor. Water that had once flowed gently into the Saco River now plunged steeply to reach the river in the notch. The picturesque waterfalls that now flow into Crawford Notch from both sides are the result of these so-called **hanging valleys.**

The forest you walk through is northern hardwoods. Many young sugar maples and birches are growing up along the trail. When you approach the falls, note how the cool water and shady gorge make you feel like you just walked into a **refrigerator.** This feeling is particularly pronounced (and welcome) on a hot day.

If you have time, climb up the left side of the waterfall and explore above the falls (but not too close to the brink). You'll get away from the crowds and also find a few pretty pools in which you can **swim.**

Mount Willard
A Bird's-Eye View of Crawford Notch

- **3.2 miles round-trip, 900-foot elevation gain**
- **3–4 hours**
- **challenging for kids**

My nephew's reaction to Mount Willard when he was eight years old is a perfect example of what it is sometimes like to hike with children. All the way up the trail he complained about the steepness of the hike: "This is stupid!" he said. "I can't understand why we're doing this. Why are you torturing me? Grumble, grumble...." In all fairness, the hike up this 2,815-foot spur of the Willey Range is pretty steep, and you really don't see much along the way because you are in a tunnel of trees. But at the top of Mount Willard, looking at the incredible panorama of Crawford Notch displayed before him, his mood changed instantly and he declared, "Oh this was *really* worth it!" The *AMC White Mountain Guide* agrees with that last statement. It says that "probably no other spot in the White Mountains affords so grand a view as Mount Willard for so little effort."

Take a windbreaker for the summit. On certain days, the wind gets funneled through the notch and really blasts away at the open ledges. The dense cover of conifers provides some shelter near the top, but proper attire will enable you to enjoy the view a little longer.

Attempts have been made in recent years to reintroduce peregrine falcons to the cliffs beneath the summit. Depending on the progress of nesting, the trail may be closed in late spring and early summer.

What's in it for kids

- A short steep climb to a wonderful view.
- One crossing of narrow-gauge railroad tracks.
- One log bridge crossing.
- Detour to Hitchcock Flume, if you dare.

Getting There

The trailhead for the Mount Willard Trail is located at the Gateway of Crawford Notch by the old Crawford Depot off U.S. 302. From the Jackson-North Conway area, follow U.S. 302 west at Glen where it splits from N.H. 16. U.S. 302 passes through Bartlett, then heads north through Crawford Notch. At the top of the notch, roughly twenty miles from the junction of N.H. 16 and U.S. 302, the road then goes through a narrow pass between two cliffs. The parking area for Crawford Depot is a few hundred yards up the road on the left.

From Twin Mountain, take U.S. 302 east. The parking area for Crawford Station is on the right just beyond the turnoff for the AMC's Crawford Notch Hostel, about eight miles south of the junction of U.S. 3 and U.S. 302.

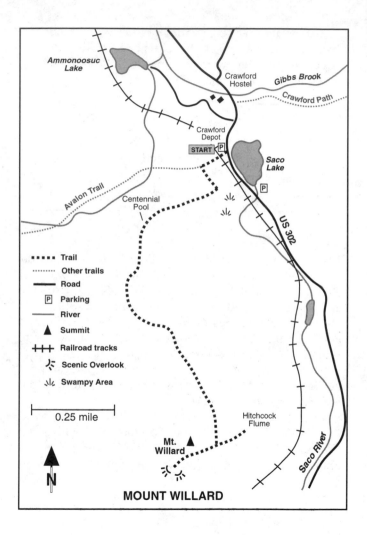

MOUNT WILLARD

The Trail

The Mount Willard Trail starts out with the Avalon Trail across the railroad tracks of the old Maine Central Line. In 0.1 mile at a display board, the Mount Willard Trail goes off to the left and the Avalon Trail continues straight ahead. The Mount Willard Trail is marked with blue blazes. The trail goes uphill at a steady pace, nowhere terribly steep or rocky, but nonetheless relentless. Where it follows the old carriage path, the Mount Willard Trail is wide enough for parents and children to walk two abreast.

The trail crosses several streams soon after leaving the Avalon Trail, the first of which is on a single log bridge. After 0.5 mile (fifteen to twenty minutes), Centennial Pool will be to the right. This is a small flume with a pretty "mini waterfall" about ten to fifteen feet high. There are nice lunch or snack rocks there, if you want a breather on the way up. At 0.7 mile, the trail turns right and follows the old carriage path the rest of the way.

Not far from the top (1.5 miles), the spur trail to Hitchcock Flume, an impressive chasm in the side of Mount Willard, departs to the left. This is a rough 0.2-mile detour steeply downhill with lots of roots, so avoid it in wet conditions, if you are not up for the extra time and effort, if you suffer vertigo, or if you have younger hikers. Allow yourself twenty to thirty minutes for this detour.

The open ledges near the summit of Mount Willard are 0.1 mile past the side trail to Hitchcock Flume. The return to Crawford Depot is a pleasant forty-to-sixty-minute walk.

Highlights

The **view from the ledges of Mount Willard** is one of the most famous in the White Mountains. Before you is a breathtaking panorama of a deep, broad notch bounded by steep-sided mountains. Crawford Notch is one of the best examples of a glacially carved U-shaped valley anywhere in the world. Because Crawford Notch runs north and south, it was a perfect channel for the continental ice sheet that covered this area as recently as 10,000 years ago. The glacier advanced along the course of a river, scouring the sides of the mountains and gouging out rocks. What had formerly been a V-shaped valley with a river at the bottom was transformed into a U.

In preglacial times, Silver and Flume cascades, which you pass on U.S. 302 just below the Gateway of

The view of Crawford Notch from Mount Willard.

the Notch, flowed gently into the river at the bottom of Crawford Notch. By steepening the sides of the Crawford Notch, the glacier left the original valleys of the two streams hanging high above the floor of the notch. The two cascades now plunge steeply down the glacially scoured side of the notch, and their courses are aptly termed hanging valleys.

Another prominent feature of the view from Mount Willard is the impressive evidence of **rock slides** on Mount Webster and Mount Willey. Many landslides and avalanches have occurred in Crawford Notch. The most famous occurred in August 1826, when several days of heavy rains caused a huge slide onto the homestead of the unfortunate Willey family. The entire family was killed. Moving accounts of the tragedy are in Lucy Crawford's *History of the White Mountains* (AMC Books) and in the Reverend Benjamin G. Willey's *Incidents in the History of the White Mountains* (available in some libraries—see bibliography).

The rocky ledges at Mount Willard support an interesting array of plants that can tolerate the exposure and thin soil. Three-toothed cinquefoil and mosses grow very neatly in cracks in the rocks where small amounts of soil accumulate. There are also patches of meadowsweet, raspberries, bluejoint grass, sedges, and hay-scented fern.

The view from the end of the **Hitchcock Flume Spur Trail**, though not as sweeping as from the ledges at the summit, is still breathtaking. Charles Hitchcock was the New Hampshire state geologist in the latter part of the nineteenth century and carried out a geological survey of the White Mountains that did much to publicize the area and inspire hikers and vacationers to come. Hitchcock Flume is a very narrow, deep fissure in a rock. There is a sheer cliff at the bottom of this flume with a view across the notch. This is definitely a vertigo spot, with no railings to lean against, so watch the children and yourself if you are uncomfortable on heights.

Near the top of the spur trail to Hitchcock Flume, you pass scattered boulders that form caves, always fun for kids to inspect. Some of the moss-covered rocks are topped with trees.

The **forest** along the Mount Willard Trail changes as you ascend. You begin in northern hardwoods and paper birch with an understory of wood ferns, shiny club moss, ground pine, goldthread, hobblebush, shinleaf, and mountain wood sorrel. Around the point where the trail rejoins the old carriage path, watch for a transitional forest with more and more spruce and fir. The understory includes sharp-leafed aster, large-leafed goldenrod, and Canada mayflower. Near the summit, you walk through the boreal forest dominated by balsam fir with an understory comprised largely of mosses, including sphagnum, haircap, and juniper mosses.

Peregrine falcons occasionally live in the area. These falcons catch other birds by flying high up in the sky above their target, then diving through the sky at speeds as fast as 180 miles per hour, knocking the unfortunate victim to the ground. Peregrines were wiped out in the eastern United States, largely because of DDT. This pesticide was picked up by the falcons in their food and caused the birds to lay eggs with thin shells. Since DDT was banned, biologists have successfully reintroduced peregrine falcons to a number of their former eastern haunts using techniques borrowed from the ancient art of falconry. Peregrines nest on inaccessible cliffs and will even use artificial cliffs (skyscrapers) in cities. Attempts have been made to establish a nesting pair on the cliffs below the summit of Mount Willard. Don't be disappointed if you find out that the trail is closed because the peregrines are nesting. Instead, feel good about this small victory for a spectacular, but still highly endangered, species, and make a point of coming back to Mount Willard some other time.

Around Saco Lake
to Elephant Head

- **1.2 miles round-trip, 100-foot elevation gain**
- **1 hour**
- **easy for all ages**

This short walk combines two even shorter walks near Crawford Depot at the Gateway to the Notch. Saco Lake, a small, unassuming pond off U.S. 302, is the headwater for the Saco River, which flows through Crawford Notch and all the way to the Atlantic Ocean. Elephant Head is a large rocky outcropping that overlooks Crawford Notch at the east side of the Gateway. It actually looks like the head of an elephant when viewed from the highway near the Depot.

The short trail around Saco Lake is perfect for all ages. A large segment of this trail is on the shoreline of the lake and crosses several streams and an impressive jumble of large boulders with views across to the Willey Range. You are rarely out of sight of the road. Elephant Head is 0.3 mile farther and requires some uphill (not very taxing). You can, of course, skip Elephant Head and return to your car after walking around the lake, or skip Saco Lake and hike directly to the Elephant Head.

What's in it for kids _____

- A climb on top of an elephant's head (so what if it's made out of stone?).

- Walk around a lake.
- A beaver house built among huge boulders, twenty feet high.
- A viewpoint named Idlewild.
- Several streams crossing on wooden bridges or flat rocks: Test your hopping skills.
- Mushy area on Elephant Head Spur traversed by wooden planks.

Getting There

Follow directions to Crawford Depot (page 177). The trailhead for the Saco Lake Trail is at the north end of the lake just across U.S. 302 from the parking area for the AMC's Crawford Notch Hostel. There is a white sign at the trailhead that says "Saco Lake, Idlewild." If you want to skip the walk around the lake and hike only to the Elephant Head, park near the south end of the lake and follow the signs to the Webster–Jackson Trail.

The Trail

The Saco Lake Trail enters the woods and soon crosses a small stream on rocks. In about five minutes you reach the shoreline of the lake. On the shore opposite the road, a plank bridge helps you traverse a rocky area with twenty-foot boulders. A short steep spur trail leads to the Idlewild Outlook on top of these rocks. The Saco Lake Trail continues along the shore, eventually crossing over the inlet to the lake on another plank bridge and returning to the highway at the south end.

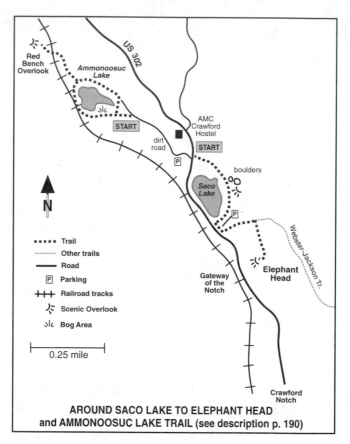

AROUND SACO LAKE TO ELEPHANT HEAD
and AMMONOOSUC LAKE TRAIL (see description p. 190)

From this point you can end your hike or continue on to Elephant Head, a round-trip of thirty minutes. To get to Elephant Head, continue toward the notch (south) along the highway to the trailhead for the Webster-Jackson Trail, just past a small field on the left. Take the Webster-Jackson Trail for a few minutes (less than 0.2 mile) to where the Elephant Head Spur diverges right, marked with a sign that says "Great View of the Notch." You pass through a damp area on wooden planks, ascend for a while, then descend slightly to the open ledge, 0.2 mile from the Webster-Jackson Trail. After admiring the view and the rocky ledge, retrace your steps back to the road and return to the Crawford Depot area and your car.

Highlights

The **walk around Saco Lake** is much more interesting than it might appear from the road. The wooden bridges, the chance to toss stones in the water, the huge rocks all combine to make this a great walk for small children. At any point along the trail, the kids can see where they have come from and where they need to go to reach the end.

The **huge rock formations** around the Idlewild Overlook are covered with rock tripe, a lichen that looks like a piece of boot leather. The rocks are topped with trees that somehow manage to cling precariously to life with very little soil. A **beaver house** is tucked in among the rocks, as if designed by a landscape architect.

From the lakeshore at this rocky area there is a **good view** across the lake to Mount Tom (4,017 feet). The view from the Idlewild Overlook is now partly overgrown, but youngsters will enjoy getting to the top of the rocks. Make sure you hang on to your children at the overlook because the railings are flimsy.

The Saco Lake Trail is a good place to study **granite.** At the bridge, inspect the coarse texture of the granite

Saco Lake and Old Crawford Depot with Mt. Webster in the distance.

for crystals of translucent quartz (grayish) mixed in with feldspar (white) and some biotite mica flakes (black or brownish). Also note that the vertical side of one of the huge boulders you pass is very flat, indicating that this rock broke off from an even larger rock along a flat joint. Another rock overhangs the trail.

In the summer, you are likely to see **swallows** flying over the lake. These small birds are very fast and adept fliers. They fly erratically with aerial pirouettes as they catch insects that fly above or emerge from the water. There are also several **wildlife trees** riddled with woodpecker holes. These dead trees provide homes for many birds and mammals.

At the inlet to the lake, poke around among the small stones for salamanders. The lake is stocked with trout, so fishing is a possibility with the proper New

Hampshire license.

Encourage the kids to spot the **Elephant Head** from the highway between Saco Lake and the Webster-Jackson Trailhead. White lines and spots of white quartz within the grayish granite give the ledge its distinctive profile. Be sure the kids get another, close-up view of the quartz and granite when they actually reach the Elephant Head. From the top of Elephant Head, you get **nice views both up and down the notch.** From this **perch** you can watch for wildlife. Beavers, ducks, and other animals reside in the wetland across U.S. 302. One time we saw an osprey flying over the wetland and then through the Gateway of the Notch, struggling against the ever-present wind the whole way.

Another thing to show children from Elephant Head are the **drainage patterns of the land.** Water in Saco Lake flows south through Crawford Notch as the Saco River, ultimately reaching the coast of Maine. Just north of the lake, above Crawford Hostel, any water that falls flows north to the Ammonoosuc River and eventually to Long Island Sound via the Connecticut River.

Note the black-eyed Susans, oxeye daisies, and goldenrods in the small field near the trailhead to the Webster-Jackson Trail. These sun-loving plants would be completely out of place in the forest. In the shade of the forest you will find mountain wood sorrel, spinulose wood fern, goldthread, clintonia, painted trillium, shiny club moss, and Dutchman's breeches. Northern white violets and sedges grow in the wet part of the trail that is traversed by the planks. These three different plant habitats illustrate the wide variety of nature you can enjoy on this short walk.

Ammonoosuc Lake

- 1 or 2 miles loop, minimal elevation change
- 1–2 hours
- easy for all ages

Ammonoosuc Lake is a surprising gem. It feels remote from civilization yet it is only a fifteen-minute walk from Crawford Depot and U.S. 302. Here you might see moose, beaver, or a wood duck, and the walk has a good assortment of White Mountain forest and wetland wildflowers. There is also a small area on the lake where you can take a cool swim on a hot day.

The Around-the-Lake Trail loops around the shore of Ammonoosuc Lake through a shady forest of evergreens. A side trail directs you to the Red Bench, a strategically placed seat in a clearing with a great view of Mount Washington and the Presidential Ridge.

It should take you no longer than an hour to hike the one-mile loop, but allow extra time for the Red Bench overlook. Make sure you have insect repellent handy, particularly if you are hiking at dawn or dusk. In damp weather or early spring, expect the trail to have some muddy spots.

What's in it for kids_____

- A loop trail around a pretty pond with an outlet dam you walk over.
- Maybe you'll see a moose.

- A swimming area (but the water may be over the heads of some children).
- A rest stop in the woods on a red bench.
- You can hunt for some snowberries, fireweed, and swamp candles.

Getting There

Park for Ammonoosuc Lake at the Crawford Depot at the head of Crawford Notch off U.S. 302. To get to Crawford Depot from the Conway-Jackson area, take U.S. 302 west about twenty miles west of the junction of N.H. 16 and U.S. 302 in Glen. From Franconia Notch and Twin Mountain, Crawford Depot is about eight miles south of the junction of U.S. 3 and U.S. 302 in Twin Mountain. The area is very well marked.

After parking your car, walk north on the service road between the AMC's Crawford Hostel on the right and a field to your left. Shortly beyond the hostel, you pick up the first sign for the Around-the-Lake Trail, which takes you left down a dirt road, then into the forest.

See page 186 for a map of this hike.

The Trail

The Around-the-Lake Trail diverges left from the dirt road that was an old vehicle access to the lake. In a few minutes, you reach the start of the loop. We suggest you follow it to the left in a clockwise direction. The trail crosses over a wet area on a board bridge and reaches the lake at a pretty fern glen. Walk along the west shore of the lake, past a mossy area with a spring, then cross another bog bridge.

In about fifteen to twenty minutes, you reach the turnoff (left) to the Red Bench overlook. This side trail to a pretty vista takes fifteen to twenty minutes in each direction. Follow the side trail through the woods away from the lake. It jogs right at the old railroad tracks, crosses over another wooden bridge by a pretty gorge, and then reaches a clearing in the forest with a red bench conveniently placed for admiring the view. Retrace your steps to return to the lake.

When you get back to the Around-the-Lake Trail, turn left. A short spur trail takes you down to the water's edge for a particularly nice view of the lake. In about ten minutes, you cross the outlet of the lake, which flows through a small culvert in a small dam. The concrete dam has been "improved" by beavers who probably don't trust their human counterparts to make a structure that will last. The best swimming is by the dam. Beyond the dam, you pass a small meadow on your right and then walk up the dirt road. If you are in a hurry, you could save a minute or two by continuing up the dirt road directly back to Crawford Depot. The Around-the-Lake Trail heads right from the road and eventually reaches the end of the loop, where you turn left to get back to your car.

Highlights

Ammonoosuc Lake is a beautiful, peaceful lake. Its spruce and fir-lined shore is the quintessential image of the northern wilderness. The scene seems right for a moose, and in fact you just might meet one here, particularly if you are hiking at dawn or dusk. You may also see ducks, including the gaudily colored wood duck, or a great blue heron feeding in the shallows. Green frogs croak with a sound like a banjo string, and salamanders hide among the stones along the streams.

At the start or the end of your hike, take a moment to admire the view of Mount Tom (4,047 feet) and examine the field across from the Crawford Hostel. Mount Tom, in the Willey Range, was named for Thomas Crawford, who built the original Crawford House. The field provides a sunny contrast to the shaded forest. In midsummer, small, deep crimson flowers with five petals and a black ring at the center are bound to catch your kids' eyes. These are maiden pinks, a nonnative inhabitant of roadsides and fields. Other nonnative eye-catchers are garden lupines, whose multicolored spikes of pealike flowers put on a gorgeous display along the left side of the dirt road that takes you into the forest. Garden lupines have "escaped" from gardens and now grow along roadsides in the area.

In early to mid-May evenings, this field hosts the bizarre courtship flight of the woodcock. Woodcocks look like little cartoon characters, with dumpy, rusty-colored bodies and long straight bills. At dusk, you first hear strange beeping noises that sound like a cross between a child's trumpet and an insect. This is followed by a somewhat musical twittering. Finally, when your eyes adjust to the half-light of dusk, you might actually see the males, who make the beeping sound and then take off straight into the sky until they almost disappear.

They then tumble to earth, making the twittering sound with specialized feathers on their wings. If you are lucky, a bird may land right near you and then repeat the ritual. If you go, get the kids to figure out where one is going to land, once it has taken off.

The **forest** near the lake is mostly red spruce, balsam fir, and paper birch. In wet areas and at the pond's edge the understory has red-berried elders, sheep laurel, northern wild raisin, leatherleaf, and Labrador tea. The easiest place to find these is on the short side trail down to the lake on the north side. Much of the path around the lake is lined with snowberry, a small plant with tiny,

Labrador tea grows on the shore of Ammonoosuc Lake.

rounded leaves attached to wiry stems that hug the ground. The leaves have a pleasant wintergreen smell when crushed. It is usually hard to find any of the snow-white berries that give this plant its name, but try your luck. There is lots of mountain wood sorrel, Canada mayflower, and clintonia growing around the lake, and you may find trillium and trailing arbutus there, too.

At the turnoff to the Red Bench, look for a good patch of goldthread as well as hobblebush. Along the Red Bench Trail show the kids how the spruce and firs give way to deciduous trees—beech, sugar maple, and yellow birch—probably because the soil is drier.

The **view from the Red Bench** of Mounts Washington (including the Cog Railway), Clay, Jefferson, and Eisenhower is definitely worth the extra time. And it's extra special because you generally have it all to yourself in a small clearing in the forest. Another plus is that the open clearing usually provides you with some relief from the blackflies and mosquitoes that can be a problem on this walk.

The children will appreciate the **small gorge** you pass near the Red Bench. It is lined with ferns and has trees growing out of its rocky walls.

The **swimming area** is at the south end of the lake by the dam. Guests from the Crawford House would come down to Ammonoosuc Lake for a swim and use a bathhouse that was located where the meadow on the shoreline presently is.

In this meadow you may find **fireweed.** Fireweed is a tall (generally three to six feet) wildflower with a very leafy stem and large, showy pink flowers with four petals. It is called fireweed because it is one of the first plants to colonize an area after a forest fire. Fireweed is not limited to burned-over areas—any new clearing will do. You'll find this wildflower along roadsides and ski trails as well as burned and logged areas. Fireweed only lasts a few years in any site before it disappears, replaced by shrubs, trees, and other plants with longer staying power (unless the area is kept open).

The wetter parts of the meadow near the shore of the lake harbor yellow loosestrife, whose bright yellow flowers in spires one to three feet off the ground in mid- to late summer give rise to its other name, **swamp candles.** If you explore around the wet meadow, be careful where you step, since it's easy to trample this kind of vegetation.

When you complete this hike, stop in at the Crawford Hostel for a snack, to use their library to look up any critters or unusual plants, or to plan your next hike.

Zealand Pond, Falls, and Hut

- **5.6 miles round-trip, 700-foot elevation gain**
- **3–4 hours**
- **moderate for kids**

The Zealand Trail takes you along a stream, over wooden bridges, past beaver meadows, along a pond where moose may lurk, and eventually to Zealand Falls and the AMC's Zealand Falls Hut. The hike is relatively easy, following the bed of an old logging railroad for most of its length except for a steep climb to the hut in the last 0.1 mile. Plan on spending a full day, since there is much for the whole family to see and do.

Zealand Falls Hut is one of the AMC's eight back-country facilities that can be reached only by hiking. Overlooking Zealand Notch at about 2,700 feet, it offers overnight lodging with breakfast and dinner (reservations essential). Since sleeping accommodations are in two large rooms with eighteen bunks each, the hut is not as comfortable for families with young children as Lonesome Lake Hut. (The AMC encourages families with children under three to stay only at those huts that have small, family sized bunk rooms, such as Lonesome Lake.) But even a day trip to Zealand Falls Hut is more than worth the effort. It has one of the most exquisite views in the White Mountains right from the front porch, and you can easily spend hours at the falls and river nearby. If you do stay overnight, the hut is a base for a number of wonderful day hikes.

Rumor has it that the area was named "Zealand" after New Zealand as a testament to its remoteness. When you are there, contemplating the serene forest with delicate wildflowers and the melodies of birdsongs wafting gently through the air, you would never imagine that at the turn of the century the Zealand Valley was ravaged by logging and two immense forest fires. Miraculously, it all came back.

What's in it for kids

- Hike along a river with wooden bridges for part of the trail.
- Beaver meadows, one crossed by an elevated boardwalk.
- Chance to see a moose.
- Zealand Pond and Falls.
- Swimming and wading in the river and falls near the hut.

Getting There

The trailhead for Zealand Trail is near Twin Mountain and Bretton Woods. From the Conway-Jackson area, take U.S. 302 west through Crawford Notch. Turn left on Zealand Road at the Zealand Campground, about 6 miles north of the AMC's Crawford Hostel. Follow Zealand Road for about 3.5 miles until its end and park in the lot. The trail is straight ahead, beyond the gate.

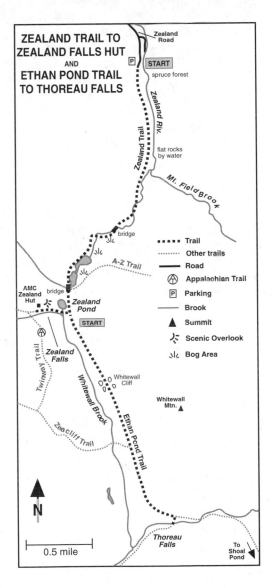

ZEALAND TRAIL TO
ZEALAND FALLS HUT
AND
ETHAN POND TRAIL
TO THOREAU FALLS

Zealand Road

P START

spruce forest

Zealand Trail

Zealand Riv.

flat rocks
by water

Mt. Field Brook

bridge

A-Z Trail

AMC
Zealand
Hut

bridge

Zealand
Pond

START

Twinway Trail

Zealand
Falls

Whitewall Brook

Whitewall
Cliff

Whitewall
Mtn.

Zeacliff Trail

Ethan Pond Trail

N

To
Shoal
Pond

Thoreau
Falls

0.5 mile

Legend:
- ▪▪▪▪ Trail
- ·········· Other trails
- ▬▬▬ Road
- Ⓐ Appalachian Trail
- P Parking
- ─── Brook
- ▲ Summit
- ⅄ Scenic Overlook
- ⅊ Bog Area

199

Zealand Road is closed to vehicles from mid-November to mid-May.

From Franconia Notch: Take U.S. 3 north to Twin Mountain. Turn right (east) on U.S. 302 and follow it for two miles. Turn right at the Zealand Campground and follow Zealand Road till its end as above.

From points north: Follow either U.S. 3 or N.H. 115 south to Twin Mountain. Turn left (east) on U.S. 302 and follow the directions given above.

The Trail

The Zealand Trail is easy and well marked with blue blazes. Be aware that a winter ski trail crosses back and forth over the hiking trail. It does cross some soggy terrain, and despite wooden bridges and planks, it can still be a bit wet in the spring or during wet weather.

The first part of the trail is a slight uphill through a dense red spruce forest with very young trees lining the trail. Most of the rest of the walk is through northern hardwoods. Along the way ask the kids to notice where they are walking on the bed of the logging railroad and where they are not.

After about twenty minutes, the first of many wooden bridges crosses a wet area. At 0.8 mile, you approach the Zealand River, where several flat rocks are perfect for having a snack or lunch. In 1.5 miles the trail crosses the river. You pass through a very pretty balsam fir and white birch woodland with an understory of mountain wood sorrel, clintonia, and hobblebush.

After about fifty minutes (1.8 miles), the trail crosses an open beaver swamp. The Forest Service is in a constant battle with the beavers to keep the Zealand Trail above water, and the new elevated wooden walkway here is their latest response to beaver development projects. The trail then reenters the forest and skirts open wetlands and wet meadows. At 2.3 miles (about 1.5 hours) the A-Z trail enters from the left, just beyond a beautiful grassy beaver meadow with a view across to Mount Tom. The trail crosses the inlet to Zealand Pond, follows the shore of the pond, then ends at the junction of the Ethan Pond and Twinway trails. Turn right on the Twinway Trail to reach Zealand Falls Hut in another 0.3 mile. The last 0.1 mile is rough and steep but stone steps aid your ascent. The bottom of Zealand Falls is to the left near the base of this steep part.

If you have the time and energy for a good day hike from the hut, try the Ethan Pond Trail through Zealand Notch to Thoreau Falls (page 207).

Highlights

The Zealand Valley is one of the best places in the White Mountains to see **wildlife,** either directly or through signs of their activities. **Beavers** have had a major influence on the area. Their mud and stick dams alter the flow of the rivers, flooding the forest and creating a pond and wetland that serves not only the beaver but other wildlife as well. Black ducks and wood ducks may be in any of the ponds. Listen for green frogs, which sound like someone plunking the string of a banjo. Dragonflies patrol for insects over the water. Tall meadow rue, a plant with fuzzy white flowers, is abundant on the shoreline.

Beavers are one of the largest members of the rodent family, which also includes mice and squirrels. Their webbed feet are perfect for swimming and their scaly flat tails, when slapped on the water, warn other beavers of danger. Beavers use their large front teeth to feed on the nutritious inner bark of trees, favoring aspens, birches, alders, willows, and maples. The kids should be able to find stumps of beaver-chiseled trees along the Zealand Trail. Grasses and other vegetation are also part of their diets.

Beavers are one of the few animals (along with humans) that modify their entire habitat to suit their needs, building dams and conical houses of sticks and mud. A family of parents, kits, and one-year-olds occupies a lodge. Two-year-olds are booted out and may start their own colony nearby.

In winter, these rodents stockpile small branches underwater, then remain in their lodges for the most part, venturing out the underwater entrance only to grab something from their food cache under the ice.

In the first few centuries of European settlement of this country, beavers were trapped in vast numbers for their valuable fur. In many areas they disappeared. In the past twenty years, however, they have made a remarkable comeback and have been reintroduced successfully by wildlife management agencies in much of their former range.

Although you can find ample evidence of their presence, beavers themselves are hard to spot. The best time to look is in the half-light of early dawn or dusk.

Before passing the junction with the Twinway Trail (2.3 miles), note the newly built beaver lodge in the pond on the left. A few years back, the old beavers had disappeared, the dam fell into disrepair, and the pond turned into a meadow. New residents restored the dam and reflooded the area again. In the late nineteenth century, this was neither a pond nor a meadow but a railroad yard servicing the logging industry.

Moose like to feed on tender submerged plants, so the beaver ponds are good places to look. If the kids are not lucky enough to actually see one, have them look for evidence of their presence. Moose tracks, resembling large deer tracks, are likely to be in muddy areas around any of the wetlands; rounded droppings may also be there. The sharpest-eyed member of your group may also find moose teeth marks on bark; they look like someone stripped the bark off the tree with a giant comb (see page 35).

Along the shore of Zealand Pond you will see neat stacks of logs, and you might wonder what sort of animal put them there and why. The wood is used to heat the hut in winter.

Zealand Falls Hut is popular with **bird lovers.** In June and July, you can hear the songs of winter wrens, hermit thrushes, and white-throated sparrows right from the porch of the hut. These birds, along with purple finches, black-throated blue warblers, black-throated green warblers, redstarts, ovenbirds, and red-eyed vireos, will be singing and calling along the trail, but spotting them in the dense forest is tough. It's easier to see ducks, blue jays, swallows, and perhaps even a goshawk over the open areas around the beaver ponds.

The **view from Zealand Falls Hut** of Zealand and Carrigain notches is one of the most magnificent in the

White Mountains. **Zealand Notch,** the closer of the two, is a classic U-shaped glacially carved valley. It is bounded on the left (east) by the impressive cliffs of Whitewall Mountain. Rock slides, logging, and fires have left much of Whitewall Mountain barren. The straight horizontal line you see on the mountainside is a former logging railroad that now is the Ethan Pond Trail (page 207). "Skid marks" heading down the mountain are sites where logs were dragged to the railroad. The west side of Zealand Notch is bounded by Zealand Ridge, which can be reached by following the Twinway Trail very steeply beyond the hut. Carrigain Notch in the distance has an aura of remoteness.

The Zealand Valley was completely ravaged by **logging** from about 1880 to 1903. During this short period

View from Zealand Falls Hut, one of the finest in the White Mountains.

Boardwalk on Zealand Trail.

of time, there was a town with a sawmill, school, post office, and railroad yard just west of the present-day Zealand Campground. Loggers stayed at logging camps near the falls and sent the logs to the sawmill on the railroad. At the hut, show the kids the old photographs on the wall from this period. They'll agree that the loggers left Zealand Valley looking like a moonscape.

Although the forest has come back, the impact of logging is still evident. The area probably had much more spruce before logging than it currently does, since that was the primary tree sought. Paper birch, which is one of the first species to colonize a disturbed area, still covers large areas that had been clear-cut.

While you are at the hut, stop in and ask for information on the **self-guided nature walk.** This takes you to eight stations that illustrate the geology and ecology of the area.

Just in front of the porch at the hut are a few **red-berried elders.** This distinctive shrub of wet areas and streamsides has compound leaves in pairs along branches. Red-berried elders produce clusters of small white flowers, which turn into small, colorful (but inedible) berries.

The kids will enjoy walking out on the rocky riverbed of Whitewall Brook (except during extremely high water), a few yards beyond the hut. On a hot day, you will immediately feel the cool breeze streaming down the mountain by the brook. This **natural refrigerator** allows **alpine plants** to grow at a lower elevation than usual. The showiest is mountain avens, a wildflower with bright yellow flowers and rounded scalloped leaves that is found virtually nowhere else in the world but in the White Mountains. Mountain cranberry, a low plant with small, dark green evergreen leaves also is there, wherever there is enough soil for a roothold. Other plants growing around the brook include three-toothed cinquefoil, meadowsweet, mountain ash, balsam fir, and red spruce.

Many people enjoy sitting on the flat rocks by Whitewall Brook above Zealand Falls. There are a number of pools within the brook that are deep enough for **swimming** or **wading,** particularly if you walk upstream. Hearty polar bears will jump right in; others will join them if the weather is hot enough. The screeches you hear are decidedly human.

Zealand Falls Hut to Thoreau Falls via Ethan Pond Trail

- 5.2 miles round-trip from the hut, 400-foot descent
- 2.5–3 hours
- moderate for kids

This hike is best for families that have stayed overnight at the Zealand Falls Hut. It could, however, be combined with the Zealand Trail to make a very long day hike for those with lots of energy and time.

You get to Thoreau Falls by hiking the Ethan Pond Trail through Zealand Notch. The trail is on the same old railroad bed that the Zealand Trail follows to the hut, and like the Zealand Trail, it takes you through an area once heavily logged. The trail skirts the side of Whitewall Mountain in Zealand Notch, passing through an impressive open area of rock slides with great views across the notch. A short stint on the Thoreau Falls Trail takes you to the cascade named after the famous naturalist and philosopher. It is an ideal place to wade or simply hang out. If you have enough time, consider extending the hike to Shoal Pond, a shallow pond with lots of bog bridges.

The trail is easy and level, except for the initial 0.1 mile descent from the hut. The few areas of rock slides should present no major difficulties. The open area of

Whitewall Mountain can be quite sunny and hot, so bring a sun hat, sunglasses, and a canteen, particularly if it is a steamy summer day.

What's in it for kids

- Waterfall with pools to wade in.
- Hike through a jumbled rockfall.
- Walk on an old railroad bed.

Getting There

The Zealand Falls Hut is reached by a 2.8-mile hike on the Zealand Trail from the end of Zealand Road. See page 199 for a map of this hike.

The Trail

From the Zealand Falls Hut, descend the Twinway Trail on the steep stone steps to the intersection with the Ethan Pond and Zealand trails (0.3 mile). Turn right (south) onto the Ethan Pond Trail. If you are hiking this as a day trip from Zealand Road, continue straight on the Ethan Pond Trail at the end of the Zealand Trail (2.5 miles from the parking area).

The Ethan Pond Trail goes through a northern hardwoods forest with large numbers of paper birch for about twenty to forty minutes and then reaches an open area of rock slides on the side of Whitewall Mountain. The trail is level, and the only challenge is a few places where rocks have tumbled across. After about fifty to sixty minutes (1.6 miles), the Zeacliff Trail departs right.

The trail enters a spruce-fir forest and reaches the junction with the Thoreau Falls Trail (2.4 miles, approximately one hour and fifteen minutes from the hut).

Take the Thoreau Falls Trail right 0.2 mile to the top of the falls. At high water this crossing may be difficult, and you should walk upstream. At low water this is a good spot to stop, have lunch, and enjoy the view before retracing your steps. There are some good wading pools upstream.

We do not recommend that you try to reach the base of the falls by continuing down the Thoreau Falls Trail. The trail descends steeply after the river crossing, but when it bottoms out, you need to bushwhack back along the stream to reach the bottom of the falls.

If you have extra time, you could continue on to Shoal Pond. This boggy beaver pond is surrounded by a pretty conifer forest and provides views of Mount Carrigain and the Zealand Ridge from its shores. From Thoreau Falls, return to the Ethan Pond Trail and turn right (east). About 0.2 mile from the trail junction, cross the North Branch of the Pemigewasset River on a wooden bridge. In another 0.3 mile, follow the Shoal Pond Trail to the right. Shoal Pond is 0.8 mile farther, although you start traversing bog bridges sooner. Plan on an extra two hours to include Shoal Pond in this hike.

Highlights

This is a great hike to show children how a forest has recovered from old-style **logging** and forest fires. Between 1880 and 1903, the logging company of J. E. Henry devastated this remote valley. In addition to the

Rockslide on Whitewall Mountain.

logging itself, two massive fires, fed by dead branches, stumps, and other "waste" left by the loggers, swept through this area, leaving behind a charred, barren landscape. When the loggers left, nature began slowly repairing the valley through the process of ecological succession. First came smaller plants like fireweed, then raspberries, blueberries, and other small shrubs. The first trees to come back were paper birch. Large patches of the forest in Zealand Notch are still dominated by this tree, its striking white bark giving a very light, airy woodland feeling. Show birch to the kids (but don't let them peel the bark, because it leaves a permanent, ugly scar). Eventually, northern hardwood species will take over from the paper birch, but it is not clear if the red spruce—the trees loggers sought most eagerly—will ever again dominate this area.

Fortunately for admirers of paper birch (like myself), there will always be a place in the forest for this beautiful tree. It needs lots of sunlight to get started, so in the absence of human impacts, it depends on natural disturbances, such as windstorms, disease, and lightning-induced fires to create sunny openings within mature forests.

After passing through the forest, you reach the starkly beautiful open area at the base of Whitewall Cliff. The **large piles of rocks,** or **talus,** fell here for two reasons. Recent landslides and avalanches were due in part to the loss of trees during the logging period. Rocks have also tumbled down from Whitewall Cliff in a more

Mountain cranberry on a rockslide on Whitewall Mountain.

gradual process, plucked from the cliff by the freezing and thawing of water.

In this open area the kids will enjoy picking **blueberries,** which, like the paper birch, thrive in open areas recently cleared. Look for **mountain cranberry,** a low, broad-leafed plant with small, dark green evergreen leaves and bright red berries. Mountain cranberries are sweeter if they have had a chance to freeze over the winter. Around Memorial Day, the flowers of rhodora, a small rhododendron, add a wonderful splash of pink to the still barren mountainside.

Thoreau Falls is a good place to have lunch and wade in the river. Use the wide flat ledges or walk up the river to some smaller cascades and pools or carefully down toward the base of the falls. The kids will love the **potholes,** some no bigger than a foot across. How much exploring the kids can do will depend on water levels and their own agility.

Henry David Thoreau did make two excursions to the White Mountains and climbed Mount Washington on two separate occasions (in 1839 and 1858), but he never actually saw the waterfall that bears his name. Moses Sweetser, who wrote *The White Mountains, A Handbook for Travelers* in 1876, named the falls in tribute to Thoreau with the thought that the waters of the North Fork do flow eventually into the Merrimack, one of Thoreau's favorite rivers. Even when Sweetser made it there in the 1870s, Thoreau Falls was considered a remote, difficult place to reach. It is ironic that one legacy left behind by the loggers who destroyed the natural beauty of this area is the trail system that gives hikers easy access, now that the forest has returned.

Sugarloaf Trail

- **3.4 miles round-trip to both peaks, 600-foot elevation gain to North Sugarloaf and 900-foot elevation gain to Middle Sugarloaf**
- **3–4 hours**
- **challenging for kids**

Several parents told me that the first "real" mountains their children (roughly five years old) climbed were the Sugarloaves. You get great views from the summits for relatively modest effort. The Sugarloaf Trail ascends both North and Middle Sugarloaf (2,310 and 2,539 feet, respectively) from Zealand Road near Twin Mountain, and your hike could include one or both of these small mountains. If you only have time for one, the hike to North Sugarloaf takes one to one and a half hours and the hike to Middle Sugarloaf is slightly longer.

The views of the surrounding mountains from both summits are great, but that's not all this trail has to offer. You pass by huge glacial erratic boulders, and on North Sugarloaf, there is an abandoned quarry where smoky quartz used to be mined. Amateurs are still allowed to collect specimens.

The U.S. Forest Service has produced a brochure that describes the Sugarloaf Trail and has a sketch that identifies the mountains you see from Middle Sugarloaf. It is available at the trailhead or at the Ammonoosuc Ranger Station (off U.S. 3 between Franconia and Twin Mountain).

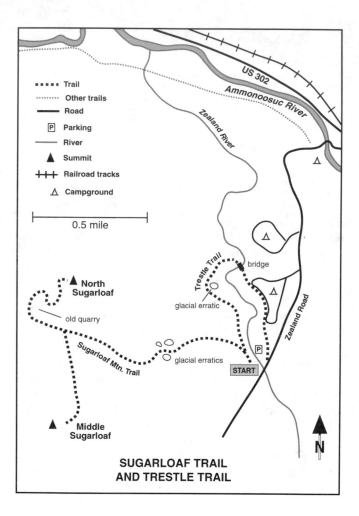

Legend:
- ▪▪▪ Trail
- ⋯ Other trails
- ▬ Road
- P Parking
- ▬ River
- ▲ Summit
- +++ Railroad tracks
- △ Campground

0.5 mile

US 302

Ammonoosuc River

Zealand River

Trestle Trail

bridge

glacial erratic

▲ North Sugarloaf

old quarry

△

Sugarloaf Mtn. Trail

glacial erratics

P

START

Zealand Road

▲ Middle Sugarloaf

SUGARLOAF TRAIL AND TRESTLE TRAIL

N

The Trestle Trail, an easy walk, can be a nice extension to the trip.

What's in it for kids _____

- This may be their first mountain climb.
- Two mountain peaks in one day (for the hardy ones).
- Great views on summit ledges.
- Huge boulders to walk between in the forest.
- The opportunity to look for smoky quartz at an abandoned quarry.
- Blueberry picking on Middle Sugarloaf.

Getting There

The trailhead is on Zealand Road, which branches off south from U.S. 302 at the Zealand Campground, about two miles east of Twin Mountain and about six miles northwest of the AMC's Crawford Notch Hostel at the head of Crawford Notch.

Follow Zealand Road for one mile from U.S. 302. Park just before the bridge over the Zealand River and look for the trailhead just past the bridge on the right.

The Trail

The Sugarloaf Trail coincides with the Trestle Trail for its first 0.2 mile, following the west shore of the Zealand River. It then branches to the left, while the Trestle Trail continues along the river.

The trail then ascends moderately steeply, first through a balsam fir forest and then through an area dominated by yellow and white birch. At about 0.5 mile, it passes by some large glacial erratics and at 0.9 mile reaches a T junction in the col (saddle) between North and Middle Sugarloaf. Turn left for Middle Sugarloaf (0.5 mile) or right for North Sugarloaf (0.3 mile). If you have enough time, climb both peaks and admire the different vistas. The walk from one peak to the other takes thirty to forty-five minutes. Make sure in scaling North Sugarloaf that you follow the trail to the very end, since there is an open area with a vista just before the actual summit that you could mistake for the summit.

Highlights

The first highlight you'll find are the **huge boulders** in the forest. These "glacial erratics" were picked up and carried southward for miles by the advancing glacier. When the ice from the glacier melted, the rocks were left behind in this forest. They are termed "erratics" because they are originally from somewhere else and were dumped here "erratically" by the glacier. As you wind your way around these immense boulders, even grown-ups will feel like tiny ants.

Note the lush covering of mosses, rock ferns, and lichens on the boulders. One of the common lichens, **rock tripe,** forms flat, leathery lobes with dimples. When it's dry, the kids may mistake it for a black piece of shoe leather or rubber from a boot. When damp, this lichen turns greenish and even begins to resemble a living organism. It is supposedly edible, but bring

Exploring glacial erratics along the Sugarloaf Trail. Nancy Schalch.

along plenty of mayonnaise or mustard. **Rock fern** (also called Virginia polypody) is a small evergreen fern that thrives on shady cliffs and boulders. Have the kids examine the round dots on the underside of its fronds with a hand lens. These are reproductive structures.

The **summit of Middle Sugarloaf** provides a fine view of Mount Hale, North Twin Mountain, the Presidential Range (including a good view of the Cog Railway on Mount Washington), and smaller peaks nearby.

You can see evidence of logging on the Rosebrook Range and North Sugarloaf. If you have binoculars, try looking for a moose in a small pond and wetland in a logged area off Zealand Road.

The **granite** rock under your feet is speckled with black and white minerals. The white is a feldspar and the black is hornblende and biotite mica. Because granite solidifies slowly when first formed, individual minerals such as feldspar and hornblende have time to form distinct crystals.

The ledgy summit of Middle Sugarloaf provides some good **blueberry picking.** Other plants to note are three-toothed cinquefoil, balsam fir, and sheep laurel.

When you walk between the two Sugarloaves have your kids count the number of **downed trees** with their shallow root systems exposed to view. The soil is thin, since much of the trail here is on bare rock, so the trees are very susceptible to being tossed over by high winds. There are some rich areas of **wildflowers,** particularly on the way to Middle Sugarloaf. These include mountain wood sorrel, clintonia, red and painted trillium, goldthread, red-berried elder, wild sarsaparilla, Solomon's seal, sharp-leafed aster, and goldenrods.

The **abandoned quarry** on North Sugarloaf is on your right and slightly up the slope about 0.2 mile from the T junction as you ascend. It looks like an unimpressive jumble of rocks, but the kids will enjoy a moment to scramble up and poke around. Look for smoky quartz, a dusky-colored version of the familiar translucent rock. Young miners can collect for their own use but are asked to cover up any holes they make. Beyond the quarry, you pass through a pleasant red spruce forest and an interesting rock outcropping before reaching the summit.

The **summit of North Sugarloaf** is about 300 feet lower than Middle Sugarloaf. The views are also fine, particularly those of the Zealand Valley, the Presidentials, and Middle Sugarloaf. You will find another common lichen, **reindeer moss,** on this summit. This is a pale green lichen with a delicate branching structure. Lichens thrive on rocky summits with little or no soil because they have the amazing ability to revive even when completely dried out.

Birds you might see around the summits of the Sugarloaves are ravens, dark-eyed juncos, and perhaps turkey vultures. The ravens, in particular, look like they enjoy the views, too.

Trestle Trail

- **1 mile loop, little elevation change**
- **45 minutes–1 hour**
- **easy for all ages**

The Trestle Trail is an easy hike, suitable even for the youngest hikers. This loop trail is named for a foot-bridge that crosses the Zealand River at the site of a trestle of the old Zealand Valley Railroad. It's a pleasant walk, taking you through a spruce forest and northern hardwoods; along rushing, boulder-strewn waters of the river; and past a very large glacial erratic boulder. Along the way, you can search for evidence of the old logging railroad that used to haul logs from Zealand Valley to a mill at the now-extinct hamlet of Zealand.

You could easily spend a good part of the day at this pleasant spot, having a picnic lunch and wading along the river. Combine this with the Sugarloaf Trail for a longer, more rigorous outing.

A trail brochure for the Trestle Trail is available from the U.S. Forest Service. You can pick it up at their headquarters off U.S. 3 between Franconia and Twin Mountain or at the trailhead. The last part of the Trestle Trail follows a road in Sugarloaf Campground with ready access to rest rooms.

What's in it for kids

- A wooden footbridge.
- Easy walk along a pretty river with rocks and wading spots.
- Large boulder to walk by and hide under.
- Evidence of the old logging railroad.

Getting There

The trailhead for the Trestle Trail is the same as that for the Sugarloaf Trail, on Zealand Road about a mile south of its junction with U.S. 302. Pick up Zealand Road about two miles east of Twin Mountain on U.S. 302 and about six miles west (north) of the AMC's Crawford Notch Hostel at the head of Crawford Notch.

Follow Zealand Road for one mile from U.S. 302. The parking area is just before the bridge over the Zealand River. The trailhead is just after the bridge on the west (right) side of the road. See page 214 for a map of this hike.

The Trail

The first 0.2 mile of the Trestle Trail coincides with the Sugarloaf Trail. Keep going straight along the west bank of the Zealand River when the Sugarloaf Trail turns left. After passing through a red spruce forest, the trail ascends to a pretty section where you look down through the trees at the river far below. The trail then descends, crosses over a snowmobile trail, and passes the large glacial erratic, roughly the halfway point of the trail. The trail turns right and follows the snowmobile trail, making another sharp right before reaching the bridge at the site of the old trestle (0.6 mile). Shortly after you cross over the bridge, the trail comes out at campsite 10 of Sugarloaf II Campground. The trail continues along the campground road for 0.1 mile, then reenters the woods and comes out at Zealand Road by the parking area.

Highlights

The Trestle Trail takes you along a very pleasant stretch of the **Zealand River.** The kids will particularly enjoy the area around the bridge, where they can scramble on some flat rocks along the shoreline, go wading (or swimming if they're short enough), have a picnic, and poke along the shoreline for salamanders and other aquatic life. When we were there, we ran into a family that had taken a long detour downstream along the riverbed itself.

The bridge is at the exact location of the old train trestle from the Zealand Valley Railroad. As with the other trails in the Zealand Valley area, encourage the children to find the old railroad bed now within the forest. See trail descriptions for the Zealand Trail and Thoreau Falls (page 208) for more on logging in this area.

At the river, help the children find **alders,** a broadleafed shrub with rounded leaves that have toothed edges. This streamside and wetland plant has little dark, pineconelike structures on branches that contain the seeds. In sunny spots along the shoreline, you will find bluets, little sky blue or even whitish flowers with thin, straight leaves.

The **immense boulder** at the halfway point of the trail will certainly catch everyone's attention. This is a glacial erratic, carried from its place of origin to this spot by the glacier of the last Ice Age, about 10,000 years ago. This particular boulder has an overhang, so the kids can use it as a hideout or a rain shelter. Make sure to show them the dead birch tree hooked around the boulder, looking like it originally grew around the contours of this giant rock.

Between the turnoff to the Sugarloaf Trail and the large boulder, the forest is largely **red spruce,** particularly on the slopes down to the river. Red spruce is now a dominant tree at higher elevations (roughly over 2,000

Trail junction along the Zealand River. Nancy Schalch.

feet) in the White Mountains, and its presence here at 1,600 feet may mean that it escaped the loggers who decimated much of the lower elevation red spruce in this area. One particular giant spared the ax is on the downhill just before the boulder.

Common **wildflowers** in the forest include wild sarsaparilla, bunchberry, and clintonia. Shrubs include blueberries, bush honeysuckle, and northern wild raisin. Look for two types of club mosses: ground pine, which looks like a miniature spreading spruce tree; and shiny club moss, which has individual erect stalks of small, tightly bunched, dark green sprucelike leaves. Both these club mosses form colonies that are connected by underground stems, so if you tried to pick up one you'd damage them all.

There are numerous small balsam fir trees coming up along the Trestle Trail, so when the kids grow up, the forest along the Trestle Trail may look substantially different than it does today. Things never stop changing, even without the loggers.

Pinkham Notch/ Gorham Region

THE PINKHAM NOTCH/GORHAM region includes the Presidential Range, the loftiest peaks of the White Mountains. Mount Washington at 6,288 feet is the highest mountain in the Northeast, and five other summits surpass 5,000 feet. In addition to their elevation, the peaks of the Presidential Range are noted for their vast bowl-shaped ravines. The less crowded Carter Range, across Pinkham Notch from the Presidentials, rises above 4,500 feet. The region is a magnet for hikers attracted by the high elevation, rugged scenery, and broad expanse of alpine terrain with extensive vistas and unique ecological characteristics. A number of trails to ponds, waterfalls, and viewpoints are perfect for children. These are centered around the Appalachian Mountain Club's Pinkham Notch Visitor Center (PNVC) and the town of Gorham. N.H. 16 passes right through Pinkham Notch between Jackson and Gorham and provides access to many trails described here. Other trails are accessed from U.S. 2 west of Gorham.

Facilities

Pinkham Notch Visitor Center. The Appalachian Mountain Club's Pinkham Notch Visitor Center is the hub of hiking activities and natural history education in the White Mountains. It includes a visitor center (the Trading Post), a dormitory-style guest house with a library and meeting rooms (the Joe Dodge Center), a dining room, and AMC offices. Breakfast and dinner are served to overnight guests and are available to others (staff need to know in advance if you want to eat there). In the evenings and sometimes during the day, you can hear naturalist lectures and participate in other types of programs. PNVC is a great place to get current information on trails and the weather and to buy hiking guides, nature books, T-shirts, and other supplies. The visitor center also has rest rooms, showers, and even a Ping-Pong table.

While at the visitor center, do not miss the scale model of the Presidential Range along with displays on mountain geology and ecology. These give a real perspective of the area.

Supplies. Snacks, soft drinks, trail lunches, insect repellent, hot drinks, clothing, and other last-minute hiking supplies are available at the PNVC. The Wildcat Mountain Ski Area, about one mile north, has all the amenities you might expect in a ski resort: a restaurant, snack bar, rest rooms, coffee machines, and gift shop.

If you are coming from the north on N.H. 16, you pass through Gorham, which has ample restaurants, inns, motels, stores, and gas stations. If you are coming up from the south, Jackson is the nearest town for supplies.

If you are coming from the west on U.S. 2, Lowe's Store is a traditional stopping place for hikers. It has a gas station, rest rooms (for customers only, so buy a little something), snacks, cold drinks, and coffee, but no sandwiches. There is also a basketball hoop if you feel like getting a different kind of exercise.

The Androscoggin Ranger Station of the U.S. Forest Service is located on N.H. 16 just south of U.S. 2 in Gorham. Stop in for information, trail pamphlets, or to use the rest rooms.

Camping. The National Forest Service's Dolly Copp Campground is at the junction of N.H. 16 and Pinkham B Road between Gorham and Pinkham Notch. With its 176 campsites, Dolly Copp is the largest public campground in the White Mountains. Large groups can camp at Barnes Field Group Area adjacent to the Dolly Copp Campground.

The Crystal Cascade

- 0.7 mile round-trip, 200-foot elevation gain
- 30 minutes
- easy for all ages

The Crystal Cascade is a fifteen-minute walk from the Pinkham Notch Visitor Center (PNVC). You can combine a short walk to this beautiful waterfall with a visit to the visitor center, which has a number of interesting displays and books about the natural history of the White Mountains. The hike is a short section of the Tuckerman Ravine Trail and goes uphill through a boreal forest near the rushing water of the Cutler River. The understory is lush, with different types of ferns, flowers, and small shrubs. This is a great destination for all ages and will take less than an hour. Expect it to be crowded on summer and fall weekends.

What's in it for kids

- A beautiful waterfall.
- One bridge crossing an impressively rushing river.
- A really short walk for a grand reward.

Getting There

To get to PNVC from the south, follow N.H. 16 north through North Conway, Glen, and Jackson. The visitor center is on the left, about 10 miles from Jackson and 0.7

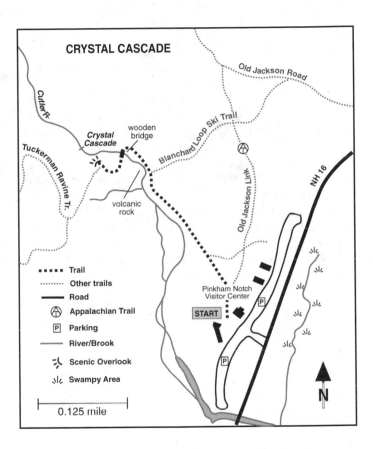

mile past the turnoff to Glen Ellis Falls. To get to Pinkham Notch from the north, pick up N.H. 16 in Gorham and go about 10 miles south. The visitor center is on the right, about a mile past the Wildcat Mountain Ski Area.

The Trail

Follow signs for the Tuckerman Ravine Trail, the most popular trail ascending Mount Washington from the east side. The signs will lead you behind the Trading Post to the trailhead. The trail splits off left from the Old Jackson Road just a little past a water fountain and a scale for weighing your pack. (Kids will naturally want to weigh their own day packs and anything else they can fit on the scale.) The "Tux" Trail is a very wide path, perfect for holding the hands of young children as you enjoy the sounds of the Cutler River. To add a bit of adventure, read all the warning signs about how potentially dangerous it is above tree line and how well prepared you should be to hike this trail (but remember, you are only going about fifteen minutes so you won't need your mukluks). After about ten minutes, you cross the Cutler River on a solid bridge and then hike a little more steeply uphill. The viewpoint for the waterfall is on the right, a few steps up from the trail. A stone fence will give a feeling of security for those worried about the steep drop-off.

On your return to Pinkham Notch, be careful to follow the Tuckerman Ravine Trail closely. Otherwise, you may end up at some far point in the parking lot, behind some of the other AMC buildings, or even on N.H. 16.

Highlights

The kids will love the **Crystal Cascade**, a very pretty waterfall on the Cutler River. While admiring the movement of water and the deep gorge, help them spot the difference between the rocks in the surrounding cliffs

Enjoy ferns and falls at the Crystal Cascade overlook. Jerry Shereda.

versus those behind the waterfall itself. Crystal Cascade tumbles over a volcanic vent that formed much later in time than the surrounding schists that make up much of the Presidentials. The volcanic rocks are basalt and are black in color even when dry. They also are more "lumpy" edged than the surrounding schists.

For a closer look at the same black volcanic rocks, there is a small outcropping just downstream of the bridge. Look near the old abandoned bridge abutment. This bridge is also a good place to stop and contemplate the sound and sight of rushing water cascading down from high up the mountain.

The persistently damp environment created by the spray of a waterfall is perfect for **ferns,** an ancient group of plants that first appeared on earth even before the debut of the dinosaurs. As you and the children look out over the stone wall, point out the ferns that cling to the sheer walls of the gorge where there is only the barest hint of any soil. The fronds of **long beech ferns** (typically about six inches long) are roughly triangular in outline, with the two bottom-most pinnae on each side pointing downward. This fern is common throughout the White Mountains in damp woods and along the sides of waterfalls—several grow at the corner of the barrier to your left as you face the falls. Another fern growing just on the other side of the stone barrier is

Long beech fern is at home at the Crystal Cascade. Nancy Schalch

oak fern. This small (about one foot in height), delicate fern has a horizontally oriented frond that is divided into three parts. The **spinulose wood fern,** common along the path to the falls, has fronds up to about two feet long and much divided into pinnae and pinnules. A distinctive characteristic of this fern is the brown scales on the stipe (stalk) of each frond.

The anatomy and habits of ferns are distinctive. Ferns consist of a frond (the individual leafy part) that is usually divided into segments called pinnae. Often these are further divided into pinnules. To get your children involved, ask them to tell you how many times the frond is divided. While they are examining a frond, see if they can find tiny brown spots (reproductive structures called sori) on the underside. A hand lens, besides being fun to look through, is particularly useful for observing intricate details of sori. Spores produced within the sori are disseminated by the wind, but they do not germinate into a new fern directly. Instead, they develop into a tiny flat mass of tissue that is more like a moss than a fern. These are very hard to find in nature; in fact, some of them are underground. In any case, this tiny organism eventually produces the fern with which we are familiar.

Pinkham Notch Visitor Center, at 2,032 feet elevation, is located in the transition zone between the lower elevation broad-leafed, deciduous forest and the higher elevation, boreal forest. As you walk up to the falls, you will see trees representative of both zones, e.g., sugar maples and balsam fir. Prominent in the understory vegetation are clintonia (bluebead lily), mountain wood sorrel, and hobblebush.

Right before you get to the bridge, look on your right for **mountain holly.** This is not a very showy shrub at first glance—its flowers are tiny, and its pale green leaves do not appear particularly distinctive. For a different perspective, encourage the children to use a hand lens to examine the tiny, sharp spine at the tip of each leaf.

The **bird feeder** outside the visitor center is worth checking out, particularly for evening grosbeaks and pine siskins. Evening grosbeaks are striking, robin-sized yellow and black finches with thick bills for cracking seeds. Pine siskins are sparrow-sized seed eaters, streaky brown with yellow patches on their wings. Both these birds are creatures of northern forests and only occasionally make their way south of northern New England.

A bird whose energetic, bubbly song can often be heard even above the din of rushing water is the **winter wren.** It is a small, rather nondescript brown bird that usually remains out of sight, but its true calling card is its voice. It's hard to believe that such a loud and cheerful succession of notes can emanate from something so small. This bird can clearly hold its own against the sound of the Crystal Cascade.

Lost Pond Trail

- **1 mile round-trip to the pond, little elevation change**
- **1 hour**
- **easy for all ages to the pond, more difficult beyond**

The Lost Pond Trail is an easy, short walk that follows the Ellis River through a rich forest and eventually ends up at Lost Pond. This pretty body of water is not far off N.H. 16 as the crow flies, yet it still feels remote and peaceful. You see much evidence of beavers along the way and may even catch a glimpse of them if you are on the trail at dawn or dusk. A wooden plank bridge over the river at the beginning of the walk and several others along the way add to the appeal of this hike. At the pond, large rocks provide great perches for enjoying the view across to Huntington Ravine and Mount Washington. Beyond the pond, there is a dramatic area of boulders.

You can combine the hike with a visit to Pinkham Notch Visitor Center (PNVC) or extend the hike to Glen Ellis Falls (see page 242) and then return via the Glen Boulder and Direttissima trails. In addition, there are a number of other trails that depart from the visitor center (Square Ledge, Crystal Cascade, Old Jackson Road to Lowe's Bald Spot) to make a longer outing.

What's in it for kids

- Several bridges with wooden planks.
- Beaver dams and lodges and maybe even a real live beaver, too.
- Beautiful clear running water with trout.
- Large picnic boulders around the lake, perfect for admiring the view.
- Stroll through a boulder field created by an avalanche.

Getting There

Park at PNVC on N.H. 16 (page 228). The trail begins across the road at the same point as the Square Ledge Trail.

The Trail

The Lost Pond Trail, together with the Square Ledge Trail, begins in a swampy area across from the PNVC and crosses the Ellis River on a wooden bridge. Both trails turn right after the bridge, but the Square Ledge Trail immediately turns left and starts to ascend. The Lost Pond Trail, which is part of the Appalachian Trail, continues straight ahead, along the east side of the river. The trail to the pond is wide with little ups and downs and a few rocks, but nothing major. After about 0.3 mile, it angles away from the Ellis River and crosses a tributary over another wooden bridge. Once you reach the north end of the pond (0.5 mile), the trail becomes rockier, passing on the east shore of the pond. The section

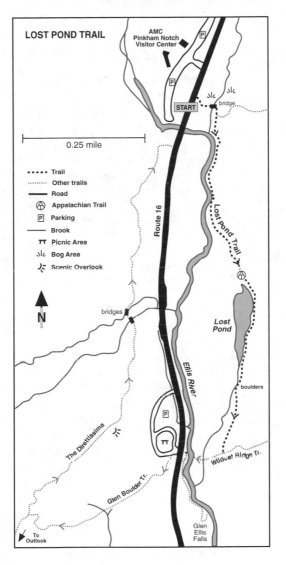

LOST POND TRAIL

AMC
Pinkham Notch
Visitor Center

P

P

START — bridge

0.25 mile

- - - - Trail
.... Other trails
——— Road
Ⓐ Appalachian Trail
P Parking
——— Brook
⊤⊤ Picnic Area
☽ Bog Area
𝆑 Scenic Overlook

N

Route 16

Lost Pond Trail

Lost Pond

bridges

boulders

Ellis River

P

⊤⊤

The Direttissima

Wildcat Ridge Tr.

Glen Boulder Tr.

To
Outlook

Glen
Ellis
Falls

237

between the south end of the lake and the Wildcat Ridge Trail passes through a riot of boulders. The trail ends at the Wildcat Ridge Trail (0.9 mile).

From here, you can retrace your steps or, if you are feeling adventurous, turn right on the Wildcat Ridge Trail and cross over the Ellis River to reach N.H. 16. This crossing can be precarious at high water, since there is no bridge so it requires stepping from rock to rock. In early spring or after a rainstorm, it is better to return the way you came than to risk injury by stepping on slippery rocks. If it is passable, you can then walk back to your car along N.H. 16 or walk over to Glen Ellis Falls and complete the loop mentioned above.

Highlights

At the beginning of this trail, you will immediately pass through a **swamp** at the height of land of Pinkham Notch. Water drains from this swamp both north to the Peabody River and south to the Ellis. Have the children look for two **"speckly" shrubs** here. Speckled alder is named for its speckled bark, which looks like it has the chicken pox. The leaves of sweet gale, which grows right next to the wooden bridge, are covered with tiny yellow speckles. Crush a sweet gale leaf in your fingers to get a strong, sweet smell that will remind you of bayberry. In August, white turtlehead flowers bloom in the swamp.

As you cross over the wooden bridge, a **beaver dam** is obvious to your left. Ask the kids to guess how it was made. The dam is composed of tree branches stripped of bark, and compacted mud. The beaver eat the bark, then use the rest of the branches as lumber for the dam.

Beavers build dams to create ponds so they can swim to their supper and have a place for their lodges safe from predators. By flooding the surrounding woodlands, they can enter their lodges underwater and swim to their major foods, the nutritious inner bark of trees, grasses, and other vegetation. Beavers are one of the few animals that thoroughly alter the habitat for a variety of other animals.

Small, graceful birds you are likely to see zooming over the swamp are **swallows.** Barn swallows have distinctive long forked tails and are bluish black on the back with reddish throats and buff-colored bellies. As the name implies, they sometimes nest in barns and under the eaves of buildings (such as the maintenance building at Pinkham Notch). Tree swallows also have dark backs but differ from barn swallows in having notched tails and in being completely white underneath. They sometimes use nest boxes. These aerial acrobats catch insects on the wing.

The Lost Pond Trail follows the Ellis River initially through a forest of balsam fir and birch and eventually through northern hardwoods with a hobblebush understory. The flow of the Ellis is greatly increased by the addition of the Cutler River flowing down from Tuckerman Ravine. Note how clear the water is in a beautiful, **deep pool** in the river you walk by. If the children stand quietly by this pool for a minute or two, they may catch a glimpse of brook trout. Water striders may also be present.

In June, look for **blooms** of Canada mayflower, clintonia, false Solomon's seal, painted trillium, and pink lady's slippers. In damp spots along the trail, wild white

Berries of painted trillium are present through much of the summer. Nancy Schalch.

violets and inflated sedges abound. Normally sedges are fairly nondescript, but inflated sedge has amusing, inflated bladders in clusters around each of its seeds.

In midsummer, **mountain wood sorrel** blooms in profusion here. The three leaves of this small plant will remind you of clover, but it is really not related. Other midsummer bloomers are goldenrods and tall meadow rue.

At Lost Pond, you will see several **beaver houses,** one along the opposite shoreline. At dusk, you stand a reasonable chance of seeing the beavers themselves cavorting about. Look for another dam at the outlet of the pond.

Along the shore of Lost Pond, look for one particularly large flat rock that just invites you to sit and quietly enjoy the peaceful scenery, perhaps with a picnic lunch. The view of Mount Washington is impressive—Huntington Ravine stands out, and you can also see Boott Spur, the Lion Head, and the Gulf of Slides from various vantage points.

Look for two different types of **water plants:** water lilies and wild celery. The leaves of water lilies float right on the surface of the water and provide the underwater parts of the plant with air through a system of gas channels. Wild celery is a great duck food with grassy, straplike leaves. Water striders skim across the surface of the pond, and dragonflies patrol the shoreline, looking for unwary insects.

As you make your way around the pond, have the kids look for water stains on the rocks and the trunks of trees at the shore. These indicate how high the water levels rose during the past spring. There is also a good display of **bunchberries,** a small relative of dogwood that produces creamy dogwoodlike flowers in the latter part of June and clusters of red berries during the summer. At one point, the kids may want to examine a tree that seemingly grows right out of a rock. Its trunk and roots form a little cave. Note also a wildlife tree laced with woodpecker holes.

If you venture beyond the pond, you will pass through an **impressive boulder field.** These were deposited here by an avalanche off Wildcat Mountain many years ago and make a fitting contrast with the peaceful pond.

Glen Ellis Falls

- **0.6 mile round-trip, short descent**
- **30–40 minutes**
- **easy for all ages**

Glen Ellis Falls is a sixty-four-foot waterfall on the Ellis River right off N.H. 16 less than a mile south of the Pinkham Notch Visitor Center (PNVC). The waterfall tumbles over a glacially carved cliff and has ample water, even in late summer. It is a popular family stop with a short, paved trail from the parking area to the falls. The walk down to the bottom of the falls is steep, but quite short.

If you want to incorporate a visit to these falls with a longer hike, park your car at the PNVC and walk to the falls via the Lost Pond Trail and a short section of the Wildcat Ridge Trail, about a one-mile hike with a river crossing at the end that can be tough if water levels are high. Either return the same way or make a loop by taking the Glen Boulder and Direttissima trails back to the visitor center. In a pinch, you can return to the visitor center by walking north for 0.7 mile along the west side of N.H. 16. There is plenty of room to walk this safely, but it is a less pleasant option because of the cars whizzing by.

What's in it for kids _____

- Great waterfall.
- Flat rocks to scramble on around the falls.

- Short walk along the Ellis River, where you can throw a leaf in the water and watch it disappear over the falls.

Getting There

The well-marked parking area for Glen Ellis Falls is on the west side of N.H. 16, 0.7 mile south of PNVC and about 9 miles north of Jackson. There are rest rooms, an information board, and a picnic area at the parking area. A tunnel underneath N.H. 16 leads to the path to the falls.

If you are hiking from the Lost Pond Trail, turn right at its terminus on the Wildcat Ridge Trail and cross over the Ellis River (difficult at high water). Follow the dirt connector path to the left on the east side of the road.

The Trail

A short (0.3-mile) path from the parking area leads you through the tunnel beneath N.H. 16 and eventually down to the base of Glen Ellis Falls. The path is gravel for much of its length, and stone steps lead down to the bottom of the falls. There are three lookouts along the way, one at the top of the falls, one about two-thirds of the way down, and a broad area at the bottom. A number of unofficial trails continue downstream from the falls along the Ellis River.

Highlights

Glen Ellis Falls is one of the most impressive falls in the White Mountains. It's worth a visit even if you have an aversion to "tourist" spots. Since there will be other families at this popular destination, your children may

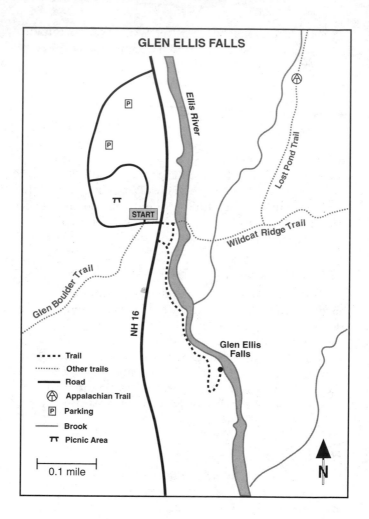

GLEN ELLIS FALLS

Ellis River

Lost Pond Trail

P

P

Wildcat Ridge Trail

π

START

Glen Boulder Trail

NH 16

Glen Ellis Falls

- - - - Trail
.... Other trails
———— Road
Ⓐ Appalachian Trail
P Parking
Brook
π Picnic Area

0.1 mile

N

even make some friends running up and down the stairs and scrambling over the rocks near the falls.

There are several signs along the trail that describe the geology of the area. The falls were created when avalanches blocked the flow of the Ellis River, causing it to change its course and tumble over the glacially carved bowl in the side of a mountain. The flow over the cliff, a minimum of 600 gallons a minute, is equal to 10 gallons a second, even during late summer when other waterfalls are just a trickle.

Each of the three lookouts provides a distinct perspective. The top one gives you a feeling of potential energy, as you see the water channeled through a

Glen Ellis Falls.
Carrie Loats.

narrow cut between boulders just before it plunges over the lip of the falls. The shape of the falls pouring over the brink may remind you of water pouring out of a pitcher, and, in fact, Pitcher Falls was the original name given to Glen Ellis Falls. Throw a leaf or a small twig in the water here and watch as it is swept along over the edge of the falls. (No rock throwing please, there are people down below.) Imagine the leaf eventually reaching the Atlantic Ocean off the coast of Maine via the Ellis and Saco rivers. Midway down, you can get dizzy watching rushing water and spray. The view at the bottom gives you the most unobstructed perspective of the entire falls. Show the kids the deep "plunge" pool cut by the erosive action of the waterfall.

The pool is bounded by lots of **flat rocks** that invite exploration. When the water levels aren't too high, you will find children and their parents scrambling around these flat rocks. Use caution because mist from the falls keeps them damp.

According to Native American legend, if you look hard into the mist created by the falls, you can see the shapes of two people hand in hand. These were lovers from different tribes who plunged to their deaths together over the falls when the woman, the daughter of the chief, was promised to someone else.

The predominant trees are red spruce, balsam fir, and yellow birch. Some of the trees hang precariously over the cliffs on either side of the river. Long beech ferns hang on the right along the side of the waterfall. The waterfall is the star attraction here, but you can still marvel at how small, fragile living things like these ferns thrive in a seemingly precarious place.

Square Ledge Trail

- **1 mile round-trip, 400-foot ascent**
- **1–2 hours**
- **challenging for kids**

Visitors to Pinkham Notch will enjoy this short trail to an overlook that has a great open view of Pinkham Notch and Mount Washington. Initially, the trail is a comfortable, slightly uphill climb wide enough for parents and children to hold hands. After passing Hangover Rock, the trail has a short but quite steep section that ends at the overlook. Hangover Rock is interesting enough on its own to be worth the trip even if you or the kids are not up to the final ascent. But the steep section extends only for about a hundred yards, so this could be a great first experience for youngsters on a steep trail. They'll feel like real hikers when they reach the beautiful view.

What's in it for kids

- A giant rock that overhangs the trail.
- A big rock for scrambling.
- A fabulous view.

Getting There

The trail begins right across the road from Pinkham Notch Visitor Center (PNVC). From the south, follow N.H. 16 north from North Conway through Glen and

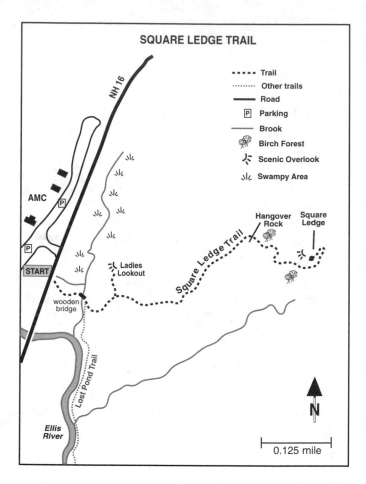

Jackson. The visitor center is on the left 0.7 mile past the turnoff to Glen Ellis Falls. From the north, PNVC is on the right about ten miles south of Gorham on N.H. 16.

The Trail

The trail runs together with the Lost Pond Trail for a short distance from N.H. 16. After crossing a wooden bridge, the two trails make a sharp right turn, after which the Square Ledge Trail makes an immediate left uphill. The trail is initially wide with a gradual uphill. Stop at Ladies Lookout (short spur trail to the left) at 0.1 mile for a view of Pinkham Notch. After the trail passes Hangover Rock, it becomes steep and has a short section with loose rocks that may make some children (and even adults) a little uncomfortable. Use caution on Square Ledge itself since there is a steep drop-off. You may want to hold your children's hands, for everyone's peace of mind.

Highlights

The breathtaking **view of Mount Washington and Pinkham Notch** from Square Ledge is the main feature of this trail. Huntington Ravine, named for one of the early explorers of the region, is in center focus. Looking across the notch to its steep headwall, carved out by a mountain glacier during the last Ice Age, kids will be amazed that there actually is a trail going up that ravine.

Your hike begins at the Ellis River, which flows into Lost Pond. This interesting section crosses a **wetland and beaver habitat** on a wooden bridge and is described under the Lost Pond Trail.

At the turnoff to Ladies Lookout there is a particularly lush growth of **striped maples.** In the White Mountains, this small tree generally remains in the understory. Children will appreciate its bright green-and-white-striped bark on branches and young trunks and its extremely large, three-lobed leaves (the latter giving rise to the name goosefoot maple). Often trees and shrubs growing in the shade have very large leaves in order to catch the small amount of light that filters down through the canopy. Striped maple is also called moosewood because moose like to eat it.

The name **Hangover Rock** has nothing to do with being a former watering hole for travelers in Pinkham Notch. Instead, it is a large boulder that projects over the trail, making a cozy place for getting out of the rain or simply hanging out.

Slow down after Hangover Rock to enjoy the grove of **paper birches.** Whoever thought of making a tree with

Inspecting paper birch and bracket fungi.
Jerry Shereda.

such white bark! Only mature trees have white bark. Young saplings and the branches of adult trees are a rich reddish brown color that has a more subdued beauty.

In addition to having the honor of being the state tree of New Hampshire, paper birches have a distinct ecological role in the White Mountains. They range from low elevations up to the tree line, thriving in disturbed areas where the former trees have been destroyed by fire, logging, wind, or other disasters. As short-lived temporary residents during the natural succession of a disturbed area from an open field back to mature forest, paper birches are eventually replaced by maples, red spruce, and other more long-lived species. Fortunately for paper birches, and for those who admire their columns of white in a sea of grayish brown and green, natural disturbance to the forest is frequent enough in the White Mountains to insure a plentiful supply of this species even in the absence of human activities.

The shagginess of paper birch along with thoughts of the birch bark canoes of Native Americans might tempt you to peel some of the bark off. Keep in mind, however, that this will leave a permanent ugly scar on the tree, so please resist the temptation.

Shiny club moss is an abundant plant of the forest floor along the Square Ledge Trail. These are low, dark green plants whose upright stems covered with small leaves resemble bottle brushes.

Upon returning to the visitor center, be sure to point out to your children the view of Square Ledge from the dining room. It will give them an appreciation for what they just accomplished.

Lowe's Bald Spot via Old Jackson Road

- **4.2 miles round-trip, 850-foot ascent**
- **3–4 hours**
- **moderate to challenging for kids**

When you tell your children the name of this destination, they might wonder: Who was Lowe and why would anyone want to hike to the top of his head? Really, though, you should take them to Lowe's Bald Spot because it is an accessible outlook with a terrific view of the Great Gulf and Mounts Adams and Madison. Along the way you will cross over streams and are likely to see some unusual mushrooms and other fungi. As to the identity of Mr. Lowe: Charles E. Lowe was one of the pioneer trail builders in the northern Presidentials in the late nineteenth and early twentieth centuries. His descendants are still prominent citizens in the Randolph area and, among other things, run Lowe's Store on U.S. 2.

Old Jackson Road was the old carriage route from the town of Jackson to the Mount Washington Auto Road, and it just happens to go right past the present site of the AMC's Pinkham Notch Visitor Center (PNVC). Now it has been incorporated into the White Mountain trail system, meeting the Mount Washington Auto Road at the latter's two-mile marker. From there, a short section of the Madison Gulf Trail leads you to Lowe's Bald Spot.

The round-trip to Lowe's Bald Spot from Pinkham Notch takes about three to four hours, depending on how fast you walk and how long you linger at the viewpoint. The trail is generally fairly gradual, with a few steep sections near the end. Younger children, and those who are not particularly enthusiastic hikers, might find it a bit long.

What's in it for kids

- An open summit with rocks on which to scramble.
- Great view at the end and a few blueberries to pick.
- Flag trees.
- Lots of fascinating mushrooms and other fungi.
- Logs over mushy areas, some pretty rivulets and swales, and a small gorge.
- Jewelweed capsules to pop.

Getting There

The trail begins at PNVC off N.H. 16. (See Crystal Cascade on page 228 for directions). Walk past the outdoor water fountain and the outdoor scale (for backpackers and kids to figure out their loads). The Old Jackson Road Trail branches off from the Tuckerman Ravine Trail right behind the visitor center.

The Trail

To reach Lowe's Bald Spot, take the Old Jackson Road Trail 1.9 miles to its terminus at the Mount Washington Auto Road and then hike up the Madison Gulf Trail (0.2

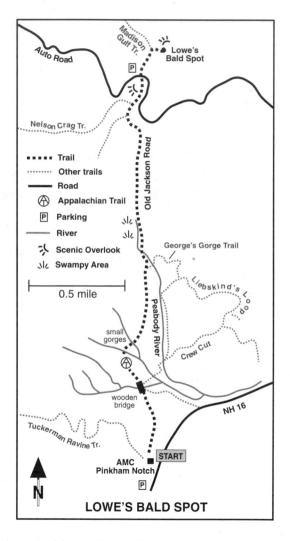

Trail

Other trails

Road

Ⓐ **Appalachian Trail**

Ⓟ **Parking**

☆ **Scenic Overlook**

⌄⌄ **Swampy Area**

0.5 mile

Madison Gulf Tr.

Lowe's Bald Spot

Auto Road

Nelson Crag Tr.

Old Jackson Road

George's Gorge Trail

Liebskind's Loop

River

small gorges

Peabody River

Crew Cut

wooden bridge

NH 16

Tuckerman Ravine Tr.

START

AMC Pinkham Notch

N

LOWE'S BALD SPOT

mile) to a short spur trail. Both these trails are part of
the Appalachian Trail and are marked with white paint
blazes. There is no sign that actually says "Lowe's Bald
Spot," but it is easy to find.

The trail begins, not on the actual Old Jackson Road
itself, but on a link that brings you shortly to the old
road. Be sure to follow the signs to the Old Jackson
Road carefully, since it crosses a maintenance road, a
ski trail (indicated by blue diamonds), and other hiking
trails.

At 0.4 mile the Old Jackson Road Trail widens out
and looks like you'd expect an old road to look. Shortly
after, the trail crosses a solid wooden bridge right at the
point where the Crew Cut Trail comes in from the right.

The Old Jackson Road then goes uphill moderately
steeply and crosses a pleasant, shady gorge with a small
waterfall. Take a moment to enjoy the cool, mossy
atmosphere and the sound of running water. Soon after,
the trail crosses another small gorge (dry in August).

After about forty minutes, the trail reaches a junction with the upper end of the George's Gorge Trail and
then levels. It crosses a pretty rivulet and passes a swale
on the left and then a damp, muddy section traversed
by double logs.

In another fifteen minutes, the trail makes a sharp
left turn and heads uphill on rock steps at a point where
an old section of trail is blocked off. You can hear cars
from the Auto Road through the trees, although you
still have about 0.5 mile to go before you cross it. The
Old Jackson Road continues straight, past the Raymond
Path, across a few small rivulets on logs, and then past
the Nelson Crag Trail.

After this, the trail ascends and opens up a bit, passing through an old gravel pit with a nice view of Nelson Crag (a shoulder of Mount Washington). The Old Jackson Road ends at a parking area on the Auto Road 1.9 miles from Pinkham Notch.

To continue on to Lowe's Bald Spot, walk across the Auto Road and follow the Madison Gulf Trail into the Great Gulf Wilderness. Five to ten minutes beyond the Auto Road, take the turnoff leading uphill to the right. In another five minutes you reach the summit of Lowe's Bald Spot.

Return the same way you came. When you get within 0.4 mile of Pinkham Notch, make sure you do not take the left fork where the Link (also Connie's Way and Go Back ski trails) comes in. If you do, you will end up on N.H. 16 about 0.3 mile north of PNVC.

Highlights

The **view from Lowe's Bald Spot** is a major highlight of the walk. You look out over a vast section of the Great Gulf Wilderness. Mount Adams, the second-highest peak in the White Mountains, is particularly impressive with its picturesque cone shape. The treeless alpine zone at the upper part of the mountain is very obvious. Show your children the distinction between the forest dominated by broad-leafed trees at the bottom of the mountain, the boreal forest (spruce and fir) midway up, and the alpine zone.

Between Mount Adams and Mount Madison is Madison Gulf, a tributary ravine of the Great Gulf. Madison Gulf is a cirque—a bowl-shaped ravine on the side of a mountain carved out by a mountain glacier. The section of the Madison Gulf Trail that climbs up this ravine is one of the most difficult hikes in the White Mountains. To the southwest, you'll see two shoulders of Mount Washington, Nelson Crag and Boott Spur. Across Pinkham Notch to the east the prominent peaks are Wildcat Mountain, Carter Dome, and the Imp Face. Endless peaks stretch out to the north.

The view isn't the only thing to see at Lowe's Bald Spot. You will probably notice a particularly gleaming white piece of **quartz** and a number of **"flag" trees** (p. 7). Using your compass, see if the kids can tell the direction of the predominant winds from the branches of these wind-sculpted trees (southeast, indicating that the predominant winter winds are from the northwest).

Plants growing at Lowe's Bald Spot include red spruce, balsam fir, mountain holly, sheep laurel, Labrador tea, crowberries, and a few scrawny blueberries.

The **rivulets and swales** (low, damp areas) at the level section of the trail about midway to Lowe's Bald Spot are home to some distinctly shaped flowers. Early in the summer look for **white bog orchids,** one-to-three-foot-tall plants with slender spikes of small white flowers. Once we spotted one of these orchids among the dense vegetation at the edge of the largest swale and then watched as a swallowtail butterfly found a number of others, as it flew from orchid to orchid, ignoring all the other plants. If you have a hand lens, give the kids a close look at one of the flowers. From a distance the flowers don't look like anything special, but close up, you will see an exotic shape typical of orchids, with a lower lip and a spur.

Flag trees at Lowe's Bald Spot reveal the wind direction.

In late summer, the white of the bog orchid is replaced by white of the **turtleheads.** It may take a little imagination to see the resemblance of this relative of the snapdragon to a turtle, but even if the kids decide that it looks more like a lizard's head than a turtle, they will definitely agree that it is a uniquely shaped flower. The flower has two lips and the top lip overhangs the bottom.

For children, the most entertaining plant of this swale is **jewelweed.** In midsummer, you can't miss its delicate orange, spurred flowers spotted with black, hanging down from juicy-looking leaves. If you are hiking in late summer, you will see the fat seedpods. When the seedpods are touched or squeezed, they explode, releasing the seeds and giving the toucher or squeezer a jolt like an electric shock. The kids can't help but jump the first few times they experience this, and they will understand why jewelweed is also called "touch me not." Jewelweed does not do this to entertain children but as a way of dispersing its seeds. After they have exploded a few of these seeds, have the children examine the springlike mechanism within the seedpod that is responsible for the seed's "explosion."

This walk is a particularly good one for seeing that mysterious group of organisms, the **fungi.** They are denizens of the forest floor, thriving in rich soils or on decaying wood.

The rich assortment of colors and odd shapes of fungi make them favorites of children. Late summer is an especially good time to look for them in the White Mountains. One of the most eye-catching is the coral fungus, which looks like someone stuck a piece of branching coral from the tropics on a log. Look for nice patches of coral fungus around the junction of the Old Jackson Road with the Link. Shelf (bracket) fungi growing out of dead trees sometimes reach monstrous sizes. Russulas (robust mushrooms with wide reddish brown or yellow caps and thick stalks), mycenas (delicate mushrooms with thin stalks and conical caps), amanitas, and many other types cover the forest floor. Admire them, but consider them all poisonous.

What you actually see of a mushroom or other fungi are their reproductive structures, which are really only a small part of their "bodies." The soil below is laced with myriad thin filaments of numerous species of fungi. Some penetrate plant roots and aid the plants in taking up nutrients. Others, such as the coral fungus and the bracket fungus, penetrate into dead wood, breaking it down to basic elements. In this way, fungi play a critical role in the ecology of the forest.

The **Indian pipe** looks like a fungus because it is all white. It is actually a flowering plant and produces white flowers. This plant has no green leaves because, unlike most plants, it "feeds" on dead organic matter in the soil rather than producing its own food. So ecologically, it is more like a fungus than a plant.

Take time to enjoy this hike. With the views, swales, mushrooms, and flowers there is much to see along the way to Lowe's Bald Spot.

Thompson's Falls Trail

- **1.8 miles round-trip, 100-foot elevation gain**
- **1–2 hours**
- **easy for all ages**

Thompson's Falls Trail is a short, easy walk to a lovely waterfall and cascades near the Wildcat Mountain Ski Area. The first part of the trail follows the route of a nature trail, the Way of the Wildcat, along the Peabody River. Above the falls, Thompson's Brook has a whole series of cascades, riffles, and pools that are bound to fascinate everyone. This is a great place to throw leaves into the water and watch them slowly make their way downstream to the ocean (well maybe not quite that far, but you get the picture). Kids will enjoy dabbling their toes in the water and picnicking on the large flat rocks in the streambed when the water is low. There are nice views of Mount Washington framed by the trees along the sides of the brook and lots of wildflowers in the spring.

The Wildcat Mountain Visitor Center is open year-round and provides various amenities before or after your walk.

What's in it for kids

- An easy hike.
- A really pretty waterfall.
- A walk along the stream.

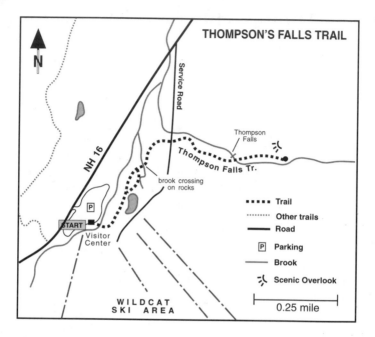

Getting There

The trail is within the Wildcat Mountain Ski Area roughly halfway between Gorham and Jackson off N.H. 16. Park in the ski area parking lot on the east side of N.H. 16 about one mile north of the AMC's Pinkham Notch Visitor Center. Walk past the information and ticket booths, cross a bridge, and follow signs pointing left to the Way of the Wildcat Nature Trail. The nature trail leads to the Thompson's Falls Trail.

The Trail

The first part of this hike, where it follows the Way of the Wildcat Nature Trail, is an easy, wide, leisurely stroll with sixteen numbered stops. A free pamphlet describing each of these stops is available in the Wildcat Mountain Visitor Center. After about a ten-minute walk, the Thompson's Falls Trail, marked with yellow blazes, leaves the nature trail at the farthest point in the loop. The trail crosses a small stream on stones (may be difficult early in the season in high water) and then crosses a service road.

The next section is still easy, with only a moderate gradient to Thompson's Falls. The distance from the beginning of the nature trail to the falls is about 0.2 mile. Since the trail steepens after the falls, those with very young children may want to turn around at this point.

After you pass the first waterfall, you need to do some moderate scrambling up rocks (no problem for older children) and then cross a stream (may be difficult in high water). The trail then levels out and provides views of Mount Washington. It follows the bank of the brook where the cascades continue to be really pretty until the trail dead-ends about 0.2 mile above Thompson's Falls.

When returning, take the right fork of the Way of the Wildcat loop to see the Peabody River.

Highlights

The main feature of the Thompson's Falls Trail is the wonderful series of **waterfalls and cascades** described above. Thompson's Falls are named for Colonel J. M.

Thompson, the owner of the first Glen House, which was located at the base of the Mount Washington Auto Road. Kids will enjoy the graceful stream of water flowing over the falls, but the pool beneath the falls is a little shady for swimming—the smaller potholes and pools above the falls in Thompson's Brook are a better bet. Make sure they note riffles and pools, two different habitats within these fast-moving mountain streams, and encourage them to explore the critters that live in each.

The view of the east side of Mount Washington is especially pretty in the fall when the trees along the brook form a colorful frame.

The walk, particularly above the first waterfall, goes through a good example of a **boreal forest.** The boreal forest floor receives very limited light because of the dense, year-round canopy of conifers. Nonetheless, one small plant that thrives in the understory and is abundant along the Thompson's Fall Trail is **goldthread.** This relative of the buttercup has three small leaflets that are roundish with scalloped edges. Delicate white flowers, one per stem with five to seven petals, appear in May at lower elevations. A golden underground stem, technically a rhizome, connects different individuals, in the same way that individual strawberry plants are connected by runners. In early days, goldthread was used medicinally to combat a variety of ailments, such as toothache.

The **pink lady's slipper** is another distinctive plant of the forest floor that you'll find along the Thompson's Brook Trail. This orchid occurs below 4,000 feet particularly in deciduous woodlands, but it is nowhere abundant. It flowers in June; hence, visitors to Thompson's

White and pink forms of the pink lady's slipper.

Falls have a better chance of catching it in bloom than the earlier spring wildflowers, such as goldthread.

The pink lady's slipper is one of the showiest wildflowers in the White Mountains and is bound to make even the most driven hiker stop for a minute. A typical pink lady's slipper has a pair of large, smooth, glossy leaves that hug the ground and a single flowering stalk with a single flower. The flower has a distinct pink, veiny pouch that resembles a shoe (more like a heavy clog than a slipper). The flower also contains three thin greenish sepals. Another name for it is moccasin flower (whoever named it had footwear in mind). A distinctive feature of the pink lady's slippers in the White Mountains is that many of them (as much as one in four) are not pink at all but are white. This leads to confusion in the name, since it is still technically a pink lady's slipper, so you have to refer to it as the "white form of the pink lady's slipper." Why the White Mountains should be blessed with so many white ones (they do occur elsewhere but much more rarely) is a mystery. Kids might have fun keeping a tally of the number of white versus pink blossoms.

The lady's slipper is a type of orchid, a large family of mostly tropical plants that are much sought after by horticulturists and florists for their beautiful, distinctive flowers. Many orchids, including the pink lady's slipper, have been dug up by collectors or others who selfishly want to savor their beauty for themselves or to sell them to unwary gardeners. This is futile for both the grower and the plant. Pink lady's slippers inevitably die in "captivity," because no one has yet been able to identify their specialized growing requirements. Orchid roots apparently require a special partnership with a fungus in order to take up nutrients from the soil, a partnership that has been impossible to replicate in a garden. So enjoy them in the woods and leave them for the next people who pass this way.

A Walk through the Alpine Garden

- **0.6–2.4 miles round-trip, 300-foot descent**
- **2–3 hours**
- **challenging for kids**

Are you curious about life above the timberline but know that the kids are not yet old enough to hike up a long and arduous trail? If you are not too proud a hiker to get in the car and drive up the Mount Washington Auto Road, then take a walk through the Alpine Garden. This is one of the most exciting things you can do in the White Mountains. You will experience an arctic outpost inhabited by rare wildflowers that normally live only in northern Canada, Greenland, or Alaska. You will see huge rock piles that look like they were put there by giants. Save this outing for a calm, sunny day, so you can savor the views as well as the flowers.

Because it is more rugged than other hikes in this book, we recommend this trail only for families whose children are at least six years old or are still small enough for a backpack. Even though the car does most of the work to get you above tree line, the hike still entails a 300-foot descent and ascent over rocky terrain.

Located on a relatively flat area on a shoulder of Mount Washington, the Alpine Garden is a haven for native alpine wildflowers and has extensive views eastward to the Carter Range. The walk begins with a short descent on the Huntington Ravine Trail. You then walk along the Alpine Garden Trail until you decide it's time to turn around and retrace your steps. The suggested trip is often used by organizations running botanical field trips, because it allows people to spend more time in the alpine zone (rather than hiking up to get there) and also opens up the alpine area to those for whom the hike up from Pinkham Notch would be too difficult.

Caution: Check at Pinkham Notch Visitor Center (PNVC) for the weather conditions on the summit of Mount Washington before beginning, since it is likely to be about twenty degrees Fahrenheit colder and much windier there than in the valley. The Alpine Garden is slightly more benign than the summit, since it is about a thousand feet lower and somewhat protected from the westerly winds. But remember, the weather here is notoriously fickle and can change rapidly even with a good forecast. Don't fool with this trail if the weather is questionable, since it is very exposed and rugged. Be prepared to turn back if the weather changes during the hike, particularly since you have to hike up from the Alpine Garden to return to your car.

Make sure everyone has sturdy shoes and extra clothes. This trail is not appropriate for anyone who is uncomfortable hiking on rocks.

The Governor Sherman Adams Summit Building at the top of Mount Washington is 1.1 miles beyond the trailhead and has rest rooms, food service, snacks, souvenirs, telephones, a post office, a museum, and lots of tourists. There are also restrooms at Glen House where the Auto Road begins.

What's in it for kids

- Some great rocks to scramble on (and make their parents nervous).
- Scenery that's really worth it.
- Rare alpine vegetation.
- Wolf spiders.

Getting There

Getting there can be half the fun, because the views from the Auto Road are phenomenal. There are so many signs for the Mount Washington Auto Road, a major tourist attraction, that you can't miss it. It is about 2.5 miles north of the AMC's PNVC along N.H. 16.

The Auto Road is not cheap. At the time of this writing, the Auto Road was charging twelve dollars for a car and driver, five dollars for each additional adult passenger, and three dollars for children five to thirteen. It is a steep, winding road, not meant for drivers with vertigo. Campers and trailers are not permitted on the road.

The Auto Road is about eight miles long and is conveniently marked off with mile markers. Park at the turnoff just below the seven-mile marker in a relatively flat area called the Cow Pasture. Look for the signs for the Huntington Ravine Trail, which descends east (left as you ascend) from the Auto Road.

The Trail

Note: Since this hike is in open terrain, there will be a great temptation to wander off on the tundra. Alpine

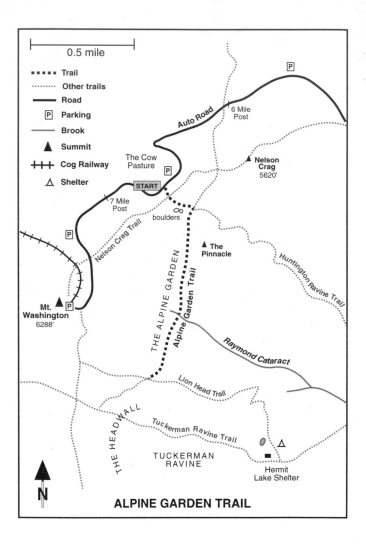

0.5 mile

Trail (dotted heavy)
Other trails (dotted light)
Road (solid)
P **Parking**
Brook
▲ **Summit**
+++ **Cog Railway**
△ **Shelter**

Auto Road

6 Mile Post

P

The Cow Pasture

P

START

Nelson Crag 5620'

7 Mile Post

P

∞ boulders

Nelson Crag Trail

▲ The Pinnacle

Huntington Ravine Trail

THE ALPINE GARDEN

Alpine Garden Trail

Mt. Washington 6288'

P

Raymond Cataract

Lion Head Trail

THE HEADWALL

Tuckerman Ravine Trail

TUCKERMAN RAVINE

△

Hermit Lake Shelter

N

ALPINE GARDEN TRAIL

vegetation can withstand the rigors of arctic conditions but cannot tolerate the pounding of hikers' feet. It is imperative that everyone stays on the trails. This is a good place to foster a sense of stewardship in the children for this and other special habitats. Tell them that alpine plants grow very slowly in these harsh conditions; therefore, it may take hundreds of years for plants to regrow in areas where they have been killed by trampling. And picking alpine plants is both illegal and extremely bad form. (You have our permission to severely chastise and report anyone engaged in such activities.) Everyone who enjoys the Alpine Garden is also responsible for protecting it.

From the parking area, descend steeply over rocks on the Huntington Ravine Trail for 0.3 mile. When it levels out, turn right (south) on the Alpine Garden Trail. Depending on how everyone is feeling you could turn around after a short walk and retrace your steps or hike completely across the Alpine Garden before turning back. Don't even think of continuing on the Huntington Ravine Trail any distance beyond this junction. The *AMC White Mountain Guide* calls the Huntington Ravine Trail the most difficult trail in the White Mountains. Instead, enjoy the relatively flat meander of the Alpine Garden Trail through alpine vegetation. The Alpine Garden Trail extends to the Lion Head Trail (1.2 miles), where you can peer down at the awesome sight of Tuckerman Ravine.

Highlights

A thorough description of the alpine area is a whole book in itself, so only a brief introduction is given here.

For a more in-depth view see the *AMC Field Guide to the New England Alpine Summits* by Nancy G. Slack and Allison Bell.

On your drive, you will share the Auto Road with all sorts of vehicles. You may feel that this is not exactly the "natural experience" you wanted in the White Mountains. Comfort yourself with the knowledge that this was the same route Henry David Thoreau used in a botanical excursion in 1858.

The Auto Road begins at 1,563 feet, reaches timberline at about 4,800 feet (between milepost four and five), passes the trailhead to the Alpine Garden at about 5,700 feet, and ends at the Mount Washington summit at 6,288 feet. It's fascinating to travel first through a dense forest, then past shorter and shorter trees until spectacular mountain vistas open up before you.

The drive up the Auto Road takes you through **three ecological zones:** the broad-leafed deciduous forest (or northern hardwoods), the boreal forest, and the alpine tundra. This is the most visible response to the change in climate with elevation. On average, the temperature drops about one degree for every 350 feet you climb, so it will be about twelve degrees cooler at the trailhead than at the beginning of the Auto Road, and a lot windier, too. By driving a mere 7 miles on the Auto Road, you have driven the ecological equivalent of about 1,000 miles north.

We think of rocks as the very essence of unyielding, enduring solidity; however, the Auto Road is a great place to show the children that even **rocks can be bent and folded.** Between milepost five and six on the small cliff faces that border the road, you can see how distinct layers of rocks have been folded. This happened about 400 million years ago when these rocks were under intense heat and pressure and actually became flexible as they were compressed between two moving continents.

As you walk down the trail to the Alpine Garden, you may wonder who piled up all of the **big boulders** in such a jumble. Will your children guess that giants used to inhabit the White Mountains? Tell them that the rocks were not put there by giants but by water. Water, freezing and then expanding in cracks in the bedrock, caused chunks of bedrock to break off into the rock pile. On the summit cone of Mount Washington nearby, boulders are piled so deep that it is hard to find the underlying bedrock.

New Hampshire may be the Granite State, but the rocks that form its highest mountain range are not granite but schists and gneisses. Schists and gneisses are metamorphic rocks, so called because they are formed by the transformation of other types of rocks. In the Presidential Range, the same intense heat and pressure that caused the folding of rocks along the Auto Road transformed sedimentary rocks (produced from compacted sand and mud under the sea) into schists and gneisses. This highest part of New England was once under the sea.

Many of the rocks are covered by yellow-green splotches that look like someone threw some paint at them. These are **map lichens,** whose scientific name, *Rhizocarpon geographicum,* also stresses their resemblance to a map. Lichens produce acids that break down the rocks upon which they reside.

The peak time to observe **flowers of the alpine tundra** in bloom is early to mid-June. This is early in the season for many hikers, but don't be disheartened, there are still many interesting plants to see all summer. A few favorites are listed here, but refer to the *AMC Field Guide to the New England Alpine Summits* for more details.

The first thing to show your children about plants in the Alpine Garden is their small stature. Most never rise more than a few inches above the ground because of the fierce winds. Taller ones are likely to be found only where they are protected from the wind, for example, in the lee of rocks. Balsam fir and black spruce grow as low, gnarled shrubs called **krummholz,** a German word meaning crooked wood.

While hiking through the Alpine Garden, you will notice cushions of dark green, tightly packed, tiny leaves that hug the ground throughout the tundra. These "pincushions" are **diapensia,** a native of North American and Scandanavian arctic realms, as well as the high peaks of New England. If you are lucky enough to be on the Alpine Garden Trail in June and the wind and temperature have been cooperative, you will be treated to a profusion of its small white flowers with five petals. The dark green leaves act as passive solar collectors, absorbing solar radiation and insuring that the plant stays warmer than the surroundings.

Insects find warmer temperatures and protection from the wind within the tight bundle of diapensia leaves. Tell the kids to put their hands down at ground level where the diapensia grows. They should feel the diminished wind compared to a few feet off the ground.

The **alpine azalea** also grows as a cushion plant. Its leaves resemble diapensia, however, its pink flowers are even smaller—no larger than the head of a matchstick. They

Diapensia and Lapland rosebay bloom in the Alpine Garden.

still put on a great show when they all bloom together.

A flower that is bound to catch your eye in June because of its relatively large magenta blossoms is the **Lapland rosebay.** The flowers may bring to mind a small rhododendron, because the Lapland rosebay is, in fact, a very small species of rhododendron.

In keeping with the theme that small is beautiful in the Alpine Garden, there are tiny willows that never get more than two inches high. In June you might find pussy willow-type "buds" coming right out of the ground. These are the male and female catkins of the **bearberry willow.**

The big yellow flowers blooming from late June throughout the summer are **mountain avens.** This plant, with relatively large scalloped leaves, grows in only two places in the world: in the White Mountains (where it is reasonably common) and on an island off Nova Scotia.

In July, delicate white flowers with five petals on small plants with thin, grassy leaves are particularly abundant alongside the trail. This is the **mountain sandwort,** a plant whose affinity for growing near trails in the White Mountains suggests that it is better adapted to Vibram soles than all others.

In July and August, the showiest flower in the Alpine Garden is the **bluebell** (harebell). This flower is common at lower elevations and may not have been native to the Alpine Garden. There is some speculation that its seeds may have been carried up the mountain in the droppings of donkeys that were used as pack animals in the nineteenth century.

You will not see many animals at the Alpine Garden. The alpine areas of the Rocky Mountains are blessed with herds of elk, deer, and bighorn sheep. In the White Mountains you will have to content yourself with **wolf spiders,** a large dark spider that scampers over the rocks, a few **butterflies,** other insects, and an occasional woodchuck or snowshoe hare. The only two species of birds that regularly build nests above the timberline are **dark-eyed juncos** and **white-throated sparrows**. The junco is a perky gray bird with a white belly that flashes white outer tail feathers when it flies. The white-throated sparrow is famous for its song, a series of clear whistles. Watch also for **ravens** cavorting in the air, with their characteristic throaty call that sometimes sounds like the snorting of a hog. Admire their ability to soar over this unique and dramatic habitat.

A Geological Field Trip to Pine Mountain

- **3.5 miles round-trip, 750-foot elevation gain**
- **2.5–4 hours**
- **moderate for kids**

Pine Mountain, at 2,410 feet, is the northeasternmost mountain in the Presidential Range. Although quite a bit lower than its more renowned cousins, it provides excellent views of the Presidential and Carter ranges for only moderate effort. It also has prominent samples of scratches carved by the last glaciers and a striking vertical dip of rocks near the summit. The hike itself is a pleasant stroll, mostly along a little-used dirt road through an airy forest dominated by paper birch.

What's in it for kids

- Great view of Mount Washington and Carter Notch.
- Rocks etched with parallel stripes on the summit.
- Steady uphill walk along a road.
- Scrambling on ledges.
- Some blueberry patches.

Getting There

Pine Mountain Trail departs from Pinkham B (Dolly Copp) Road in the town of Gorham. If you are coming

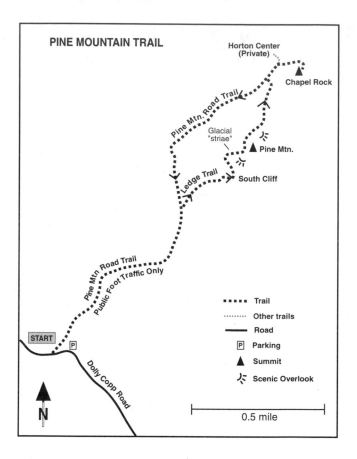

PINE MOUNTAIN TRAIL

Horton Center
(Private)

Chapel Rock

Pine Mtn. Road Trail

Glacial
"striae"

Pine Mtn.

Ledge Trail

South Cliff

Pine Mtn Road Trail

Public Foot Traffic Only

Trail

Other trails

Road

P Parking

▲ Summit

Scenic Overlook

START

P

Dolly Copp Road

N

0.5 mile

from Jackson or North Conway, head north on N.H. 16 past Jackson and Pinkham Notch. Make a left on Pinkham B (Dolly Copp) Road, about 6.5 miles north of the AMC's Pinkham Notch Visitor Center (PNVC). The trail to Pine Mountain is 2.4 miles from N.H. 16 on the right (northeast) side. There will be signs to the Horton Center (see below) as well as Pine Mountain.

If you are coming from the Twin Mountain or Franconia area, take U.S. 3 to N.H. 115 in Twin Mountain, then take 115 about 12 miles to U.S. 2. Make a right on U.S. 2 and travel about 8 miles to Pinkham B (Dolly Copp) Road (0.8 mile past the Appalachia parking area) and make another right. The trailhead is about 3 miles on the left.

The Trail

The trail to Pine Mountain is a private unpaved road (Pine Mountain Road) that leads to the Douglas Horton Center, a retreat run by the United Church of Christ near the summit of Pine Mountain. The center is not open to the public, but you are welcome to hike the trail and enjoy the views from the top.

Pine Mountain Road runs through a pleasant, relatively open woods and ascends gradually for much of its length. It is wide enough to walk several abreast, but remember to be watchful for occasional automobiles that use the road to reach the Horton Center. The road ends at the center (1.6 miles), and the trail turns right and ascends for a short distance to the actual summit (2 miles). Side trails lead to views northeast toward the Androscoggin River valley and Mount Moriah. At the summit, you will find the foundation of an old fire tower. For the best views of Mount Washington and Carter Notch, walk past the foundation to the open ledges a little beyond.

You can make an interesting loop by hiking 1 mile (about twenty to forty minutes) along the road and turning right on the Ledge Trail. The Ledge Trail offers a shorter, steeper ascent to the summit with excellent views from the south-facing cliff along the way. A little scrambling is required, but older children should have no trouble. From the summit, you can then descend along the Pine Mountain Trail back to your car. The entire loop is 3.5 miles.

Highlights

There are two important **geological stories** you can tell your kids on the summit of Pine Mountain. The first has to do with the formation of the rocks. Look behind you when you are sitting on the rock-carved bench at the summit ledges and observe vertical layers of rocks. These rocks were once horizontal beds of sandstones and muds deposited on the bottom of an ancient sea that predated the modern Atlantic. About 400 million years ago, there was a giant collision between North America and an ancient continent called Avalon. The heat and pressure of the crash metamorphosed the deposits into schists and quartzites and folded and thrust them up into their present dramatic, vertical position.

Glaciation is the second geological story. On the open ledges just down from the summit on the Ledge Trail, have the children look for the **parallel stripes** (called striae) embedded in the rock in a northwest-southeast direction. These are scratches made by the gouging action of stones under the continental glacier

Glacial scratches near the summit of Pine Mountain.

as it crept along like a frozen river southwest over Pine Mountain. The rocks, stones, and other debris at the bottom of the glacier, squeezed by the tremendous weight of ice, acted like sandpaper, etching and scouring the earth below.

Another indication of glaciation visible from the summit of Pine Mountain on a clear day is the view of Carter Notch. The beautiful U-shaped notch and the rounded summit of Wildcat Mountain are characteristic features of valleys and mountains smoothed by glaciers.

Although geology is center stage on this hike, everyone should still take note of the forest and plants. The forest along Pine Mountain Road is more open and "airy" than most others in the Whites, with beautiful ribbons of dappled sunlight penetrating to the forest floor.

Paper birches are abundant, suggesting that this area was probably logged or otherwise disturbed in recent history. (A question almost as mysterious as "why is the sky blue" is "why is the bark of a paper birch white?" I doubt it is to provide camouflage in the winter. Perhaps it is to reduce the amount of heating of the tree during summer in the open areas where this tree tends to grow. As anyone who has walked barefoot on dark pavement in the summer sun knows, dark objects absorb a lot more heat from the sun than light-colored ones.)

A common shrub along Pine Mountain Road in wet swales is the **red-berried elder.** This shrub has compound leaves that branch off in pairs along the stems. The branches themselves are covered with corky spots. The numerous flowers, produced around early June, are

Tiger swallowtail.

in showy, white pyramidal clusters. Unfortunately, the dark red berries found during the summer are often inedible, unlike those of its close relative, the elderberry.

Many **spring wildflowers** and other small plants grow along the trail, an added feature if you are hiking in May or early June. Common ones include painted trillium, Canada mayflower, clintonia, bunchberry, wild sarsaparilla, wild white violet, and starflower. Interrupted ferns and lady ferns (a variety with a red stem) thrive along the edge of the road, and you also should be able to find shiny club moss and ground pine. Ground pine will remind the children of a tiny Christmas tree. Look for pink lady's slippers in June and sharp-leafed aster in late summer.

The ledges along the Ledge Trail are home to reindeer moss, rhodora, blueberries, Labrador tea, heart-leafed white birch, and wild currants. **Reindeer moss** is a low, delicate lichen with thin, bluish gray, tangled branches that you frequently see in rocky areas with thin soil in the mountains, often around and under blueberry shrubs. It usually looks so neat and prim that it is hard to believe that it wasn't deliberately placed down by a landscape gardener.

Rhodora is a small wild rhododendron with smooth, blue-green leaves. It is common in bogs and lower summits such as Pine Mountain. Around Memorial Day in the White Mountains, its beautiful large pink flowers put on a dazzling display, as befits a rhododendron.

With its geological and botanical treasures, your outing to Pine Mountain will certainly be satisfying.

Town Line Brook Trail to Triple Falls

- **0.4 mile round-trip, 200-foot elevation gain**
- **40 minutes**
- **easy but steep for kids**

It takes about as long to hike this trail as to say "Town Line Brook Trail to Triple Falls." The walk is short and steep, dead-ending after passing three scenic waterfalls. The banks of the brook are heavily forested and dark and, combined with the mythological names of two of the three falls, create a mysterious atmosphere. Like many waterfalls in the White Mountains, these are best visited early in the season or after a rainstorm. Because it is so shady, the trail is also a relatively cool place on a hot day. Even though the trail ascends steeply, its short-ness makes it appropriate for just about any young hiker, but with one cautionary note. This is not a trail to allow your children to run off unsupervised, since there are some steep drop-offs without any protective barriers.

What's in it for kids

- Three waterfalls with the intriguing names of Proteus, Erebus, and Evans (well at least the first two are intriguing).
- Some impressively large rocks and a steep gorge with passageways and holes. Natural bridges created over a narrow gorge by large fallen hemlocks.

- A really short hike that's steep enough to feel like you have accomplished something.

Getting There

The Town Line Brook Trail starts at Pinkham B (Dolly Copp) Road. From the Twin Mountain area or points north, Pinkham B Road goes right off U.S. 2 approximately 0.8 mile east of the Appalachia trailhead parking lot. The trailhead, marked with a sign, is 1.4 miles south of the railroad crossing, on the right just past the bridge over Town Line Brook. From Pinkham Notch, Jackson, and North Conway, Pinkham B Road goes left off N.H. 16 at the Dolly Copp Campground (not the picnic area) about 6.5 miles north of the AMC's Pinkham Notch Visitor Center (PNVC). The trailhead will be on your left just before the bridge over Town Line Brook, less than a mile past the Pine Mountain Road Trail. From Gorham or the Evans Notch area, you can take your pick and reach Pinkham B Road either by going south on N.H. 16 or west on U.S. 2.

The Trail

The trail is 0.2 mile long and goes steeply uphill along a brook for most of its length. The path is in good condition, easy to follow, and covered by a soft cushion of hemlock needles. All three waterfalls are marked by signs. It takes only five minutes to reach Proteus Falls, so if the steep uphill walking is not to your liking or if you want only a *really* short walk, you can turn around there. Erebus Falls, a few minutes beyond, is the most vertigo-inducing of the

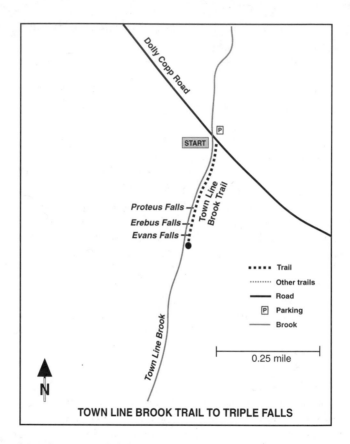

TOWN LINE BROOK TRAIL TO TRIPLE FALLS

three because of the steep drop-off at a point where you overlook the gorge. It's a long way down! The trail ends at Evans Falls, where you retrace your steps back to your car. Town Line Brook refers to the boundary between the towns of Gorham and Randolph.

Highlights

Triple Falls is really **three separate waterfalls.** It is fitting that Proteus and Erebus falls share names from Greek mythology because they are both more mysterious than Evans Falls. Both are within a shady, steep-sided gorge. In approaching Proteus Falls, you squeeze through shady passageways between big boulders. On the way up, tell the kids about the origins of these mythological names. Proteus, a Greek god associated with water, is often pictured as an old man. He has prophetic powers and can change into any shape he wants, perhaps even one of the boulders along the side of the trail or a hemlock hanging over the edge of the gorge. Erebus, the father of the Three Fates, is the dark place where souls pass on their way to the underworld.

While fantasizing about such matters, look for the dike of white quartz running across the base of Erebus Falls, an intrusion in the darker metamorphic rock of the northern Presidentials. In a couple of places, large hemlocks have fallen across the gorge, creating natural bridges. Dark, hummocky holes around Proteus and Erebus falls form little caves in which water may flow or animals hide.

Evans Falls, although smaller than the other two, is friendlier. The forest is lighter and it's a good spot for a picnic.

The **forest** along Town Line Brook Trail is predominantly northern hardwoods (American beech, sugar maple, and yellow birch) and hemlock. Hemlocks thrive in the cool, damp ravine, as they do along many streams in the White Mountains. You'll see some impressively

Coral fungus, a denizen of damp, shady forests.

large ones here. The **refrigerator effect** of the cool mountain stream tumbling down the side of Mount Madison causes a delay in the flowering times of plants that grow in the ravine (e.g., hobblebush, painted trillium, and mountain wood sorrel) compared to their neighbors in the nearby upland.

The shady dampness creates a great habitat for **ferns, mosses,** and **fungi** that cover the rocks and forest floor along the trail and in the streambed. Look for rock ferns (Virginia polypody) on boulders and rocky ledges, long beech fern right around the waterfalls, and spinulose wood fern on the forest floor. Piggyback moss and haircap moss are also common.

Is the coolness due to the mountain stream, or is it really the chilling breath of Erebus?

Waterfall Loop: Fallsway Trail to Brookbank Trail

- **1.5 miles round-trip, 400-foot elevation gain**
- **1–2 hours**
- **easy (Fallsway Trail only) or moderate (Brookbank Trail)**

This is a relatively easy loop that runs along picturesque Snyder Brook through deep, cool hemlock forests of the Snyder Brook Scenic Area. Pretty waterfalls and many flat rocks along the brook invite you to have a picnic, get your feet wet, and relax while listening to the sounds of rushing water. There are no views from this trail, so consider it on a foggy or drizzly day when no views are possible anyway. The route we recommend should take between one to two hours. A shorter, easier loop is possible by returning on the Valley Way, or you can simply retrace your steps after taking in a waterfall or two.

What's in it for kids _____

- Four different waterfalls.
- Wading in a cool (OK, frigid) mountain stream.
- Crossing an abandoned railroad track.

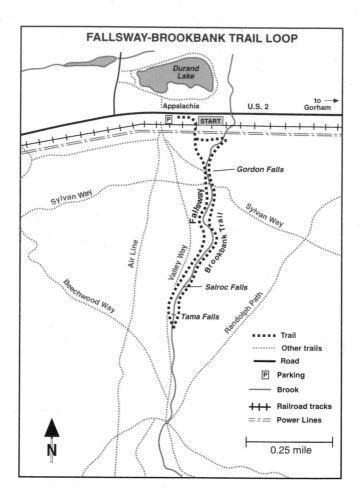

FALLSWAY-BROOKBANK TRAIL LOOP

Durand Lake

Appalachia

U.S. 2

to Gorham

P

START

Gordon Falls

Sylvan Way

Fallsway

Air Line

Valley Way

Sylvan Way

Brookbank Trail

Beechwood Way

Salroc Falls

Tama Falls

Randolph Path

- ▪▪▪▪ Trail
- ⋯⋯ Other trails
- ▬▬ Road
- P Parking
- ▬▬ Brook
- +++ Railroad tracks
- === Power Lines

0.25 mile

N

Getting There

The Fallsway Trail leaves from the Appalachia parking lot off U.S. 2 west of Gorham, about 5 miles west of the point where N.H. 16 splits off from U.S. 2 and heads north and about 0.8 mile west of Pinkham B Road (Dolly Copp Road). If you are coming from the west through the Twin Mountain area, the trailhead is about 7 miles east of the junction of U.S. 2 and N.H. 115. The parking lot is on the south side of U.S. 2.

The parking area is well marked and large, since it is the trailhead for a number of trails into the northern Presidentials. The Fallsway Trail leaves from the east side of the parking lot and is well marked. Most of the other trails, such as the Valley Way, depart from the west side.

The Trail

The first part of this loop, the Fallsway Trail, is a wide, easy uphill path through a relatively open woods along running water. It is marked with yellow paint blazes. The Brookbank Trail is a little rougher and less well traveled, but shouldn't be much of a problem.

The Fallsway Trail starts through a short section of woods before crossing an open area with power lines and an overgrown railroad track. The trail then reenters the forest of sugar maples and hobblebush, meets up with Snyder Brook, follows the west bank of the brook, then passes by Gordon Falls. This part of the White Mountains is laced with many short trails and trail junctions, but they are all well marked. Just keep following the signs for the Fallsway. After passing Lower and Upper Salroc falls, the Fallsway joins the Valley Way for a short stretch (for a shorter loop, you can return to the parking lot on the Valley Way). At the sign for Fallsway Loop, turn left and walk 0.1 mile to Tama Falls, the final destination of this hike, 0.6 mile from the parking lot.

At Tama Falls, you can pick up the Brookbank Trail and complete the loop (0.9 mile back to the parking lot). Cross over Snyder Brook on some flat rocks (no problem except in extremely high water) and start your descent. The Brookbank Trail follows the east bank of Snyder Brook, providing good access to the brook at a number of locations and a different perspective of the same waterfalls you saw on the way up. Brookbank has one short rocky section that may be slick in wet weather or high water. Eventually, you cross back over Snyder Brook at the point where the trail reaches the open area (may be difficult at high water). Walk back along the power lines to the Fallsway Trail and then to the parking lot.

Highlights

The **waterfalls** are the major attraction. The kids will enjoy it even if they just make it the fifteen minutes to Gordon Falls. At Gordon Falls, the amazing erosive power of rushing water is apparent in the channels and shoots in solid rock. Mosses and ferns thrive in the mist along the sides of the waterfalls.

Lower and Upper Salroc falls also have interesting geological features. An impressive **deep plunge pool** has been carved out of the streambed by Lower Salroc Falls. This pool will even be over the head of adults, at least early in the season. **Dikes** of basalt and pegmatite are visible in the streambed. The pegmatite appears as whitish stripes of large crystals within the granite rocks of the area; the basalt dikes are black and finely grained. The dikes were formed when molten lava from deep within the earth flowed up into cracks in the granite and then hardened. There is also an extensive flat rock, great for a picnic if it is not underwater.

If the children make it as far as Tama Falls, they will be rewarded with a sight of the largest falls of the group. The consensus is that Tama is also the prettiest— a graceful veil of water flowing down a carved granite staircase.

Bunchberry is a common flower along most trails.

Show children the **difference in the forest** immediately adjacent to and farther away from the stream. Hemlocks dominate along the banks of the stream because they favor the cool, shady, damp atmosphere. As you move away from the water into drier, warmer habitat, northern hardwoods thrive, particularly sugar maples and yellow birches. From just about any White Mountain summit, you'll see dark lines of hemlock that reveal the courses of streams. Along the Fallsway and Brookbank trails, you experience this dynamic more intimately.

Mosses abound in the cool woods along the Brookbank Trail and the damp rocks around the waterfalls. One of the most intriguing is named piggyback moss, because new moss "plantlets" grow right out of the "backs" of older shoots. Look for one nice patch of **piggyback moss** (also called fern moss) just below Tama Falls on the Brookbank Trail, near where a yellow birch is growing right out of a big boulder. Patches of **sphagnum moss** also occur.

You can teach your children a good conservation lesson by pointing out the **difference in the understory** between the well-traveled Fallsway Trail and the less well trod Brookbank. The Fallsway is largely barren of undergrowth, which has succumbed beneath the feet of too many trampling hikers wandering off the trail for views of the brook. In contrast, the Brookbank is characterized by lush growth of mosses, ferns, and small herbs because far fewer people use it. It is a great illustration of why everyone should stay on trails.

North Conway Region

THE NORTH CONWAY region is a popular area for families, both for its outdoor opportunities and for its extensive facilities. The region includes 3,000-foot mountains, bold cliffs popular with rock climbers, the Saco River, and a large number of ponds. The Green Hills, especially Black Cap, provide excellent views of the Presidential and Carter ranges for relatively little effort. There are also secluded areas that provide great wildlife observation opportunities. The communities of North Conway and Jackson are popular vacation centers with many amenities for tourists and some "theme parks" oriented to children.

Facilities

The Visitor Information Center in Intervale, north of the center of North Conway, has clean rest rooms, hot water, a place to walk your dog, and a plethora of brochures about various activities in the White Mountains. Echo Lake State Park is a popular swimming area a few miles west of North Conway. The Saco Ranger Station of the White Mountain National Forest is at the junction of N.H. 16 and N.H. 112 (Kancamagus Highway) one mile south of Conway.

Supplies. North Conway is a major tourist center with restaurants, gas stations, motels, supermarkets, craft shops, and factory outlets. Those traveling from the Pinkham Notch area pass through Jackson, Glen, and Intervale before reaching the three trails described in this region. A variety of stores that sell food, snacks, and other amenities are across N.H. 16 from the Information Center in Intervale near Hurricane Mountain Road.

Camping. The nearest public campgrounds for the trails described in this region include those along the eastern section of the Kancamagus Highway, the White Ledge Campground (six miles south of Conway on N.H. 16), the Dry River Campground in Crawford Notch State Park, and the Dolly Copp Campground north of Pinkham Notch. Each of these is about twenty to thirty minutes away from North Conway. There are a number of private campgrounds along N.H. 16 as well. Be aware that the traffic through North Conway can be painfully slow on weekends.

Diana's Baths

- **1 mile round-trip, minimal elevation change**
- **30–60 minutes**
- **easy for all ages**

Diana's Baths is a pleasant spot to relax and hang out on a summer afternoon. A short, level half-mile walk along the Moat Mountain Trail brings you to this former mill site where you can wade in one of the many pools among numerous picturesque cascades or explore the ruins of the old mill. It is a popular family destination, suitable for the youngest hikers, so you won't be alone. The shady forest and the cool water make this an ideal place to visit during the summer.

*What's in it for kids*_____

- Wading in the water among cascades with rushing water.
- Lots of flat rocks to hang out on.
- A very easy, level walk.

Getting There

Getting to the trailhead is more of a challenge than the hike itself. Actually, it isn't so difficult to find with good directions, but keep in mind that there is no sign for it on West Side Road. From North Conway, turn west on

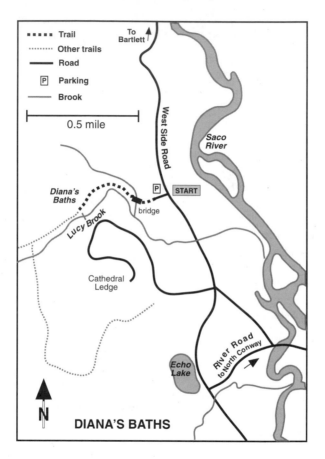

DIANA'S BATHS

River Road, which leaves N.H. 16/U.S. 302 for Echo Lake State Park at the traffic light just north of the Eastern Slope Inn. Cross the Saco River and bear right at the next two intersections. You are now headed north on

West Side Road. About 0.7 mile past the road to Cathedral Ledge (2.2 miles from N.H. 16 in North Conway), turn left on a dirt road between two fenced-in fields just after you pass a large white farmhouse on the left. The trail starts a few hundred yards down the road at the metal barrier with a sign for the Moat Mountain Trail. Park along this road as far down as you can.

From the south, pick up West Side Road in Conway Village by turning left from N.H. 16 onto Passaconaway Road at the intersection where N.H. 153 goes off to the right. Continue north (straight) as the road turns into West Side Road. About five miles past Conway, bear left where River Road comes in from the right. Pass the road to Cathedral Ledge and follow the above directions.

From Crawford Notch, travel east on U.S. 302 and turn right on West Side Road about 4 miles east of the turnoff to Bear Notch Road in Bartlett. Turn on the dirt road between the two fenced-in fields 0.4 mile south of the Conway-Bartlett town line.

The Trail

The Moat Mountain Trail between the parking area and Diana's Baths is a wide and level dirt road and completely uneventful. The trail parallels Lucy Brook, a tributary of the Saco River. In about ten to fifteen minutes you reach a clearing. The mill site is immediately to your left, and Diana's Baths is just a little ahead, also to the left. The Moat Mountain Trail continues beyond the baths, but it becomes very steep and is not recommended for families.

Highlights

Numerous cascades will immediately catch your attention when you arrive at Diana's Baths. Even with the crowds, you will still be able to find a flat rock and an interesting stretch of water that you can claim for several hours. The kids will enjoy meandering up the granite terraces to see the wonderful assortment of waterfalls, pools, and rocks upstream.

Show the kids the numerous small, round **potholes** carved into the flat granite. These were formed by the

One of the many pretty cascades of Diana's Baths.

scouring action of small stones and sand carried around by spring floodwater. Ask the kids how they think the potholes that are perched high above the current level of the water came to be. These were probably formed during the melting of the last glacier when water levels were much higher than they are now.

Some gears, pipes, and stone walls from the old mill are still present. This was a gristmill that used the waterpower of Lucy Brook to ground flour.

Diana's Baths is situated among shady hemlocks, which keep it pleasantly cool. Three interesting shrubs that grow around the water's edge are rhodora, speckled alder, and mountain holly. If you get here around Memorial Day weekend, rhodora will be in bloom, with showy pinkish flowers that are pretty enough to make you forget the blackflies, at least for a moment. Speckled alders have distinctly spotted twigs and branches, as if they have the chicken pox. Mountain hollies are particularly abundant. These shrubs have leaves with unserrated edges and tipped with a tiny spine (look carefully, using a hand lens if you have one). The leaves look pale green and delicate in contrast to its dark gray branches.

Along the trail you will see asters and silverod in mid- to late summer. Silverod is actually a type of goldenrod but with silvery, rather than yellow, flowers.

Diana's Baths are named for the Roman goddess of the hunt, who was often pictured in woodland settings surrounded by animals. Enjoy your swim, and watch out for the water sprites that legend has it used to inhabit the area.

Black Cap Path

- **2.2 miles round-trip, 700-foot elevation gain**
- **2 hours**
- **moderate for kids**

Black Cap (2,370 feet) in the Green Hills near North Conway has one of the finest views in the White Mountains for relatively little effort. On a clear day you can see Mount Washington, Kearsarge, Chocorua, and other famous peaks of the White Mountains from its summit.

The hike to Black Cap is a very popular family walk. The kids will get a real sense of accomplishment as they hike from the dense forest at the trailhead to the open vista on Black Cap. Bring along a windbreaker for this exposed summit.

What's in it for kids

- A relatively short hike that has great views.
- An open, ledgy summit that is a great place for scrambling around on rocks.
- An opportunity to contemplate White Mountain weather.
- A chance to ask why nothing grows underneath spruce trees.

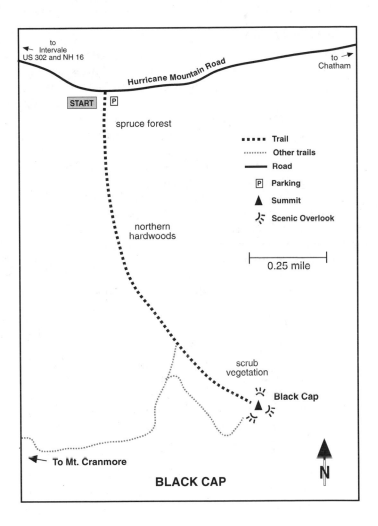

Getting There

The trailhead for Black Cap Path is on Hurricane Mountain Road, an experience in itself, between Intervale and South Chatham. From North Conway, head north on NH 16/US 302, and turn right on Hurricane Mountain Road just after passing the large Visitor Information Center and scenic overlook. From the Crawford Notch or Jackson areas, head south through Glen on N.H. 16/U.S. 302 and make a left on this road just south of Intervale. Wind your way up Hurricane Mountain Road for 3.7 miles to the height of land. Park near the yellow-blazed trees that mark the beginning of the trail.

You can also reach the trailhead from the Evans Notch area by turning right (west) off Route 113 at North Fryeburg, making the first left toward South Chatham, and then a right on Hurricane Mountain Road. The trailhead will be on your left after about 2.5 miles.

The Trail

The Black Cap Path begins in a spruce forest and is marked with orange blazes. The first 0.9 mile of the trail also has yellow blazes that identify the route to Mount Cranmore. When the Mount Cranmore Trail departs to the right from the Black Cap Path, continue following the orange blazes to reach the open ledges of Black Cap at 1.2 miles.

The trail is easy to follow and well maintained, with stone barriers that channel water off during wet weather. Because this is such a popular trail, it is heavily eroded in places, so please keep to the trail itself to preserve the woodland vegetation.

Highlights

The **view** from the summit is the highlight of this hike. Looking north, the most prominent nearby peak is Mount Kearsarge North, which has a fire tower at its summit. To the west are the steep rock faces of Cathedral and Humphrey ledges and the Moat Range, the latter containing one of the few large remnants of truly volcanic rock in the White Mountains. On a clear day, you can see Mount Washington to the northwest, Chocorua and Passaconaway to the southwest, and Mount Carrigain and Carrigain Notch to the west. Conway Lake is due south. Try taking turns with a compass and a map to identify these different peaks. The children can also hunt for the little arrow that marks the exact summit of Black Cap.

Climbing Black Cap Path. Andy Falender.

The summit of Black Cap is a great place to contemplate **White Mountain weather,** assuming of course that the weather is decent enough to allow you to contemplate anything. On the way up, look for a number of white birches blown over by the **wind** near the junction with the trail to Mount Cranmore. The shallow roots made these trees particularly vulnerable to such mishaps. In the thin soil near the summits of the mountains, roots have difficulty penetrating far into the ground. Evidence of the effect of wind is also apparent in the low scrubby vegetation that grows on the summit itself.

Clouds are another major feature of White Mountain weather. From the summit of Black Cap, you may see clouds hovering over some of the taller peaks, particularly Mount Washington, where cloud cover averages 75 percent of the year. As air from the west (where most of our weather systems originate) flows up and over these mountains, it cools. Clouds form because cooler air holds less moisture than warm air, just as the warm, moist air inside your lungs condenses on a cold morning when you breathe out. The Presidential Range has particularly severe weather because, in addition to being the highest range in the region, it is positioned at the convergence of several storm tracks.

Clouds floating in the sky above you can be harbingers of good weather or indicate that rain is on its way. If you and the kids want to try your hand at forecasting the weather, the AMC has produced a pamphlet, available at Pinkham Notch Visitor Center, that tells you how, based on cloud shapes and wind direction.

The **forest** changes from a pure stand of red spruce near the trailhead, then a northern hardwood forest, and finally to a scrubby open area around the summit. Note the **absence of any understory** vegetation within the red spruce area. This is often the case under pure stands of conifer trees, such as spruce, balsam fir, and hemlock. The dense canopy limits light to the forest floor much more completely than in the forest of broad-leafed trees. Even when the broad-leafed trees form a dense canopy, understory herbs and shrubs still get a chance at sunlight in early spring before the trees leaf out. Not so under evergreens. Also, the needles that do fall off the evergreens decompose to an acid soil rich in tannins, both factors not conducive to plant growth.

The northern hardwood forest of beech, birch, and sugar maple is much lighter than the spruce forest. Striped maple is the dominant understory shrub. Spring wildflowers include rosy twisted stalk, clintonia, painted and red trillium, and bunchberries. In the late summer and fall, look for asters.

At the summit look for heart-leafed white birch, balsam fir, mountain ash, currants (a small shrub with maplelike leaves), and some blueberries. In the spring, shadbushes bloom.

If you are interested in photographing the mountain scenery, you should hike Black Cap in the morning, since the mountain views are most striking in the north-west to southwest direction. That way you will not be shooting into the sun. A side benefit of a morning ascent is that you are more likely to have the vistas to yourself.

Mountain Pond Loop Trail

- **2.7 miles, little elevation change**
- **2–3 hours**
- **moderate for kids**

I may lose a couple of friends by including Mountain Pond here. It's in a beautiful, secluded part of the White Mountain National Forest, yet it is accessible enough to be a fine family destination. Plan at least a half day. Families with young children (two to five) can take a very pleasant short walk even if they decide not to hike the entire loop.

Mountain Pond Trail is south of the Baldface Range in the valley of Slippery Brook, east of Jackson and Wildcat Mountain. Mountain Pond, a clear, quiet body of water 0.75 mile long by 0.5 mile wide, evokes images of what a lot of ponds in northern New England must have looked like before lakeside cottages and "no trespassing" signs. There are beaver houses, loons, a dense spruce-fir forest, and jumbles of rocks along the shore. A shelter on the north side of the pond is a great place to stop for a picnic lunch. The latrine there is the only rest room in the area.

What's in it for kids

- Trees growing out of rocks.
- Animal dens.
- Chance to throw rocks in the water.

- Beaver houses.
- Plants that smell like chewing gum.
- A wooden bridge over a bog.

Getting There

From North Conway, head north on N.H. 16/U.S. 302 and turn right on Town Hall Road in Intervale (left if you are coming south from Jackson or Glen). After 0.1 mile, the road crosses N.H. 16A and becomes Slippery Brook Road, which becomes Forest Road 17. The trailhead is 6.4 miles past 16A, the last 4 of which are unpaved (but hard packed) through the National Forest. Ignore the small road going off to the right at 2.4 miles where the pavement ends. Plan on a fifteen- to twenty-minute drive after leaving "civilization." The parking lot and trailhead are on the right about 0.6 mile after F.R. 38 goes off to the left.

The Trail

From the parking lot, follow the short, wide path (0.3 mile) marked with yellow blazes to the Mountain Pond Loop Trail. The trail is deceptively long because you can easily see across the pond, yet it takes awhile to get around. Besides, it is such a lovely and interesting spot that you will naturally slow down. The trail is rocky in some sections, so expect tired feet at the end.

Although you could walk in either direction around the pond, we suggest going counterclockwise by turning right at the fork. You will quickly come to a small wetland that could be muddy during the spring thaw or

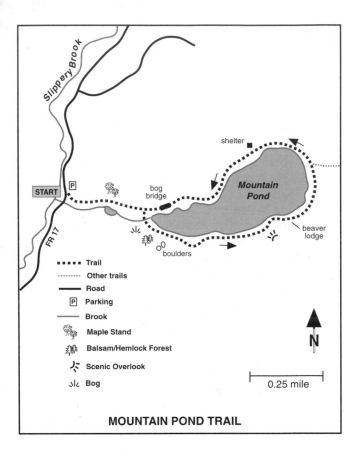

MOUNTAIN POND TRAIL

Trail
Other trails
Road
P Parking
Brook
Maple Stand
Balsam/Hemlock Forest
Scenic Overlook
Bog

0.25 mile

right after heavy rains. If passage over this damp area looks like it might start a revolution in the family, turn around and walk part of the trail in the clockwise direction. It would be frustrating to start out clockwise, walk almost the entire loop, and then get to the wetland and discover that it is too muddy to cross comfortably. The wetland should be easily passable in dry weather.

The remainder of the loop follows the pond shore. The shelter is reached at 1.7 miles and the end of the loop at 2.4 miles.

A shorter walk suitable for all ages is to go clockwise (left) at the fork, walk to the shelter, have a nice relaxing picnic, and then return the way you came (total distance about 2 miles). There are several short spurs that lead down to the shore of the pond along this section of the trail and a wooden bog bridge across a wet area.

Highlights

Mountain Pond is a great spot for showing the kids trees, wildflowers, and, with luck, wildlife. The following description highlights things to look for as you walk counterclockwise around the pond.

Maples, with their familiar three- or five-pointed lobed leaves, brilliant fall colors, helicopter-like winged seeds, and sweet sap, are perennial favorites of children. Not far from the parking lot even before you get to the loop path, you can find four different kinds. Three of them—striped, red, and mountain maple—grow around a small wet area, and the fourth—sugar maple—is a little farther down the path.

Striped maples are particularly striking and easy to identify. These small trees are named for the distinctive white striping along their bright green, young branches. Their large leaves (up to ten inches across) with three relatively small pointed lobes resemble the webbed foot

Mountain Pond.

of a goose, which is why they are also called goosefoot maples. Another name for striped maple is moosewood, a name that predates the popular vegetarian cookbook. Beneath these leaves in early summer, one can occasionally find drooping flower clusters or the familiar winged seeds of maples. The striped maples you see along the trails are usually part of the understory, not more than ten feet tall.

Unlike their smaller cousins, **sugar maples** are a tree of the forest canopy, growing up to about 2,000 feet in elevation in the White Mountains. Their leaves are smaller than those of the striped maple and have five pointed lobes. (Here is a good place to show kids how sunlight affects leaves: Understory trees like striped maples that grow in the shade have larger leaves than trees like sugar maples that get more direct sunlight. Even within the same tree, leaves in the shade will tend to be larger than those in direct sun.) Sugar maple leaves turn brilliant yellow and orange in the fall. And, of course, the concentrated sap of this tree is something all kids adore, particularly on blueberry pancakes.

Red maples are equally at home in wetlands and along mountain slopes. Their leaves are smaller than striped maples and are three-pointed with sharp angles between the lobes. Red maples turn spectacular shades of red in the fall. Their wine-colored flowers in the spring bloom before their leaves come out and add a splash of color to our wetlands early in the season.

Mountain maples are the most inconspicuous of our four maples, growing as understory shrubs. Their leaves tend to be three-pointed and rounded, and their twigs are hairy. Long clusters of flowers may be present in spring and early summer, and the familiar winged maple seeds can be seen in mid- to late summer.

Beyond the wetland, the trail is dominated by **balsam fir** and **hemlock** with large boulders strewn about. There are many holes under the rocks and along the trail, some large enough for kids to hide in. It is a great place to imagine the creatures that might be lurking in these dens. Some trees grow directly on top of the rocks with their roots snaking over the rocks to reach the soil below. Dense growth of mosses, mountain wood sorrel, and other plants of the forest floor add to the magic of the atmosphere.

Two small plants common here, **wintergreen** and **snowberry,** are distinctive for their sweet, minty odor. Both have thick glossy leaves that remain on the plant throughout winter (hence the name wintergreen). Wintergreen (also called teaberry or checkerberry) is the larger of the two plants, growing as high as two inches off the ground. The kids will enjoy crushing a leaf to evoke its pleasant aroma, reminiscent of chewing gum. As a conservation lesson, pick a leaf only where the plant is abundant. The trailing vines of snowberry really hug the ground. Its tiny rounded leaves are stalkless and seem to come off the stems in pairs. The "wintergreen" smell produced by snowberry is not as overpowering as that produced by wintergreen itself.

Mountain Pond is one of the best spots to find **water birds** in the White Mountains. Look for loons, ducks, and other water birds whenever you pass an opening along the pond shore. If you are fortunate enough to see loons, take the time to watch these large handsome birds for a while as they swim silently across the pond, dive for fish, or sound their eerie cry. In summer, the loon is unmistakable with its dark head, checkered necklace, speckled back, and large daggerlike bill.

On one visit, we ran into twelve common mergansers fishing along the shores of the pond. These diving birds are ducks, but instead of having a flat bill like Donald or Daffy, they have a thin one with serrated edges that enables the birds to more easily grasp their slippery prey. Mergansers can be fascinating to watch because small groups use teamwork to capture fish. A merganser team swims in a line to drive the fish toward shore and then dives in tandem to prevent fish from escaping.

Mountain wood sorrel.

In addition to the loons, other nesters are black ducks, hooded mergansers, ruffed grouse, hairy woodpeckers, rusty blackbirds, purple finches, and a number of warblers.

When you reach the far end of the pond, stop to appreciate the great **view** of Baldface. The bald summit of this 3,500-foot mountain is the result of past wildfires. Near the viewpoint for Baldface, there is a **beaver lodge** right by the shore.

Mountain Pond is a place you and the kids will want to come back to.

Evans Notch Region

EVANS NOTCH is the farthest east of the four major north-south notches that run through the White Mountains. It straddles the New Hampshire-Maine border for much of its length. The mountains on its western border include the Baldfaces, the Basin Rim, and the Royces, generally ranging from 3,000–3,500 feet in elevation. The hills on the east side of the notch are lower (1,000–2,900 feet), and include Caribou, Speckled, and Blueberry mountains and Deer Hill.

Evans Notch provides some excellent family hiking. It is less crowded than other regions, and the lower elevations are more manageable for children. Most of the summits have excellent views, flowing water abounds, and there are ample places for picking blueberries.

ME. 113 provides access to most of the hiking trails. Approaching from the south, you pick up ME. 113 in Fryeburg, Maine. Fryeburg is approximately eight miles east of Conway and North Conway along N.H. 113 or U.S. 302, respectively. Keep in mind, particularly when returning to New Hampshire, that N.H. 113 and ME. 113 are two different roads. After leaving Fryeburg, ME. 113 passes through Chatham, North Chatham, and Stowe. From the north, ME. 113 is reached by traveling east on U.S. 2 about ten miles from Gorham to the former logging town of Gilead.

Facilities

A major center for hiking in Evans Notch is the AMC's Cold River Camp, located off ME. 113 about 5.5 miles north of Stowe. The camp has rustic cabins for rent, a communal dining hall, and occasional programs on natural history. An excellent, detailed hiking map of Evans Notch and the Cold River Valley, published by the Chatham Trails Association (CTA), is available at the camp.

The Basin is a National Forest Recreation Area named for a glacially carved bowl between West Royce Mountain and Mount Meader. Basin Pond offers fishing, canoeing, picnicking, swimming, and a great chance to spot a moose and other wildlife. The most accessible rest rooms in the notch are there, too. Other public rest rooms are at the campgrounds.

The Androscoggin Ranger Station on N.H. 16 in Gorham and the Evans Notch Station in Bethel have pamphlets on a number of the trails in Evans Notch, as well as information on rock-collecting opportunities for young miners.

Supplies. The towns you pass through along your way to Evans Notch—Chatham, North Chatham, and Stowe—are small, so you may want to pick up supplies you need for your hike at the larger communities farther away (e.g., Bethel, Fryeburg, Gorham). The Corner Store in Stowe has baked goods, lunches, and ice-cream cones (the latter of truly monstrous proportions and an excellent pre- or post-hike treat for everyone).

Camping. There are four National Forest campgrounds in and around Evans Notch: the Cold River, Basin, Hastings, and Wild River campgrounds. The Cold River and Basin campgrounds are both at the Basin. The Hastings Campground, with twenty-four sites, is located between the two ends of the Roost Trail just off ME. 113. It has limited accessibility for people with disabilities. The Wild River Campground, also with twenty-four sites, is reached by a five-mile drive down Wild River Road, a dirt road off ME. 113.

Deer Hill and
Deer Hill Spring

- **3.2 miles round-trip, 850-foot elevation gain**
- **3–4 hours**
- **moderate for kids to Deer Hill**
- **1 hour, easy for kids to Deer Hill Spring**

The hike up Deer Hill (1,367 feet) from AMC's Cold River Camp is a pleasant half-day outing that starts in New Hampshire and ends in Maine. It crosses Cold River on a dam, enters the state of Maine, and then heads uphill through forests of maples, beech, birch, and hemlock. The 850-foot rise in elevation is definitely manageable for most families but still enough to make you feel like you have gotten a good bit of exercise. Blueberries are abundant and the views are great. There are a number of interesting things to see along the way, so this hike is worthwhile even if you decide not to complete the entire walk.

Deer Hill Spring Quicksand is a bizarre phenomenon that should not be missed. Water constantly bubbles up through a potion of sand, much like one of those muddy hot springs at Yellowstone National Park. Although the sand looks like it might be solid, you certainly do not want to walk on it. You can get there by extending your hike to Deer Hill or as a separate, short outing. If you have two cars available or are willing to hike about two miles back to your car along a road, it is possible to hike from Deer Hill to Deer Hill Spring.

What's in it for kids_____

- A great bridge over the Cold River.
- Great views from two ledgy summits.
- Blueberries.
- Wildlife trees.
- The bizarre Deer Hill Spring Quicksand.

Getting There

The trailhead is at the AMC's Cold River Camp. From the North Conway area, follow ME. 113 north from Fryeburg, Maine along the Maine-New Hampshire border. Cold River Camp is on the right about 6.3 miles north of the village of Stowe, Maine. For those approaching from Gorham or Bethel, take ME. 113 south from U.S. 2 in Gilead.

Park your car in the hiker's parking area of the Cold River Camp off Route 113. Walk past the main dining building then through the overnight guest's parking lot and downhill along a wide path at the far right end. The first trail sign for Little Deer Hill isn't until you cross the river, pass into Maine, and cross an old logging road.

The Trail

After leaving the parking lot, descend to the Cold River (0.1 mile) on a very wide path, passing through a stand of white pine, hemlock, birches, and oaks. At the river's edge, the Conant Path goes off to the right and the Tea House Path to the left. The children will enjoy crossing over the river on a bridge with a spillway in the middle.

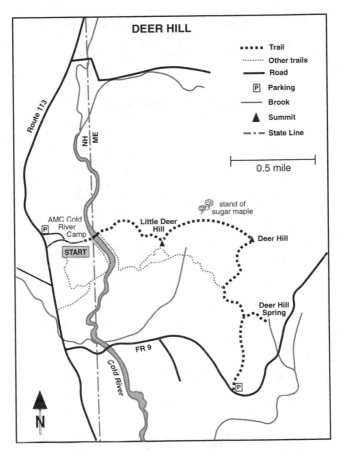

If your time is limited or your children are very young, you can enjoy the river and the dam for a while and then return to Cold River Camp via the Tea House Path. This short loop back to Cold River Camp (ten to thirty minutes), is named after a screened-in gazebo a short distance up the trail. The Tea House is a very pleasant place to have a picnic lunch safe from mosquitoes and blackflies, and the area is rich in wildflowers.

For Deer Hill, bear right at the double yellow marker after crossing the bridge, pass the stone that indicates the border of New Hampshire and Maine, then look for the sign for Little Deer Hill after the old logging road. Yellow blazes mark the trail as it goes uphill through a northern hardwoods forest, eventually passing over several ledges with blueberries and nice views, and reaching Little Deer Hill (0.6 mile). The views and blueberries are great here, so it is another possible turnaround spot. The summit of Deer Hill is another 0.6 mile (twenty to thirty minutes) beyond. The trail descends about 100 feet into the col between Little Deer and Deer hills in a forest dominated by sugar maples, crosses a stream, then ascends about 400 feet to the summit of Deer Hill. Deer Hill Spring is about a half hour farther down the trail.

The trail is in relatively good condition and is easy to follow with some moderately steep, rocky sections and a few sections with roots. A heavy layer of leaves in some steep sections may make the trail slippery when wet.

Highlights

The **border of New Hampshire and Maine** is noted with an impressive stone bench marker. Not many can resist the temptation to have one foot in New Hampshire and the other in Maine. Painted trillium, clintonia, and hobblebush grow abundantly here.

Beyond the bridge show the kids how the river has formed flat parallel **terraces** at different heights above its current banks. Each terrace was built up when the river flooded its banks and deposited sand, silt, and mud along its shores. During the melting of the last glacier about 10,000 years ago, the Cold River was much deeper and wider than it is today. As a result, the terraces that it formed then are now stranded high above the present water level.

Several dead **wildlife trees** stand along the trail between Cold River and Little Deer Hill. Show the kids the softball-sized holes in these trees and the large wood chips at the base, both the handiwork of pileated woodpeckers.

About halfway up the trail to Little Deer Hill on the right side, look for a **hemlock with four separate trunks** united at the base. More than likely, the original trunk was damaged by insects or wind, and none of the four branches could dominate and take over. Other trees in the area have double trunks for the same reason.

Many **wildflowers** grow alongside the trail, but unfortunately for summer visitors, most bloom in May and June. In the woods, you can see clintonia, painted trillium, Canada mayflower, Indian cucumber root, pink lady's slippers, wild anemone, dwarf ginseng, partridgeberry, and wild sarsaparilla. The dominant understory shrub is hobblebush. Trailing arbutus and flowering wintergreen are common where the woods thin out near ledges. Blueberries are abundant on the ledgy areas, as are chokeberries and reindeer moss. The trail is also a good one to learn to identify the different types of

Inspecting a woodpecker hole.

conifer trees: hemlock, red spruce, balsam fir, white pine, and red pine.

The **summits of Little Deer Hill and Deer Hill** are great for scenic vistas, picnics, and midsummer blueberry picking. From Little Deer Hill, the bare summits of the Baldface Range and the impressive cliff face of the Basin are to the west. Cold River Camp is partially within view, so the kids can see how far they've hiked. The best vista from Deer Hill is about fifty yards east of the true summit. Looking eastward you'll see hills, lakes, and bogs of Maine. With binoculars, you may get lucky as we did and see a Maine moose in one of the bogs.

Deer Hill Spring is a must for children. It is in a shady hemlock grove where you are likely to be serenaded by the beautiful flutelike song of the hermit thrush or the energetic bubbling of the winter wren. Before you actually see it, there is nothing to alert you that something odd is nearby. Then you notice a porridge of boiling yellow sand contrasting sharply with the dark surroundings. Water bubbles out of the side of the mountain with enough force to keep sand constantly in suspension. Finer particles pass out of the spring with the outflow. Rumors abound that a horse once fell into the quicksand, and its remains still lie somewhere below. Even if the story is not exactly true, it is not hard to imagine that something must have fallen into the spring at some point.

You can get to Deer Hill Spring by hiking the Deer Hill Trail twenty to thirty minutes (0.7 mile) beyond Deer Hill and turning left at the short, 0.2-mile spur trail to the spring. This requires some prior planning, since you then either have to retrace your steps back to Cold River Camp over Deer Hill (about 2.5 miles), spot a second car on Deer Hill Road near the spring, or walk 2 miles back to Cold River Camp along roads. An alternative is to drive south on N.H. 113 from Cold River Camp for about 0.75 mile, turn left on Deer Hill Road (Forest Road 9) for 1.3 miles, and park where you see the signs for the trail on the left. Walk along the old logging road 0.7 mile, and then turn right on the short spur trail to the spring. That walk should take about thirty minutes and is pleasant, relaxing, and easy.

Prospecting for Minerals at Lord Hill

- **2.6 miles round-trip, 650-foot elevation gain**
- **2–3 hours**
- **moderate for kids**

Lord Hill is a real find. The excursion to its summit on the Horseshoe Pond and Conant trails combines a relatively short uphill walk with an excellent view and a visit to an abandoned mine where amateur rock hobbyists are still permitted to collect for their personal use. The view from the 1,257-foot summit includes Horseshoe Pond immediately below, the long, sinuous Kezar Lake a little farther, and the hills and forests of this easternmost section of the National Forest. Lord Hill is a little off the beaten track, but it is a great place to escape the crowds and get a sense of what the White Mountains were like in earlier times.

The White Mountain National Forest owns the northern and western shorelines of Horseshoe Pond, so this hike can be combined with a picnic at the pond. You can fish for bass, pickerel, and trout, or go for a swim.

At a leisurely pace it should take about an hour to reach the summit of Lord Hill. With an hour or more of enjoying the view and poking around the mine and another hour back, plan on a half day or more, especially if you bring a picnic and spend some time around Horseshoe Pond.

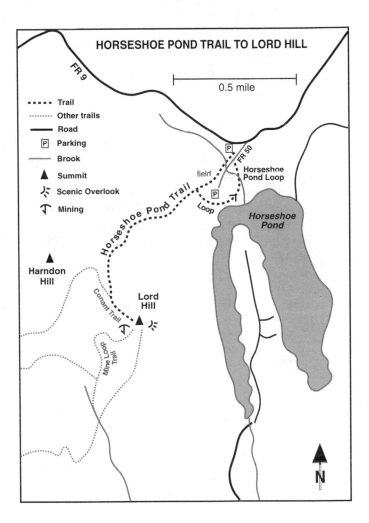

HORSESHOE POND TRAIL TO LORD HILL

0.5 mile

- - - - Trail
.... Other trails
▬▬▬ Road
P Parking
▬▬ Brook
▲ Summit
⚹ Scenic Overlook
⚒ Mining

FR 9

FR 50

field

Horseshoe Pond Loop

Loop

Horseshoe Pond

Horseshoe Pond Trail

Harndon Hill

Conant Trail

Lord Hill

Mine Loop Trail

N

What's in it for kids _____

- Rock collecting.
- A relatively short climb to a summit.
- Nice view from the summit.
- Swimming at Horseshoe Pond.

Getting There

From the Conway/North Conway area, take U.S. 302 to
Fryeburg, then head north on ME. 113. Turn right (east)
on Deer Hill Road (F.R. 9) approximately 5.5 miles
north of the little village of Stowe, with its notable Corner Store. After 4.7 miles on Deer Hill Road, take a very
sharp right onto an unpaved road (F.R. 50) and park at
the open area a short distance beyond.

If you are approaching from the north or west, take
U.S. 2 through Gorham and turn south (right) on ME.
113 about 10 miles east of the junction of U.S. 2 with
N.H. 16. Turn left on Deer Hill Road approximately 0.75
mile south of the AMC's Cold River Camp and follow
above directions.

The Trail

The Chatham Trails Association Map provides the best
detail of this walk. Pick up the Horseshoe Pond Trail at
the cairns in the field adjacent to the parking area, and
head uphill (left). Later on, you can take the trail in the
other direction to Horseshoe Pond itself. The path,
marked by yellow metal rectangles, is a gradual uphill
through a mixture of fields, open woodlands, and ever-

green forests. After about one mile, the Horseshoe Pond Trail ends at a T intersection with the Conant Trail (also called the Pine-Lord Loop Trail or the Pine-Lord-Harndon Loop). Turn left and follow the Conant Trail for about 0.2 mile. At the summit go left to reach the best views from open ledges. Take the Mine Loop Trail to the right for the short walk to the abandoned mine.

On your way back, if you want to visit the pond, turn right at the Horseshoe Pond Loop when you reach the open field. Follow this somewhat overgrown trail for about 0.2 mile to the western shore of Horseshoe Pond. Keep following the yellow blazes for a number of nice viewpoints on the pond, and eventually make your way back to F.R. 50 and turn left to reach your car.

The White Mountain National Forest has produced a flyer on looking for minerals at Lord Hill and Deer Hill. Stop in at the Evans Notch Ranger Station in Bethel (on U.S. 2) or other ranger stations for a copy.

Highlights

Visiting the **old mine** on Lord Hill is a dream come true for a young rock hunter. Many early explorers of the White Mountains came seeking riches from minerals locked up in the rocks. Although there is little commercial mining in the White Mountains now, in the past mining probably ranked number two behind lumbering in local commerce. Lord Hill is one of a number of mines in western Maine, some of which are still in commercial operation. The region is still a major source of amethysts and other semiprecious gems.

A young explorer visits the digs at Lord Hill.
Jan Collins

The White Mountain National Forest allows you to dig for common minerals for your own use without a permit (except for smoky quartz in the Saco Ranger District). Power tools and explosives are forbidden, and a prospecting permit is required if you plan to sell the minerals.

The Lord Hill mine is actually an open depression in the hill, rather than a deep, dark shaft. It can be hot and sunny there on summer days, so bring sun hats and plenty of water. The floor of the hole is littered with small pieces of rock, the remnants of past blasting. Have the kids search for the minerals among these rock fragments or in the wall that borders one side of the mine.

Miners at Lord Hill were particularly interested in the **large chunks of muscovite,** a silvery mica that can be divided into paper-thin crystals like the pages of a book. These crystals were used for capacitors. Although mica crystals are common in the granitic rocks throughout the White Mountains, the large, striking "books" at Lord Hill are particularly impressive. The opaque, whitish feldspar is not as striking, but at one time this mineral was mined here for use as a porcelain-like material for sinks and bathtubs.

Two gems found at Lord Hill are **beryl,** a greenish quartz that is high in the element beryllium, and **topaz.** Beryl crystals ten to twelve feet long have been found in this part of Maine—one is now at the American Museum of Natural History in New York City. You might initially mistake the clear topaz for a quartz since it is also uncolored and translucent, but notice the difference in the arrangement of the angles of the crystals. Topaz has a smoother feel to it. Smoky quartz is also common at Lord Hill, and purple amethysts can be found as well, although the latter are more common at a mine nearby at Deer Hill.

These beautiful crystals were formed beneath the earth within the granite that makes up much of the White Mountains. Eons ago, molten rock bubbled up through cracks in the granite, forming pegmatite dikes of feldspar. Within the feldspar, crystals of the minerals formed, becoming large because they cooled very slowly. Later, erosion from water and ice and scouring by glaciers broke up the rock, revealing the minerals to future generations.

The **scenery** at the summit of Lord Hill is also striking. The view from the ledge at the summit includes Horseshoe Pond nearby and part of Kezar Lake in the distance. You also look out to a ridge that includes Speckled Mountain (2,906 feet), Red Rock Cliff, and Blueberry Mountain.

Watch for interesting **forest dynamics** along the Horseshoe Pond Trail up the hill. Stone walls indicate that the area was farmed at one time, and if the kids are alert, they may find an old house foundation in the woods. The forest returned after the farms were abandoned. In December 1980, an intense windstorm hit the area. The storm was very selective in its effects, so the forest now alternates between older stands of white pines, hemlock, and sugar maples and newer patches of aspens and birches. Have the kids on the lookout for these changes. Sweet fern, a small, sun-loving shrub with fernlike leaves, grows in the open patches. (Crush a leaf and you will understand why it is named sweet fern.)

Lord Hill also is a good low elevation spot for **red spruce,** a tree that at one time covered much of the lower elevations in the mountains before it was intensively logged. If the kids are daring, they can make **spruce gum** out of globs of the resin sticking to the bark. This used to be a popular treat before Mr. Wrigley. They'll need to work it over in their mouths, spitting out the grit. Eventually it will soften up and look like regular chewing gum.

If their gustatory inclinations are less adventurous, raspberries grow in open areas near the base of the hill and some blueberries around the summit.

Look for **piles of hemlock bark** that somehow never made it to the tannery. Hemlocks, identified by their short flat needles (only one per bunch), were extensively logged for tannins before the advent of synthetic substitutes. After trees were cut, the bark was stripped and placed in piles in the woods before being transported to tanneries. Tannins extracted from the bark were used to preserve leather.

At the summit of Lord Hill there is a nice stand of **red pine,** a tree with distinctive reddish bark in "plates" and two long needles per bunch. This pretty tree is often planted as an ornamental.

Keep your eyes open for the evidence of **pileated woodpeckers** that live in the area. If you are lucky, you might catch a glimpse of this crow-sized woodpecker with the flaming red crest. If not, there are a number of trees with softball-sized holes chiseled out and large flakes of wood piled up on the ground below. One of these pileated woodpecker trees is located near the junction of the Horseshoe Pond and Conant trails.

Young miners and foresters will enjoy finishing this expedition with a visit to the pond.

Blueberry Mountain via Stone House Trail

- **4.5 miles round-trip, 1,200-foot elevation gain**
- **3–5 hours**
- **challenging for kids**

The name of this trail conjures up images of an August afternoon blissfully spent picking sweet blue morsels from low shrubs while looking out over a pretty valley and surrounding mountains. The next morning there's a feast of blueberry pancakes around a campfire. Well, that aptly describes this trail. Blueberry Mountain, 1,781 feet in elevation, is loaded with blueberries and commands great views of the Baldface Ridge and the hills around the Cold River valley. In addition to the blueberries and the vista, the first part of the Stone House Trail passes a gorge and a deep pool in Rattlesnake Brook.

The complete Stone House Trail is a moderately challenging hike. Most of the trail is a soft, gradually ascending path, but the upper part is steeper and has a few rocky sections. A 0.7-mile loop around the summit gives you access to several outlooks. Plan on at least a half-day outing to hike the entire walk plus the loop. It can be a full day if you stop at the gorge and the pool, have a picnic lunch, and do some serious blueberry picking on the summit. If you do not have much time, or if your energy levels are down, you could hike as far as Rattlesnake Pool and still have a satisfying one-to-two-hour outing.

The Stone House Trail provides the easiest ascent of Blueberry Mountain and is the most suitable for children, but there are several other ways to hike up or down. The Stone House Trail can be combined with the Blueberry Mountain and White Cairn trails to make a loop, but be aware that the White Cairn Trail has longer steep, rocky sections and is decidedly more challenging. Check the *AMC White Mountain Guide* or the Chatham Trails Association (CTA) map of Cold River valley and Evans Notch if you want to explore more.

What's in it for kids

- Blueberries and huckleberries.
- Great vistas from ledges.
- Rattlesnake Flume and Pool.
- Wooden bridges.
- The Stone House (private—but interesting to look at).
- Wonderful scents of sweet fern and wintergreen.
- Beechdrops.

Getting There

If you are coming from N.H. 16 in Conway or North Conway, pick up ME. 113 in Fryeburg, Maine, either by taking U.S. 302 or N.H. 113 and head north. From Gorham, New Hampshire, or Bethel, Maine, take ME. 113 south from its junction with U.S. 2.

The trailhead for the Stone House Trail is off an unmarked dirt road (Forest Road 16) that heads east

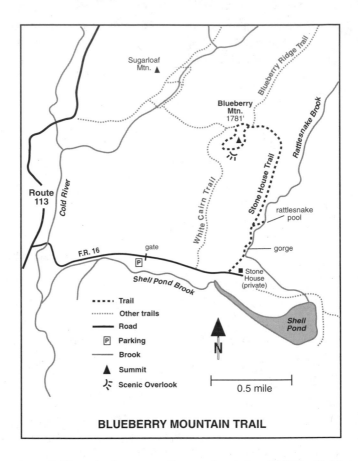

BLUEBERRY MOUNTAIN TRAIL

from ME. 113 about a mile north of the AMC's Cold River Camp, seven miles north of the Stowe Corner Store, and about a mile south of the Basin Campground and Picnic Area.

F.R. 16 crosses a small stream and then makes a sharp right and then a sharp left. Park on the side of the road at a closed gate about 1.1 miles from ME. 113. Continue walking on the road, past the trailhead for the White Cairn Trail (0.3 mile) until you reach the Stone House Trail going off to the left, about a half mile from the gate. The road continues on as the Shell Pond Trail, past the Stone House and a private airstrip.

The Trail

The Stone House Trail is well marked with CTA signs and some yellow blazes. As you ascend, keep in mind that you are walking on private land for the first mile, so stay on the main trail marked by the CTA signs and blazes except for the detours to Rattlesnake Flume and Pool.

The first part of the trail is wide, like an old jeep road, and is a very gradual uphill. After 0.2 mile, a private path from the Stone House enters right. A few paces beyond, a spur trail to the right marked with an arrow leads you to the gorge. It is definitely worth the thirty-yard detour to the little wooden bridge over Rattlesnake Flume. There is a whole network of trails beyond that bridge that could easily get you lost, so return back to the main trail the way you came and continue uphill.

After 0.5 mile, the trail crosses a small wooden bridge and then passes a sign saying "Stone House Trail to Blueberry Mountain" Shortly after, another spur trail on the right leads you 0.1 mile to Rattlesnake Pool.

After the Pool, return to the main trail. This is a logical place to turn back if you have had enough hiking. If not, continue uphill on the Stone House Trail, being sure to stay left at a fork as indicated by a CTA sign.

At about 0.8 mile, the trail enters the Caribou-Speckled Mountain Wilderness and becomes steeper, passing through a thick forest of beech. Near the summit of Blueberry Mountain, red spruce and balsam fir take over. Make sure to follow the yellow blazes carefully at this point. The trail reaches the junction with Blueberry Ridge Trail 1.5 miles from the start of the trail (1.9 miles from your car).

For the best vistas and blueberries, take a left (west) on the Blueberry Ridge Trail and follow it past a few small cairns for about fifty yards to its junction with the Overlook Loop. The Overlook Loop goes off to the left, winding past ledges and a small bog for 0.5 mile before ending back at the Blueberry Ridge Trail. Turn right for the 0.2-mile walk back to the Stone House Trail and your descent.

Highlights

Rattlesnake Flume is the first highlight of the Stone House Trail. Here the kids can stand on a wooden bridge and watch the waters of Rattlesnake Brook rushing through a narrow gorge with straight walls rising about twenty-five feet above the water. Rock ferns and rock tripe cover the damp walls of the flume. On the opposite side of the brook, look for the exquisite flowers of trailing arbutus (in May) and twinflower (in July). Like the well-known Flume of Franconia Notch, Rattlesnake Flume was created by the erosion of a narrow dike of softer rock that had intruded into the granite.

Rattlesnake Pool is actually a series of small pools connected by cascades and chutes. The setting is a shady woods of hemlocks, beech, yellow birch, and striped maple. This is a good spot for a snack, lunch, or if you are truly daring, a plunge into the icy waters. The first pool is fairly deep (probably about fifteen feet) and is remarkable for its very clear water. The pools farther downstream are shallower and more suitable for young children, but be prepared for some scrambling over boulders that may be slippery.

The **Overlook Loop** around the summit of Blueberry Mountain has great views from a number of open rocky ledges. We first visited the summit on a magical day in the fall when the scene was at first muted and dull because of fog. Then the fog began to lift, unveiling incredibly vivid fall foliage. The peaks of the Baldface Range slowly came into view and eventually loomed over everything. Special days like that can make you forget all the damp days of hiking in the mist when you cannot see much past your own nose.

The **Stone House** was built from granite carted down from Baldface Ledge by oxen about 200 years ago. Think what a job that must have been when you are at the summit of Blueberry Mountain looking across to Baldface Cliff.

The most abundant plants around the Overlook Loop are **blueberries**, huckleberries, and sheep laurel. Low-bush blueberry shrubs are everywhere on Blueberry Mountain, so bring containers for your mid-July-through-late-August hike. The kids' patience for collecting these tasty treats will probably be a lot shorter than yours, so if you really want to do some serious picking,

Low-bush blueberry.

factor in a number of breaks or prepare to have one adult entertain them while the other attends to the business at hand. Do not ignore the darker, blue-black huckleberries—they are "seedier" but also quite tasty. The huckleberry can also be distinguished from the blueberries by their leaves; huckleberry leaves are covered by small yellow resin dots on their undersides (easier to see if you have a hand lens).

Other plants to note around the ledges are rhodora, which has beautiful large pink flowers around Memorial Day weekend, three-toothed cinquefoil, red pine, white pine, and red spruce.

The **small bog** along the Overlook Loop provides a good illustration of why bogs form where they do. The water that collects in this depression is stagnant, having no flow of water to replenish nutrients once they are used up by plants. The sphagnum mosses that grow so abundantly in the bog make life even more difficult for plants and for the fungi and bacteria that decompose dead leaves and recycle nutrients because they increase the acidity of the water. As a result, plants that live in bogs have to be able to survive on very low levels of nutrients.

One beautiful tree that manages to grow quite well in this and other bogs is **larch,** a conifer whose gracefully curved branches and light, airy appearance make it seem lacy and oriental. Have the kids look for **cotton grass,** with its unmistakable white cottony balls at the top of leafless, grasslike stems. Bog bilberry, rhodora, and mountain holly also grow in this bog.

Beechdrops is a unique plant that grows only under beech trees. All you ever see of this six- to eighteen-inch plant are its small white flowers with reddish brown splotches scattered along a colorless stalk. It has no green leaves because it gets all its nutrition by parasitizing the roots of beech trees. Beechdrops do no obvious damage to their host beech trees. Have the kids look around whenever you find some beechdrops, because there are bound to be some beeches present.

If you are listening for birdsongs as you ascend in June and July, you are likely to hear the flutelike songs of hermit thrushes as you start the trail and Swainson's thrushes higher up. Also, keep your eyes open for a guild of forest birds, including chickadees, nuthatches, downy woodpeckers, a blue jay, and some finches. Ravens, dark-eyed juncos, and snowshoe hares are all possible at the summit.

The Roost

- **2.1 miles round-trip, 500-foot elevation gain**
- **1–1.5 hours**
- **moderate for kids**

The Roost is a small hill (1,374 feet) north of Evans Notch that provides terrific views of the Wild River and Evans Brook valleys. It is reached by a short, steep trail off ME. 113 near the Hastings Campground at the abandoned village of Hastings. The ascent takes only about a half hour from the north trailhead, so it rewards you with great views for relatively modest effort. (When you are walking up, you will probably question the use of the term "modest," but it is quick.) Either return the way you came or complete a loop by hiking the 1.2-mile trail and then walking back to your car 0.7 mile along ME. 113.

What's in it for kids

- Great views.
- Trail is short but offers a sense of accomplishment.
- Learn about the history of the "ghost town" of Hastings, Maine.
- A bouncy narrow suspension footbridge over Wild River is nearby.

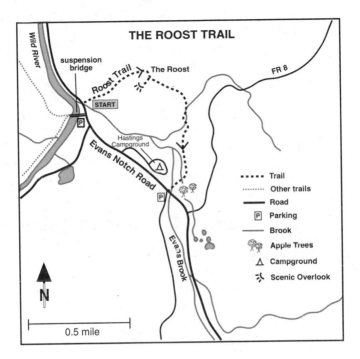

THE ROOST TRAIL

Wild River

suspension
bridge

Roost Trail

The Roost

FR 8

START

P

Hastings
Campground

Evans Notch Road

P

Evans Brook

- - - - Trail
.... Other trails
———— Road
P Parking
——— Brook
🌳 Apple Trees
△ Campground
� Scenic Overlook

N

0.5 mile

Getting There

The Roost Trail forms a semicircle with two trailheads on
the east side of ME. 113. The north trailhead is about 2.7
miles south of U.S. 2, just north of the bridge over Evans
Brook and the junction of ME. 113 with Wild River Road.
There is only space for a car or two opposite the trailhead, so you may need to park at the more substantial
turnoff on the south side of the bridge. The south trailhead is 0.7 mile south of the north trailhead on ME. 113,
about 0.1 mile north of its intersection with F.R. 8.

The Trail

The distance to the summit of the Roost is 0.5 mile from the north trailhead and 0.7 mile from the south trailhead. From the north trailhead, the trail immediately climbs some stairs that will definitely get your pulse rate up. After about twenty minutes of hiking through a forest of mostly paper birch and aspen, you reach the summit. The summit has only a restricted view, so follow the sign "to the scenic view." This leads you downhill to the right on a rather steep side path 0.1 mile to open ledges that overlook the Wild River and the Evans Brook valleys.

After climbing back up to the main trail, either return the way you came or turn right for the rest of the loop. The trail descends through birch, beech, and sugar maple forest and then crosses a stream 0.3 mile from the summit. Like most streams in the White Mountains, this one could be trouble early in the season when water levels are high. The trail then turns right on a dirt road, crosses a second stream, and passes through an area of junior-sized balsam fir. The main road is just after an old apple grove. Turn right on ME. 113 for the walk back to your car.

Highlights

The Roost is strategically situated right above the confluence of Evans Brook and the Wild River, enabling you to see both valleys. The Wild River valley, angling off to the southwest, is broader, looking as if glaciers did not carve it quite so deeply as they carved the Evans Brook valley. The tall peaks on the west slope of the

Wild River valley are the Carter-Moriah Range. Since the panorama is to the west of the Roost, hike this trail in the morning if you want to take photographs without looking into the sun.

Walk down the ledges as far as you safely can for the best view of the Evans Brook valley toward Evans Notch. You'll be rewarded with a view of a number of small ponds and an oxbow (very sharp curve) in Evans Brook.

From the Roost look down and see the leaves of **trembling aspens** shimmering in the breeze. These trees have smooth, light grayish green bark, but their most notable feature is their leaves. A very gentle wind that hardly even ruffles the leaves of other trees induces aspen leaves to shake violently and evoke the sound of the wind. To show kids why aspen leaves are so shaky, find some aspen leaves on the ground and point out that the leaf stalk is flattened rather than rounded as in most trees. The flattened stalks enable aspen leaves to bend more readily during even the slightest breeze. What function this serves for the aspen is anybody's guess, but what it does for us is to make us aware of even the slightest breeze.

Aspens, like paper birch, are early colonizers of land where the trees have been cut or blown down. The aspens on the Roost probably moved in after the area was heavily logged from 1891 to 1917. You can read about the history of this area in *The Wild River Wilderness* by D.B. Wight (Courier Press, 1971) and *Logging Railroads of the White Mountains* by C.F. Belcher (AMC Books, 1980).

The floodplain of the rivers that you see below from the Roost is one of the few level areas in this mountain-

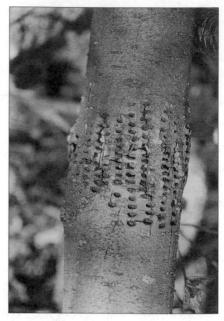

These holes were created by a yellow-bellied sapsucker, a type of woodpecker.

ous region. In the midnineteenth century it had been farmed by a runaway slave who, as legend has it, had to abandon his farm and flee the area when his former master came looking for him. Then the loggers came.

Before 1890, logging operations had been small. Logs were either floated down the Wild River or dragged by teams of horses to a mill at the village of Gilead. In 1891, the Wild River Railroad was completed to bring wood products down the valley, and logging efforts began in earnest. Hemlock bark was taken for tanneries and red spruce for pulp. The village of Hastings, with a population of over 300, sprang up almost overnight in the V between the two rivers. The village had sawmills, a school, a post office, houses for workers, and a plant that produced wood alcohol. The Wild River Railroad ran alongside the Wild River about fifteen miles south into the valley, following the course of present-day ME. 113 south from Gilead, Wild River Road, and Wild River Trail. Like Zealand Valley, there were a number of logging camps, trestles, railroad yards, and spur lines along the railroad. And like Zealand, the logging activity removed many acres of trees and spawned fires and erosion, causing devastation where a few years before a wilderness had existed.

Bridge over the Wild River near the Roost. Nancy Schalch.

Disaster came in 1903 when the Wild River lived up to its name. A tremendous flood between March 11 and 20 inundated Hastings and destroyed much of the Wild River Railroad. This was followed in 1904 by a very dry year with many forest fires.

When the loggers left, the wilderness returned and prevails today. Now, looking down from the Roost, it is hard to imagine that a thriving village had been there. Have the kids find the **apple grove** near the south trailhead, one of the few reminders of that once thriving community.

Note the difference in the **forest** in the north and south parts of the trail. As you ascend from the north trailhead, you pass through a diverse forest of beech, sugar maple, paper birch, white ash, hop hornbeam (note vertically scraggly bark), and aspens. There is a red spruce forest near the summit; then, when you descend south, typical northern hardwoods, dominated by yellow birch, beech, and sugar maple. Along the dirt road, you pass some very big white pines, hemlocks, and red spruce.

Take a detour along ME. 113 to walk out on the 180-foot **suspension bridge** over the Wild River near the parking area for the north trailhead. This narrow footbridge bounces with your steps, which is either very exciting or terrorizing depending on your particular point of view. There is a good sitting log near the water on the opposite side of the river, a great place to end your hike.

North Country Region

THE NORTH COUNTRY lies north of the major White Mountain areas, above U.S. 2 and Gorham. It tends to be less crowded than the busy notches farther south, probably because it is a longer drive for visitors from the south, its mountains are not as tall as the Presidential or the Franconia ranges, and the area is still a center of logging operations. Nevertheless, the North Country has a certain mystique for backpackers and others who want to escape the crowds. It is the White Mountains as they might have been fifty years ago. Much of the area is wild and less developed for tourists. Several peaks in the Kilkenny Range, which forms the central "spine" of this region, are over 4,000 feet.

Facilities

The South Pond Recreational Area (see below) has a bathhouse, rest rooms, and picnic tables.

Supplies. Berlin is the largest city in this section of the White Mountains. Pick up supplies there or in other towns you pass through on your way up, such as Gorham, Lancaster, or Twin Mountain. Stark, several miles west of the access road, is the nearest community to the South Pond Recreation Area.

Camping. There are no National Forest campgrounds in this region. The Nay Pond Campground is in West Milan off N.H. 110. Moose Brook State Park in Gorham has forty-two tent sites.

South Pond Recreation Area and the Devil's Hopyard

- **2 miles round-trip, little elevation change**
- **1–2 hours**
- **easy for all ages to the base of the Hopyard and challenging for kids in the Hopyard**

The South Pond Recreation Area is ideal for families—an easily accessible, developed Forest Service recreational area with picnic tables, a swimming beach, a bathhouse, and boater access. South Pond itself hosts lake trout and loons and serves as a jumping-off point for a short walk to a narrow, deep gorge called the Devil's Hopyard or for longer backpacking trips along the Kilkenny Ridge.

The beginning section of the trail to the Devil's Hopyard is a wheelchair-accessible path, which means it is also ideal for strollers and very young walkers. Within the Devil's Hopyard itself, the trail requires some scrambling on rocks, so this section is not recommended for families with young children (two to five years). Caution is required at all times for everyone because the rocks in the shady gorge are wet and slippery most of the time. The Devil's Hopyard is an exquisite spot, however, and it is certainly worth the walk even if you don't get very far into it.

The recreation area is open roughly from 9:00 A.M. to 8:00 P.M. during the summer season, and an entrance fee is charged. During the off-season, a barrier blocks the access road about a mile from the parking area. Hikers can go around the barrier but need to walk about twenty minutes to get to the pond itself and the Hopyard trail.

The trail should take about an hour but add more time if you walk farther into the Devil's Hopyard or if you need to park at the gate. A family can spend a whole day in the area, hanging out at the beach and picnic area for part of the time and hiking for the remainder.

What's in it for kids _____

- A wooden bridge over a stream.
- A very easy walk along the edge of a pond.
- Exciting scramble through a narrow gorge.
- Determining who has the best answer to the question, "What is a devil's hopyard?"
- A swim in South Pond when you get back.

Getting There

Take N.H. 16 north from Gorham 4.5 miles to Berlin. Bear left on N.H. 110 heading north (to West Milan). It is a little tricky following N.H. 110 as it winds its way through Berlin, since the directional arrows are rather tiny. It makes a left on Madigan Street and then a right on Wight Street. Stay on N.H. 110 past Ducky's Minimart and the Nay Pond Campground through West Milan. South Pond Road is on the left 14.7 miles after turning onto N.H. 110 in Berlin. There are a number of

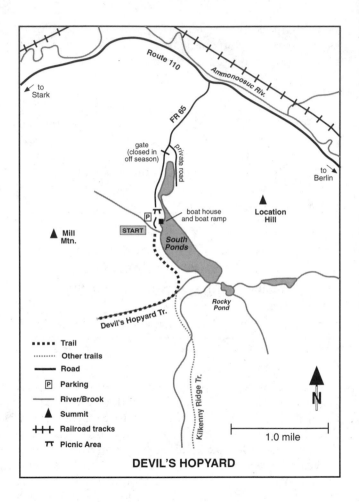

Trail ▪▪▪▪▪
Other trails ·········
Road ▬▬▬
Parking P
River/Brook ──
Summit ▲
Railroad tracks +++
Picnic Area TT

DEVIL'S HOPYARD

mailboxes and a hiking sign at the intersection, but the sign for the South Pond Recreation Area may not be there in the off-season. Bear right in 0.7 mile where South Pond Road forks. If you visit when the barrier is across the road a short distance after the fork, you will need to leave your car there and walk the remainder of the distance to the pond (about a mile).

From Franconia Notch or Twin Mountain, take U.S. 3 north about 25 miles past Twin Mountain to its intersection with N.H. 110 in Groveton. This drive will take you near the town of Guildhall, Vermont, notable as the ancestral home of the Crawford family before they settled in the notch that now bears their name. Follow N.H. 110 through Stark, another 8 miles or so, and turn right on South Pond Road about 1.7 miles past a historic marker along the road.

The Trail

This is a dead-end trail and you don't have to walk to the very end to enjoy it. Walk past the bathhouse at the South Pond Recreation Area, following signs to the Kilkenny Ridge Trail and the wheelchair-accessible trail. These start out together along South Pond as a very level, flat gravel path that for several hundred yards is perfect for a stroller. Along the way there are benches where you can stop and admire the pond, pull out a fishing rod, or throw stones in the water. The trail extends as a path beyond the handicapped trail. At 0.6 mile, the trail to the Devil's Hopyard forks off to the right and the Kilkenny Ridge Trail continues on straight for 13 more miles (save that one until the kids are older). At 0.8 mile, the trail crosses a stream on a bouncy log bridge and, shortly beyond, enters the Devil's Hopyard itself. Here, the trail changes from a flat woodland path to a rocky scramble.

If you have young children, we recommend you walk only a short distance into the gorge before turning around. Once in the Devil's Hopyard itself, the trail becomes increasingly steep before ending at 1.3 miles and climbing about 400 feet. The gorge is shady and remains damp long after rainstorms have passed. Use your judgment about how much farther everyone should clamber before turning around.

Highlights

The two main features of this trail are South Pond and the Devil's Hopyard. The rich woodland provides a number of other delights.

Along the lake, the trail passes through a rich deciduous forest, the type that dominates the lower elevations of the White Mountains. Trees to show the kids are **American beech, sugar maples,** and **yellow birch.** Beech trees have distinct smooth gray bark that looks like it was meant for someone to carve their initials into (of course you won't do that!). Sugar maples have the familiar palm-shaped leaves. The bark of yellow birch is yellowish brown, marked with short horizontal lines, and peels naturally.

Two shorter woody plants common along this part of the trail are **striped maple** and **hobblebush.** Striped maple is a small tree with large lobed leaves that look like a goose's foot and distinctly green-and-white-

Hobblebush in mid-summer. Nancy Schalch.

striped bark. Hobblebush forms impenetrable thickets that will hobble anyone who dares to lumber through. It has large rounded leaves that come off the long skinny branches in pairs. In May, it produces striking, flat-topped clusters of white flowers, larger showy ones on the outside of the cluster and smaller ones inside.

The flowers of the hobblebush show a fascinating division of labor. The showy, outer flowers are all show but no business. They serve to attract insects to the cluster but are themselves sterile. The innocuous-looking flowers in the center of the cluster lack the showy petals but have the stamens and pistils needed to produce fruits and seeds. Insects attracted to the cluster by the showy flowers brush up against the inner ones, pollinating them. Later on in the season, clusters of bluish fruits show that this unique arrangement does work.

This is a good place to show children the two different ways leaves arrange themselves around branches. Hobblebush and maples have "opposite" leaves, because two leaves are attached to branches in pairs at the same point. Yellow birch and beech are "alternately" leaved, because individual leaves are attached singly and alternate along the stem.

Opposite or alternate-leaved patterns are generally consistent within groups of plants. All maples and all viburnums (of which hobblebush is a representative) have opposite leaves. Beech, birch, all oaks, and blueberries are always alternately leaved. The white ash, which grows along South Pond, not only has opposite leaves, but the leaves are compound, i.e., broken up into seven or so leaflets.

The small, delicate fern that covers much of the forest floor is **New York fern,** a misnomer since it is easily as common in New England as it is in New York. Note that its frond (the upright stem and leaflet combination) tapers sharply at the top and bottom.

Shiny club moss is abundant in the forest floor at the junction of the Devil's Hopyard and Kilkenny Ridge trails. It resembles an upright moss with erect, 6-inch stems. These are covered by tightly whorled "leaves" each from 1/8 to 1/4 inch long. They are easily overlooked, but millions of years ago their distant relatives were as large as trees. Much of the coal we burn for fuel came from the fossilized ancestors of the little club mosses.

The kids will enjoy the **wooden bridge** just before the gorge. Beyond the bridge, the gradient steepens, and the stream alternates between **fast-moving riffles and calm pools.** Aquatic animals, including insects, show distinct preferences for either riffles or pools. Water striders, for example, will seek out the calmer pools, whereas blackfly larvae prefer the faster-moving riffles.

The **Devil's Hopyard gorge** is really the highlight of this walk. Make sure the children feel how cool it is, like they just walked into a **refrigerator.** The cooler temperature results from the cold water of the rushing stream and the dense shade within the steep walls of the gorge. Even in midsummer, the kids may be able to find ice lingering in holes between the rocks.

At times you might feel that you are walking on top of the stream, and indeed you are. The stream is often hidden underneath a jumble of large rocks that are part of the trail. Gurgling sounds from holes between the rocks reveal that the stream has gone underground.

Mosses abound in this cool, damp habitat. One of the most abundant here is the **common fern moss,** so named because of its delicate, ferny appearance. This moss is also called piggyback moss because the new delicate ferny branches ride directly on top of the old.

As for the name Devil's Hopyard, the kids' guess is as good as ours. Someone must have considered the dark, misty gorge a sinister place, appropriate for a devil. That same person must have thought that labeling it a hopyard, after a cultivated vine nowhere to be found in the White Mountains, was a more powerful symbol than naming it a mossyard.

Quick Reference Chart:

Region	Hike	Page Number	Difficulty Level (for kids)	Distance (miles RT)
Franconia Notch	Bald Mountain	40	moderate	1.5
	Lonesome Lake	48	challenging	3.2
	Pemi Trail	56	moderate	4 one-way
	Basin-Cascade Trail	63	easy/mod./ challenging	0.4/1.2/2.4
	The Flume	69	easy	2.0
	Lost River	75	easy	0.75
	Coppermine Trail	82	moderate	5.0
Waterville Valley	Welch/Dickey Loop	91	challenging	4.4
	Smarts Brook Trail	99	easy	2.6
	East Pond	107	moderate	5.2
	Cascade Path	115	moderate	3.0
Kancamagus	Greely Ponds	123	moderate	3.2/4.6
	Sabbaday Falls	131	easy	0.6
	UNH Trail/ Hedgehog Mtn.	136	challenging	4.8
	Rail 'n River Nature Trail	143	easy	0.75
	Champney Falls	149	moderate	3.5

Hikes and Highlights

River or Brook	Falls or Gorge	Lake or Pond	Scenic Vista	Rocky Ledges	Wooden Bridges	Blue-berries	Special Geology
			✓	✓		✓	✓
		✓	✓		✓		
✓		✓	✓		✓		
✓	✓				✓		
✓	✓				✓		✓
✓	✓				✓		✓
✓	✓				✓		
✓			✓	✓		✓	
✓							
		✓					
✓	✓				✓		
		✓			✓		
✓	✓				✓		
			✓	✓			
✓							
✓	✓		✓				

Region	Hike	Page Number	Difficulty Level (for kids)	Distance (miles RT)
Kancamagus	Rocky Gorge Lovequist Loop	155	easy	0.9
	Boulder Loop Trail	162	challenging	3.1
Crawford and Zealand	Ripley Falls	171	moderate	1.0
	Mount Willard	176	challenging	3.2
	Elephant Head Saco Lake	184	easy	1.2
	Ammonoosuc Lake	190	easy	1.0/2.0
	Zealand Falls and Hut	197	moderate	5.6
	Thoreau Falls	207	moderate	5.2
	Sugarloaf Trail	213	challenging	3.4
	Trestle Trail	220	easy	1.0
Pinkham and Gorham	Crystal Cascade	228	easy	0.7
	Lost Pond Trail	235	easy	1.0
	Glen Ellis Falls	242	easy	0.6
	Square Ledge Trail	247	challenging	1.0
	Lowe's Bald Spot	252	mod./chall.	4.2
	Thompson's Falls	261	easy	1.8
	Alpine Garden	267	challenging	0.6–2.4

River or Brook	Falls or Gorge	Lake or Pond	Scenic Vista	Rocky Ledges	Wooden Bridges	Blue-berries	Special Geology
✓	✓	✓			✓		
			✓	✓			✓
✓	✓						
	✓		✓	✓			✓
		✓	✓	✓	✓		✓
			✓	✓			
✓	✓	✓	✓		✓		
✓	✓		✓			✓	✓
			✓	✓		✓	✓
✓					✓		
✓	✓						
✓		✓	✓		✓		
✓	✓						
			✓	✓			
	✓		✓	✓	✓	✓	
✓	✓						
			✓	✓			✓

Region	Hike	Page Number	Difficulty Level (for kids)	Distance (miles RT)
Pinkham and Gorham	Pine Mountain	277	moderate	3.5
	Triple Falls	284	easy but steep	0.4
	Fallsway Trail/ Brookbank Trail	289	easy/moderate	1.5
North Conway	Diana's Baths	297	easy	1.0
	Black Cap Path	302	moderate	2.2
	Mountain Pond	308	moderate	2.7
Evans Notch	Deer Hill Deer Hill Spring	319	moderate easy	3.2 1.8
	Lord Hill	326	moderate	2.6
	Blueberry Mountain	334	challenging	4.5
	The Roost	342	moderate	2.1
North Country	Devil's Hopyard	350	easy/chall.	2.0/2.4

River or Brook	Falls or Gorge	Lake or Pond	Scenic Vista	Rocky Ledges	Wooden Bridges	Blueberries	Special Geology
			✓	✓			✓
✓	✓						
✓	✓						
✓	✓						
			✓	✓			
		✓					
✓			✓			✓	✓
			✓				✓
	✓		✓	✓		✓	
			✓	✓			
✓	✓	✓					

Selected Bibliography

Natural History Guides

Appalachian Mountain Club. *AMC Field Guide to Mountain Flowers of New England*. Boston: Appalachian Mountain Club Books, 1977.

Bliss, L. C. *Alpine Zone of the Presidential Range*. Edmonton, Canada, 1963.

Borror, Donald J., and Richard E. White. *A Field Guide to the Insects of America, North of Mexico*. Boston: Houghton Mifflin Co., 1970.

Burt, William Henry, and Richard Philip Grossenheider. *A Field Guide to the Mammals*. Boston: Houghton Mifflin Co., 1964.

Cobb, Boughton. *A Field Guide to Ferns and Their Related Families of Northeastern and Central North America*. Boston: Houghton Mifflin Co., 1963.

Conant, Roger. *A Field Guide to Reptiles and Amphibians*. Cambridge, MA: The Riverside Press, 1958.

DeGraaf, Richard M., and Deborah D. Rudis. *New England Wildlife: Habitat, Natural History, and Distribution*. United States Department of Agriculture, Forest Service, Northeastern Forest Experiment Station, General Technical Report NE-108, 1987.

Grieve, M. *A Modern Herbal: The Medicinal, Culinary, Cosmetic and Economic Properties, Cultivation and Folk-Lore of*

Herbs, Grasses, Fungi, Shrubs and Trees with their Modern Scientific Uses. Vols. 1 and 2. New York: Dover Publications, 1971 (originally published in 1931).

Johnson, Charles W. *Bogs of the Northeast.* Hanover, NH: University Press of New England, 1985.

Jorgensen, Neil. *A Guide to New England's Landscape.* Barre, MA: Barre Publishers, 1971.

Marchand, Peter. *North Woods: An Insider's Look at the Nature of Forests in the Northeast.* Boston: Appalachian Mountain Club Books, 1987.

Newcomb, Lawrence. *Newcomb's Wildflower Guide.* Boston: Little, Brown & Co., 1977.

Pacioni, Giovanni. *Simon & Schuster's Guide to Mushrooms.* New York: Simon and Schuster, 1981.

Pease, Arthur Stanley. *A Flora of Northern New Hampshire.* Cambridge, MA: New England Botanical Club, 1964.

Peterson, Roger Tory. *A Field Guide to the Birds of Eastern and Central North America.* Boston: Houghton Mifflin Co., 1980.

Peterson, Roger Tory and Margaret McKenny. *A Field Guide to Wildflowers of Northeastern and North-central North America.* Boston: Houghton Mifflin Co., 1968.

Petrides, George A. *A Field Guide to Trees and Shrubs.* Boston: Houghton Mifflin Co., 1972.

Phillips, Roger. *Mushrooms of North America.* Boston: Little, Brown & Co., 1991.

Pyle, Robert Michael. *The Audubon Society Field Guide to North American Butterflies.* New York: Alfred A. Knopf, 1981.

Raymo, Chet and Maureen Raymo. *Written in Stone: A Geological History of the Northeastern United States.* Chester, CT: Globe Pequot Press, 1989.

Steele, Frederic L. *At Timberline: A Nature Guide to the Mountains of the Northeast.* Boston: Appalachian Mountain Club Books, 1982.

Stokes, Donald W. *A Guide to Observing Insect Lives.* Boston: Little, Brown & Co., 1983.

Nature with Children

Cornell, Joseph. *Sharing Nature with Children.* Nevada City, CA: Dawn Publishing Co., 1979.

Gertz, Lucille N. *Let Nature Be the Teacher.* Belmont, MA: Habitat Institute for the Environment, 1993.

Sheehan, Kathryn and Mary Waidner. *Earth Child: Games, Stories, Activities, Experiments & Ideas About Living Lightly on Planet Earth.* Tulsa, OK: Council Oak Books, 1991.

White Mountains Guides and Histories

Allen, Linda Buchanan. *Short Hikes & Ski Trips Around Pinkham Notch.* Boston: Appalachian Mountain Club Books, 1991.

Appalachian Mountain Club. *AMC White Mountain Guide* 25th ed. Boston: Appalachian Mountain Club Books, 1992.

Belcher, C. Francis. *Logging Railroads of the White Mountains.* Boston: Appalachian Mountain Club Books, 1980.

Billings, Marland P., Katharine Fowler-Billings, Carleton A. Chapman, Randolph W. Chapman, and Richard P. Goldthwait. *The Geology of the Mt. Washington Quadrangle, New Hampshire.* Concord, NH: State of New Hampshire, Department of Resources and Economic Development, 1979.

Bolnick, Bruce, and Doreen Bolnick. *Waterfalls of the White Mountains: 30 Trips to 100 Waterfalls.* Woodstock, VT: Backcountry Publications, 1993.

DeLorme Publishing Company. *Trail Map and Guide to the White Mountain National Forest.* Freeport, ME: DeLorme Publishing Co., 1992.

Morse, Stearns. *Lucy Crawford's History of the White Mountains.* Boston: Appalachian Mountain Club Books, 1978.

Randall, Peter E. *Mount Washington: A Guide & Short History.* Woodstock, VT: The Countryman Press, 1992.

Reifsnyder, William E. *High Huts of the White Mountains: Nature Walks, Natural History, and Day Hikes around the AMC's Mountain Hostels.* Boston: Appalachian Mountain Club Books, 1993.

Smith, Steven D. *Ponds & Lakes of the White Mountains: From Wayside to Wilderness.* Woodstock, VT: Backcountry Publications, 1993.

Waterman, Laura, and Guy Waterman. *Forest and Crag: A History of Hiking, Trail Blazing, and Adventure in the Northeast Mountains.* Boston: Appalachian Mountain Club Books, 1989.

Wight, D.B. *The Wild River Wilderness.* Littleton, NH: Courier Press, 1971.

Willey, Benjamin G. *Incidents in White Mountain History.* Boston: Nathaniel Noyes, 1856.

About the Author

ROBERT BUCHSBAUM has both a professional interest in and a passion for the natural history of New England. He received a bachelor of science degree in natural resources from Cornell University and a Ph.D. in marine ecology from the Boston University Marine Program at Woods Hole. A native New Yorker, he moved to New England in 1978 and has since spent many of his free weekends and vacations exploring the White Mountains. As an AMC Volunteer Naturalist since 1986, Buchsbaum has presented programs in the huts and elsewhere in the Whites on a wide variety of topics, including botany, alpine ecology, birds, and geology.

Ed Quinlan

Buchsbaum resides in Beverly, Massachusetts with his wife Nancy Schalch and their daughter Alison. He works for the Massachusetts Audubon Society as a staff scientist and co-director of their North Shore office. He has written numerous magazine articles on conservation and has published extensively in technical journals and books.

368

About the Appalachian Mountain Club

THE APPALACHIAN MOUNTAIN CLUB pursues an active conservation agenda while encouraging responsible recreation. Our philosophy is that successful, long-term conservation depends on firsthand experience of the natural environment. AMC's 64,000 members pursue interests in hiking, canoeing, skiing, walking, rock climbing, bicycling, camping, kayaking, and backpacking, and—at the same time—help safeguard the environment.

Founded in 1876, the club has been at the forefront of the environmental protection movement. As cofounder of several leading New England environmental organizations, and as an active member working in coalition with these and many other groups, the AMC has successfully influenced legislation and public opinion.

Conservation

The most recent efforts in the AMC conservation program include river protection, Northern Forest Lands policy, Sterling Forest (NY) preservation, and support for the Clean Air Act. The AMC depends upon its active members and grassroots supporters to promote this conservation agenda.

Education

The AMC's education department offers members and the general public a wide range of workshops, from introductory camping to intensive Mountain Leadership School taught on the trails of the White Mountains. In addition, volunteers in each chapter lead hundreds of outdoor activities and excursions and offer introductory instruction in backcountry sports.

Research

The AMC's research department focuses on the forces affecting the ecosystem, including ozone levels, acid rain and fog, climate change, rare flora and habitat protection, and air quality and visibility.

Trails Program

Another facet of the AMC is the trails program, which maintains more than 1,400 miles of trail (including 350 miles of the Appalachian Trail) and more than 50 shelters in the Northeast. Through a coordinated effort of volunteers, seasonal crews, and program staff, the AMC contributes more than 10,000 hours of public service work each summer in the area from Washington, D.C. to Maine.

In addition to supporting our work by becoming an AMC member, hikers can donate time as volunteers. The club offers four unique weekly volunteer base camps in New Hampshire, Maine, Massachusetts, and New York. We also sponsor ten-day service projects throughout the United States, Adopt-a-Trail programs, trails day events, trail skills workshops, and chapter and camp volunteer projects.

The AMC has a longstanding connection to Acadia National Park. Working in cooperation with the National

Park Service and Friends of Acadia, the AMC Trails Program provides many opportunities to preserve the park's resources. These include half-day volunteer projects for guests at AMC's Echo Lake Camp, ten-day service projects, weeklong volunteer crews in the fall, and trails day events. For more information on these public service volunteer opportunities, contact the AMC Trails Program, Pinkham Notch Visitor Center, P.O. Box 298, Gorham NH 03581; 603-466-2721.

Alpine Huts

The club operates eight alpine huts in the White Mountains that provide shelter, bunks and blankets, and hearty meals for hikers. Pinkham Notch Visitor Center, at the foot of Mt. Washington, is base camp to the adventurous and the ideal location for individuals and families new to outdoor recreation. Comfortable bunkrooms, mountain hospitality, and home-cooked, family-style meals make Pinkham Notch Visitor Center a fun and affordable choice for lodging. For reservations, call 603-466-2727.

Publications

At the AMC main office in Boston and at Pinkham Notch Visitor Center in New Hampshire, the bookstore and information center stock the entire line of AMC publications, as well as other trail and river guides, maps, reference materials, and the latest articles on conservation issues. Guidebooks and other AMC gifts are available by mail order 1-800-262-4455, or by writing AMC, P.O. Box 298, Gorham NII 03581. Also available from the bookstore or by subscription is *Appalachia*, the country's oldest mountaineering and conservation journal.

Index